WRITING THE MODERN CITY

Literary texts and buildings have always represented space, narrated cultural and political values, and functioned as sites of personal and collective identity. In the twentieth century, new forms of narrative have represented cultural modernity, political idealism and architectural innovation. This book explores the diverse and fascinating relationships between literature, architecture and modernity and considers how they have shaped the world today.

This collection of thirteen original essays examines the ways in which literature and architecture have shaped a range of recognisably 'modern' identities. It focuses on the cultural connections between prose narratives – the novel, short stories, autobiography, crime and science fiction – and a range of urban environments, from the city apartment and river to the colonial house and the utopian city. It explores how the themes of memory, nation and identity have been represented in both literary and architectural works in the aftermath of twentieth-century conflict; how the cultural movements of modernism and postmodernism have affected notions of canonicity and genre in the creation of books and buildings; and how and why literary and architectural narratives are influenced by each other's formal properties and styles.

The book breaks new ground in its exclusive focus on modern narrative and urban space. The essays examine texts and spaces that have both unsettled traditional definitions of literature and architecture and reflected and shaped modern identities: sexual, domestic, professional and national. It is essential reading for students and researchers of literature, cultural studies, cultural geography, art history and architectural history.

Sarah Edwards lectures in English Studies at the University of Strathclyde. Her publications include articles in *Women's Writing, Journal of Gender Studies, Life Writing, Journal of Popular Culture, Adaptation* and *Review of English Studies*. She is currently completing a monograph, *The Edwardians Since 1910*, and is the leader of an ESRC seminar series, *Nostalgia in the 21st Century* (2010–11).

Jonathan Charley works and lives, with his family, in Glasgow where he is currently Director of Cultural Studies in the Department of Architecture at the University of Strathclyde. He studied architecture in London and Moscow and works mainly on the political and social history of buildings and cities.

WRITING THE MODERN CITY

Literature, architecture, modernity

*Edited by Sarah Edwards
and Jonathan Charley*

Routledge
Taylor & Francis Group

LONDON AND NEW YORK

First published 2012
by Routledge
2 Park Square, Milton Park, Abingdon, Oxon OX14 4RN

Simultaneously published in the USA and Canada
by Routledge
711 Third Avenue, New York, NY 10017

Routledge is an imprint of the Taylor & Francis Group, an informa business

British Library Cataloguing in Publication Data
A catalogue record for this book is available from the British Library

Library of Congress Cataloging in Publiction Data
Writing the modern city : literature, architecture, modernity / edited by Sarah Edwards and Jonathan Charley.
p. cm.
Includes bibliographical references and index.
1. Architecture and literature. 2. Space (Architecture) in literature. 3. Architecture and philosophy. I. Edwards, Sarah, 1973- II. Charley, Jonathan, 1959- III. Title: Literature, architecture, modernity.
PN56.A73W75 2012
809'.93357--dc23
2011024286

ISBN: 978-0-415-59150-8 (hbk)
ISBN: 978-0-415-59151-5 (pbk)
ISBN: 978-0-203-14996-6 (ebk)

Typeset in Bembo
by GreenGate Publishing Services, Tonbridge, Kent

MIX
Paper from
responsible sources
FSC www.fsc.org FSC® C004839

Printed and bound in Great Britain by
TJ International Ltd, Padstow, Cornwall

This volume is dedicated, in loving memory, to:

Margaret Edwards
John Edwards
Julie Hirst

CONTENTS

FIGURES

CONTRIBUTORS

Gary A. Boyd is Senior Lecturer in Architecture at University College Cork. His first book *Dublin 1745–1922: Hospitals, Spectacle and Vice* (2006) examined connections between medical institutions and the city's urban and social development. Current publications and research activities include systems and manufactured landscapes; housing design and its histories; and the relationship between war, architecture and space.

Inga Bryden is Reader in Literature and Culture and Head of Research in the Faculty of Arts at the University of Winchester. She has published on Victorian literature and culture; urban space and representations of the city; domestic space, and visual and material cultures.

Mark Mukherjee Campbell is a PhD candidate in the Department of Architecture at the University of Strathclyde. His thesis examines the history of residential architecture in Kolkata and the representation of its domestic cultures in literature and cinema. He has presented at conferences across architecture, urban geography and literary studies.

Jonathan Charley lives and works, with his family, in Glasgow where he is currently Director of Cultural Studies in the Department of Architecture at the University of Strathclyde. He studied architecture in London and Moscow and works mainly on the political and social history of buildings and cities.

Peter Clandfield teaches in the Department of English Studies, Nipissing University, North Bay, Ontario. He is working on a project about representations of urban redevelopment, and has published recent essays on Scottish 'architectural crime' fiction and on the depiction of Baltimore development in *The Wire*.

Sarah Edwards lectures in English Studies at the University of Strathclyde. Her publications include articles in *Women's Writing, Journal of Gender Studies, Life Writing, Journal of Popular Culture, Adaptation* and *Review of English Studies*. She is currently completing a monograph, *The Edwardians Since 1910*, and is the leader of an ESRC seminar series, *Nostalgia in the 21st Century* (2010–11).

David T. Fortin is a registered architect in Canada. He teaches design studio, architectural history and theory at Montana State University. He is the author of *Architecture and Science-Fiction Film: Philip K. Dick and the Spectacle of Home* and is currently researching design strategies for housing in Nairobi.

Victoria Rosner is an Associate Dean at Columbia University, where she teaches courses on modern literature and gender studies. She is the author of *Modernism and the Architecture of Private Life* (Columbia UP, 2005), as well as editor (with Geraldine Pratt) of *The Global and the Intimate: Feminism in Our Time* (Columbia UP, 2011).

Stefanie Elizabeth Sobelle is Assistant Professor of English at Gettysburg College and obtained her PhD from Columbia University. Her current research projects include an examination of architecture in postmodern novels and a survey of the poetics of mobility in American literature.

Renée Tobe is Director of Architecture at the University of East London. Before entering academia she was in professional practice for ten years after training at the AA. She is currently working on two publications for Ashgate: one as author entitled *Architecture, Film and the Spatial Imagination* and one as editor with Professor Nicholas Temple (U Lincoln) and Professor Jonathan Simon (UC Berkeley) entitled *Architecture and Justice*.

Brian Ward is a lecturer at the Dublin School of Architecture, DIT. Between 2005 and 2007 he was editor of *building material*, the journal of the Architectural Association of Ireland. He is currently conducting research at University College Dublin on the democratisation of the design process in town planning discourse at the beginning of the twentieth century.

PREFACE

Jonathan Charley and Sarah Edwards

Our intention in putting together such an anthology of essays was to offer what we hope are new perspectives on familiar journeys. Although there is a growing body of scholarship on the cultural significance of modernity in relationship to architecture, the city and literature,[1] there has been relatively little that explores the relationship between all three and that which does tends to focus on 'high modernist' literary icons.[2] Building on this legacy we have endeavoured to push the debate into new territory by challenging the categories of architecture and literature while examining the ways in which they have defined and articulated the experience of modernity in the twentieth century. By modernity we are referring to the transformation of everyday life that occurred in the final decades of the nineteenth century, in the wake of the profound intellectual and social revolutions that defined the enlightenment and the development of capitalism.[3] This was the historical context that both modern architects and writers were to respond to and narrate. In this task, they were faced with nothing short of a rupturing of all that was familiar, the emergence of new concepts of time and space, of hitherto unimaginable technologies, of strange new aesthetic sensibilities, of revolutionary political ideologies, and of equally profound shifts in the way in which we understood and viewed the human psyche.

The collection focuses specifically on the relationships between key embodiments of modernity in literature and architecture. The essays focus, then, on the cultural connections between a variety of prose narratives that include the novel, short story, autobiographical, political, architectural and science-fiction writings and a range of urban environments, both planned and unplanned, from the hut to the colonial city, and from the housing estate to a simple staircase. We have structured the book around thematic headings that we argue are common to discourses on both architecture and literature. Each section begins with an editorial essay which provides a conceptual overview of key issues and debates, as well as outlining other works that might be read alongside our authors' essays.

In Part I, *Memory, Nation, Identity*, the essays focus on the political and cultural ideas that informed individual and collective constructions of national identity during the first half of the twentieth century. These happened in the context of colonial expansion and retreat, in which questions regarding the meaning of family, gender and ethnicity were thrown sharply into focus in both private and public domains. It begins with Brian Ward's essay on the transatlantic conversations on utopia, wilderness and urban planning of Whitman, Carpenter and Raymond Unwin, before moving on to Mark Campbell's investigation of hybrid identity and socio-spatial transgression in Calcutta, explored through the work of the Indian writer Tagore. The section ends with Victoria Rosner's exploration of the colonial experience of 'home' in the 'Rhodesian' autobiographies of Doris Lessing.

Part II, *Movement, Culture, Genre*, takes us to the dark side. These three essays in their different ways ask critical questions about notions of canon, value, hierarchy, politics and how we might periodise cultural history. These issues have increasingly preoccupied both literary and architectural scholars in the later twentieth century, as the impact of critical theory and postmodernism has forced both disciplines to reassess the cultural categories of literature and architecture. We start with Peter Clandfield's essay on the evolution of modern crime novels in which architecture has become the 'object of crime'. From there we enter the strangely familiar urban spaces of Philip K. Dick described by David Fortin, before encountering the world of marginal drugged pornography in Gary Boyd's essay on Alexander Trocchi.

In Part III, *Narrative, Form, Space*, we embark on an equally bizarre trio of excursions. These essays focus more specifically on the formal strategies of what might be termed 'postmodern' narratives, and look at the ways our bodily and psychic inhabitations of the contemporary city are shaped and represented whilst reconsidering the usefulness of twentieth-century literary and cultural theory, in particular Walter Benjamin's concept of urban 'traces' and Roland Barthes' idea of the pleasurable text. Renée Tobe's essay on the novels of Millet and Camus invites us to rethink everyday urban spaces as opportunities for casual sexual encounters, Stefanie Sobelle looks at how Perec recasts the Parisian tenement as a grid and puzzle of over-layered characters, whilst Inga Bryden explores the different ways writers cut pathways through urban space to create story lines that quite literally make streets 'tell tales'. This is where our particular travelogue temporarily stops, wedged somehow appropriately between a town plan, a hut, a city, a building site, a canal, a suburb, an office, a staircase and a motorway.

Notes

1 Compared with the paucity of literature forty years ago on the city and modernity, there is now a wealth of debate. Besides the well-known texts highlighted in the essays that follow by writers like Georg Simmel, Walter Benjamin and Henri Lefebvre would appear the following: Harvey, David, *The Condition of Postmodernity*, Wiley Blackwell, 2004, and *Paris: Capital of Modernity*, Routledge, 2003; Frisby, David, *Cityscapes of*

Modernity, Polity, 2007; Soja, Edward, *Postmodern Geographies – The Reassertion of Space in Critical Social Theory*, Verso, 1989, and Jameson, Frederic, *Postmodernism, Or, The Cultural Logic Of Late Capitalism*, Verso, 1991. These have been accompanied by a flurry of rich anthologies that interrogate modern urban life such as Hermansen, C. and Hvattum, M. (ed.), *Tracing Modernity – Manifestations of the Modern in Architecture and the City*, Routledge, 2004; Leach, N. (ed.), *Rethinking Architecture – A Reader in Cultural Theory*, Routledge, 1997, and *The Hieroglyphics of Space: Reading and Experiencing the Modern Metropolis*, Routledge, 2002; and Borden, I., Kerr, J., Rendell, J. and Pivaro, A. (eds) *The Unknown City*, MIT Press, 2001.

2   There are a number of notable texts that broke new ground in the discussion about the relationship between architecture, literature and modernity, most notably works by Williams, Raymond, *The Country and The City* (1973); Berman, Marshall, *All That Is Solid Melts Into Air* (1989); and Moretti, Franco, *Atlas of the European Novel 1800–1900* (1999). Useful additions to the bibliography are Varey, Simon, *Space and the Eighteenth-Century Novel* (1990), the analysis of Joyce and Dos Passos in Harding, David, *Writing the City: Urban Visions and Literary Modernism* (2003), and Frank, Ellen Eve, *Literary Architecture: Essays Towards a Tradition* (1979) that looks at Proust and Henry James. Other previous works that studied the relationships between literature and architecture have focussed on poetry: these works include Eriksen, Roy, *The Building in the Text* (2001) and Johnson, A. W., *Ben Jonson: Poetry and Architecture* (1994), which examine compositional analogies in relation to Renaissance civic, political and socio-economic issues. Morrissey, Lee, *From the Temple to the Castle: An Architectural History of British Literature 1660–1760* (1999) similarly examines the cultural and civic role of poet–architects such as Pope and Vanbrugh.

3   See Marshall Berman, Mica Nava and Alan O'Shea (eds) *Modern Times: Reflections on a Century of English Modernity*, Routledge, 1996, who argue that that various political, cultural and technological developments in the final decades of the nineteenth century combined to produce new ways of viewing the human psyche and organising social life, such as Freudian psychoanalysis, the 'new' imperialism and the beginnings of first-wave feminism.

ACKNOWLEDGEMENTS

We would like to thank our colleagues and students in the Departments of Architecture and English Studies at Strathclyde University for their continual support; the British Academy, for supporting our 2008 conference, Architexture: Textual and Architectural Spaces, which led to the commencement of this book project; the invaluable and unfailing encouragement and advice of our editors at Routledge, Alex Hollingsworth and Louise Fox, and of the original reviewers; and the love and support of our families and friends.

1

TIME, SPACE AND NARRATIVE

Reflections on architecture, literature and modernity

Jonathan Charley

> The city spread over a plain into distances further than the eye could see. Whichever way he turned there was no end to it, nothing but houses and apartment blocks, streets, squares, towers, old and new quarters of town, mildewy storm-battered rented barracks and skyscrapers faced with modern marble, main roads and alleys, factories, workshops, gasometers and the clumsy looking great hall that he recognised from her as the slaughterhouse. And chimneys, chimneys everywhere …
>
> *Karinthy 2008: 111*

Intangibility and the poets of modernity

It is with an image of the limitless concrete geometries from the top of the Banespa Bank in Sao Paulo and the ziggurats and leaping flames from the opening clip of *Blade Runner* that I begin my course every year on the History of the Modern City. Like my vain attempt to draw Borges' metaphor for the universe, the indefinite and infinite Library of Babel, it is a vision of a metropolis that has no centre and no end. And as it drifts and stumbles outwards to the periphery before disappearing into the hazy smog of the horizon, it is as if it is demonically possessed with a speed and complexity that mocks our efforts at comprehension, and defies our knowledge of earthbound demographics, semiotics and urban economics. As dusk falls over this city of twenty million souls, and millions upon millions of lights flicker and illuminate a nocturnal kaleidoscope of objects and bodies, the scene is almost indistinguishable from the Asimovian mega cities beloved of the fantastic imagination that have bled and bled until they enclose the entire surface of the globe. The first generation of modern writers were likewise shocked and astonished as they gazed in awe at the hypnotic antinomies and creatively destructive patterns of

FIGURE 1.1 'The unknowable and impossible city', Sao Paulo

the nineteenth-century capitalist metropolis. It is why Walter Benjamin, Marshall Berman and many others have found such lyrical power in one of the greatest poets of modernity, Baudelaire, who on his urban drifts through Paris tells us that modernity is best understood as 'the indefinable … the transient, the fleeting, and the contingent'[1] (Baudelaire 2006: 399).

Equally poetic in his depiction of modern life was Marx, who if legend is to be believed drafted the Communist Manifesto in the Swan Bar in Brussels' Grand Place. Surrounded by the ornate guild houses and exotic town halls that reinforce Belgium's claim to be one of the first industrial nations, and having fled from one European capital city to another, he was understandably mesmerised by the forces unleashed by capitalist production. In a phrase that he could well have penned from the top of the Banespa, he tells us that: 'In scarce one hundred years the bourgeoisie has created more massive and colossal productive forces than have all preceding generations together.' But he also warns us. The bourgeois world is haunted. It is stalked by illusions, spectres and ghosts that have conspired not only to create, but to destroy a society that is characterised by nothing less than the 'constant revolutionising of production, uninterrupted disturbance of all social conditions, everlasting uncertainty and agitation' (Marx 1990: 223). It was a sight at which Lukacs simply threw his arms up in the air and from the pulpit announced: 'And the nature of history is precisely that every definition degenerates into an illusion:

history is the history of the unceasing overthrow of the objective forms that shape the life of man' (Lukacs 1983: 186).

It is this ephemeral and dynamic world, in which space splinters, time accelerates and technological wizardry is layered over lo-fi urban misery, that the modern writer and architect attempt to make sense of.[2] But it is no easy task. The modern city would soon shake with the unfamiliar noise of machinery and early automobiles, ring to the shrill tones of telephones, spin with the whirr of a movie camera, and erupt in abstract splashes of colour and shape. Not only this but capitalist modernity appeared to have created a peculiarly dialectical reality, in which the world had been split into multiplications of increasingly fuzzy but powerfully evocative binary metaphors: civilisation and barbarism, capitalist and worker, coloniser and colonised, black and white, man and woman, sane and mad.

Inevitably these transformations in the structure and patterns of everyday life were reflected in what Bakhtin referred to as the *chronotopic* (literally 'space-time') organisation of literary texts.[3] In fact the novel undergoes a profound chronotopic shift that is exemplified by the difference between Tolstoy's *War and Peace* (1869) and Dostoevsky's *Crime and Punishment* (1866). Whereas the former, despite its metropolitan encounters, still feels with its idealised portraits of peasant life like a novel run on agricultural time, the latter, one of the first great urban thrillers, beats with the distinctly modern rhythm of boulevards, pavement footsteps and murderous anti-heroes.

Like a fading memory, the pre-capitalist world of villages, churches and fields, of priests, lords and peasants, living a life governed by seasons, tithes and calls to prayer, retreats into the literary hinterland. In its place comes the chronotopic vocabulary of modern capitalism and the battle cries of bourgeoisie and working class. Together they inhabit a new city made up of arcades, mills, factories, terraces, mines and railway stations in which time is governed according to quite new and strange rules. The day is now regimented by the click of the clocking-in card, the siren of the factory, piece rate wages and the speed of the production line. It all amounted to nothing less than a full-blown temporal revolution engineered towards the perpetual speed-up of everyday life, economic efficiency and the maximisation of profits. This then, is the space–time terrain in which the narratives of modern literature and indeed the plots of modern architecture unfold, meet and merge.

By the turn of the twentieth century this metropolitan experience had become ubiquitous in advanced capitalist societies such that the creative imagination of the majority of both writers and architects had become almost completely urbanised. The city was no longer 'a paradox, a monster, a hell or heaven that contrasted sharply with village or country life in a natural environment' (Lefebvre 2003: 11). It had become the norm. As Raymond Williams commented, for many writers, 'there seemed little reality in any other mode of life,' such that 'all sources of perception seemed to begin and end in the city, and if there was anything beyond it, it was also beyond life' (Williams 1985: 230).

Nation, empire and a very urban revolution

The revolutionary process of capitalist urbanisation with all the social contradictions and psychological traumas that it engendered was no respecter of boundaries and sentiment. It was as unstoppable as it was invasive and would come to provide the contextual framework for all writers and architects, even those in remote garrets harbouring romantic dreams of autonomy from political diktat and economic servitude.[4] Laughing at their delusions were characters like Peotr Petrovich who revelled in the demise of the old world. Holding court in a salon he declares in the spirit of Hegel that:

> something definite has been accomplished; new and useful ideas have spread, new and useful writings disseminated in place of the old dreamy and romantic ones; literature has assumed a tinge of maturity; many harmful prejudices have been uprooted and held up to ridicule – In a word, we have irrevocably severed ourselves from the past and that, in my opinion, is something worthwhile, sir.
>
> *Dostoevsky 1989: 167*

Petrovich's self-conscious modernity was typical of the urban raconteur in the latter half of the nineteenth century who, caught in the slipstream of the European

FIGURE 1.2 'Enlightenment, modernity and national identity', Bibliothèque Ste. Geneviève, The Panthéon, Paris

Enlightenment, and familiar with the ideas of thinkers like Descartes, Kant, Hegel and Adam Smith, was deeply conscious of the seismic consequences of the 1789 and 1848 revolutions and considered the construction of a new world view based on scientific reason and rational philosophical enquiry to be the epitome of what it meant to be modern.

There is no precise starting date for the advent of modernity. For some it is synonymous with the enlightenment and the political and cultural revolution of the early bourgeoisie. Alternatively we might argue that it begins whenever the first generation of liberated serfs clamber over the walls of the demesne, and migrate as 'free' wage labourers to the gaping pits and smoking chimneys that bored though the earth and clashed with church spires. In Dostoevsky's Russia this was not to happen until the emancipation of the serfs in 1869, but it was a process that began in Britain much earlier, as migrant workers travelled to the sites of the industrial revolution, and to the sources of power, energy and raw materials, around which the first great modern industrial cities like Manchester and Glasgow were to develop. And it was in the midst of these new social and spatial formations that the epic battle between capitalist and worker commenced; new classed, gendered and racialised identities were formed; and a new vocabulary of social freedom and individual liberty was discovered.

Newly professionalised architects were confronted with a vast expansion in building typologies, new categories of clients, militant construction trade unions and revolutionary contracting procedures such as competitive tendering.[5] Many devoted their lives to designing the institutions on which capital accumulation depended, magnificent stock exchanges dedicated to the circulation of money that rivalled the temples of antiquity; asylums, prisons and workhouses to classify and discipline mind and body; and staggeringly palatial neo-classical courthouses and seats of government to maintain law and order. Others however, motivated and appalled by the violent and transparent disparities in wealth and property, recast themselves as servants of the people and embraced the idea of an architecture of social commitment. What had begun in the architectural programmes of Utopian Socialists like Robert Owen and Charles Fourier, that had mutated into the architecture of philanthropic concern,[6] was transformed again by the foundation of the first Local Authority Architect's Departments that built networks of public libraries, schools, baths and housing at the turn of the twentieth century. It was a socialisation of architecture that culminated in the 1920s in the manifestos of politically motivated modernists across Europe who aspired to nothing less than the synthesis of a revolutionary social and technological programme.[7]

The modern novelist fills this new construction and architectural landscape with a glittering array of new rogues and heroes. Disgruntled aristocrats in their country houses, angry women imprisoned by antiquarian morals in rural towns, righteous suburban families semi-detached from the city, down-trodden workers in slums and ghettos, and lonely individuals lost in the urban crowd. These were just a few of an intricate cast of new characters that began to occupy the pages of a whole new literature of redemption, reconciliation, suffering and struggle. Literature might well attend to the trials and tribulations of the aristocracy and middle class, but it could also illuminate the ordeals of the poor and the insurgent in which location and architecture were everything. Through the modern novel the reader could now visit the grimy blackened towns and pits of Zola's *Germinal* and Dickens' *Hard Times*, encounter the *People of the Abyss* with Jack London, gaze with horror through the doors into the bloody meat factory of Upton Sinclair, express solidarity with the workers in Gorky's factories, join the Wobblies in Dos Passos' *U.S.A.* or empathise with the victims of Steinbeck's dust bowl migrations. After what Lukacs had labelled the crisis of bourgeois realism, the historical novel appeared to have been reborn as a weapon in the class struggle, a literature that was 'grand, dramatic, and rife with deep conflict in every phase', and which aimed to present 'the movement of popular life in history in its objective reality'.[8]

More broadly this socio-spatial narrative revolution was indicative of a new geographical imagination that was required to describe and map not only the transformation of relations between home and workplace, town and country, regions and nation state, but importantly between the nation state and an evolving integrated world system. Imagined or otherwise the marked development in forms of national consciousness and identity in the nineteenth century formed part of a more general cultural and ideological project that was reflected in the idea of a national architecture and literature. Fierce debates ensued on the character of the vernacular and on the meaning of national tradition and custom. Political symbolism to reinforce national identity became a powerful ideological device in which architecture and literature could merge. A prime example of this was the burial of the heroes of French literature, Zola, Hugo and Voltaire in the Panthéon, and the heralds of the modern English novel, Dickens and Hardy in Westminster Abbey.[9]

This dramatic geo-political shift in the production and representation of first national and then international space, which was driven by the first global migrations of capital and labour, was to accelerate with the pan European restructuring of cities that followed the 1848 revolutions. From hereon, whilst the European architectural and literary imagination was still formed by its immediate historical and geographical contexts, it was increasingly determined by its reflexive relationships with a global network of colonies and empires. Architecturally it was explicit in the fact that without slavery, colonial expansion and imperialism, the palatial and triumphant buildings of the Victorian city that underpinned the seemingly immutable power of capital and the British State, would have been impossible. Equally as Edward Said argued, without empire there would be no European novel as we know it, such that not only do the absences, silences and oblique references of nineteenth and early twentieth-century literature echo with the traces of other peoples and other worlds, but more obviously there would have been no *Heart of Darkness*, *Passage to India* or *Kim*.[10]

New chapters in the history of science, alienation and realism

None of these spatial revolutions could have occurred without successive scientific–technological revolutions that produced extraordinary innovations in transport, communication and our ability to manipulate and transform matter. Our knowledge of nature and the cosmos seemed somehow to expand exponentially as everything from machinery to the circulation of information and capital seemed to accelerate whilst simultaneously our conceptions of spatial distance seemed to shrink. It is a history in which the individually handcrafted books and buildings of the late eighteenth century within the space of 200 years would be exiled by the cogs of vast industrial machines pumping out bestsellers and flat pack houses in their thousands. It is a history in which the image of the machine and scientific rationality evokes a vision of both a *liberated* and a *tyrannised* humanity in equal measure, a truly explosive cocktail with which to propel both the literary and architectural imagination. But as the process of capitalist commodity production became more and more generalised, many concluded in the wake of Marx that humankind had entered a new crisis-ridden economic history in which human beings, if not completely tyrannised, had become estranged from each other, from nature and from the objects of labour.[11]

FIGURE 1.3 'The city as a complex commodity and landscape for capital accumulation', New York

It was a world that appeared to be governed by a terrifying logic; the transformation of every aspect of the built environment, every last leaf of nature, and every last atom of the human body into a gigantic extended landscape for capital accumulation. It was a ruthless and emotionless process, whereby the use value of a commodity, like the cultural and social worth of a building or book, became secondary to the maximisation of its exchange value. By the latter half of the twentieth century, many a pessimistic intellectual had concluded that the trajectory of capitalism had but one ending – the world remade into a grotesque one-dimensional complex commodity in which real freedom and liberty had been virtually extinguished.[12] Not surprisingly, such a shift in the economic and moral foundations of human life not only reinvigorated ancient literary themes such as adventure, avarice, greed and tragedy but twisted them into a new distinctly modern literature of existential angst, nihilism and alienation – the shattered mirror image of the bourgeois utopia.

Philosopher novelists were spoilt for choice in how to address this crisis of subjectivity and the psychological damage of what Simmel had detected as the deepest problem of modern life, the struggle to maintain the independence and individuality of existence in the midst of a social world in which the circulation of money had transformed life into an 'arithmetical problem and formula' (Simmel 1997: 69). They could return to Hegel's 'Alienation of the Spirit' and Marx's 'Estrangement from our Species Being' or engage with Nietzsche's critique of nihilism, a mourning for a world in which we were simply 'weary *of man*'.[13] Alternatively the novelist could travel through the repressed memories of Freud or stumble through Sartre's discourse on Nothingness. In short modernity had brought in its wake a rich array of new theoretical ideas about how to understand humankind.

Again this created an astonishing new set of characters in bizarre locations, such that the twentieth century began to resonate with tales of outsiders, non-conformists and deviants. We could now descend into the courtrooms of incomprehensible bureaucracies in Kafka's *Trial* (1925) or climb to a sanatorium with a character stricken by a deathly comedy in Mann's *Magic Mountain* (1924). We could take Bataille's lead and insert a bull's eye into an orifice or visit Ellison's *Invisible Man* (1952) residing in a darkened basement where the electricity supply has been cut. We could flee the droogs stalking the concrete underpasses of Burgess's *Clockwork Orange* (1962) or hallucinate in the warped zone of Burroughs's *Naked Lunch* (1959). And as the millennium dawned Cipriano Algor travels with his daughter to enjoy the good life in a fully serviced condominium fitted with all the most up-to-date labour-saving technology and comfort that modern architecture can offer; only to realise as he had suspected all along, that it wasn't paradise, but the end of civilisation, a suspicion that is confirmed when he discovers Plato's cave in the basement (Saramago 2003).

Wherever in fact we look into the history of either literature or architecture it is self evident that the writer or the architect, knowingly or not, is engaged in a constant dialogue with the social world. There may not be any singular process of determination in the production of literary and architectural ideas, but the writer and the architect are nevertheless immersed in the swirling vortex of philosophical tensions, political, economic and social relations that define any historical moment, and which are impossible to evade or ignore.[14] It could not be otherwise for two simple reasons: no architect or novelist can stand outside of history, and the human mind cannot imagine anything completely and unutterably new with regards to the organisation of time, space or social life. The *novum*, or rather the idea of complete novelty, is a myth in that what might appear as new and innovative is always built upon accumulated knowledge. This goes as much for the 6,000-year history of building construction and technology as it does for the development of language. Even the literature of the absurd, the surreal and of science fiction, that stretch and deform concepts of social reality and which superficially transport us to other worlds governed by different chronotopic rules can be thought of as narratives of an exaggerated present that explore themes however alien or otherworldly that are prefigured in the world that exists.[15]

It is in any case somewhat absurd to think that the content of works of art, such as a novel or an architectural drawing or photograph of an urban scene can ever be real in the same sense as social reality.[16] Like Adorno, Bakhtin argued that,

> There is a sharp and categorical boundary line between the actual world of representation and the world represented in the work. We must never forget this, we must never confuse – as been done up to now and is still often done – the represented world with the world outside the text (naïve realism) …
>
> *Bakhtin 1986: 49*[17]

Although this may be true, by the same token, all works of art are necessarily an ideological engagement with the reality of social existence, however partial, camouflaged, or distorted this relationship may be.[18]

Hostile to the disintegrating montage tricks of modernism, Lukacs was in no doubt as to what kind of art and literature was best able to achieve this, when he wrote that, 'only the major realists are capable of forming an avant-garde'.[19] However we can just as easily turn this statement on its head so that it reads: 'only the modernist avant-garde is capable of producing a genuinely *critical* realism'.[20] Such a proposition would argue that literary modernism like Dos Passos' *U.S.A.* that combines layered individual stories, newsreels and 'streams of consciousness', political satire like Bulgakov's *The Master and Margarita*, Popova's abstract *Space– Time Construction* paintings, Kurt Schwitters' *Merzbau* constructions and Vertov's cinematic montage, *Man with a Movie Camera*, were far more convincing representations of the real experience of urban modernity as something fractured, disjointed and explosive, than the banal idea of providing what purports to be a real and accurate portrait of the city through conventional figurative methods. But it was exactly this type of vulgar realism that was to triumph in the dictatorships of the 1930s. The German propaganda machine and the commissars of the USSR required an art, architecture and literature 'that the people could understand' and identify with. The modernist avant-garde was exiled and deeply reactionary cultural programmes were launched that were constructed around hagiographic mythologies whose only reality was the 'realism of social deception'.[21]

Chronotopic fusion and anthropomorphism

If, as Franco Moretti suggests, it is only in recent times that the geographical, spatial and architectural dimensions of literature have been acknowledged as a primary force in the development of the novel, it is if nothing else strange to say the least. It seems somehow obvious 'that locality serves as the starting point for the creative imagination' and that 'without a certain kind of space, a certain kind of story is simply impossible'.[22] In fact it is probably safe to say that there is no work of literature that does not have some spatio-temporal dimension nor any building that doesn't possess a plot. Both architects and novelists in this sense are jugglers of space, time and narrative.

FIGURE 1.4 'Time and space take on flesh', Dostoevsky in front of the Lenin Library, Moscow

Zola could never have written *The Kill* (1871) if Napoleon the Third had not contracted Baron von Haussmann to bulldoze old Paris and open it up to the urban speculator, sightseer, *flâneur* and machine gun. Dickens would have been unable to drag us into the seamy underworld and urban poverty of London, if enclosures had not forced agricultural workers off the land, and if an unregulated factory system, anti-combination laws and a speculative house-building industry had not been unleashed on an unsuspecting urban population. On closer analysis it seems both predictable and inevitable that canonical novels, iconic buildings and urban developments operate side by side in a symbiotic relationship, and the more in fact we look, the stronger and clearer this interdependence between time, space and narrative becomes. Epic works like Naguib Mahfouz's masterly exposition of the tensions of modern urban Egypt in the *Cairo Trilogy* (1956–7), played out on the streets of the old Islamic quarter, naturally emerged out of the explosive collision between the old world and the modern, religious faith and secularism, and between the country's colonial past and post-colonial future. Equally the narrative of Chinua Achebe's *African Trilogy* (1958–64) is inconceivable outside of the ideological consequences of the impact of the political and urban strategies of British Imperial rule on indigenous patterns of social life and spatial organisation. Then there are authors whose almost entire creative output is built upon particular spaces and narratives of urban development. J. G. Ballard's novels like *Drowned World* (1962), *Concrete Island* (1974), *High Rise* (1975) and *Super-Cannes* (2000) are as much about the social contradictions thrown up by late twentieth-century forms of urbanisation – the motorway, the tower block, the shopping mall and the fortified condominium – as anything else.

On occasions the chronotopic character of a novel can be so powerful that it assumes the identity of a character. To paraphrase Bakhtin, time really does thicken, take on flesh, and become artistically visible, just as space becomes charged and responsive to the movements of time, plot and history. Indeed, one of the reasons why novels like Bely's *Petersburg* (1913) and Joyce's *Ulysses* (1922) have become modern icons is because of the manner in which their 'cut-up' narrative techniques somehow mimic the frenetic disjunctures and fragmentary experience of urban modernity. St Petersburg and Dublin seem literally to pulse with life.[23] In fact so dramatic are the architectural and spatial metaphors in Bely, and so evocative his depiction of modern life – the rush, the speed, the noise, the crowd, the geometry – that the city becomes an individual in its own right and assumes anthropomorphic qualities, as if it is heaving, breathing and struggling for breath; a city in which 'The sidewalks conversed in whispers and shuffled beneath the gang of stone giants – the houses' (Bely 1983: 272).[24] A few years later, Yevgeny Zamyatin was to push this relationship between city and text even further. In his novel *We,* the structure, narrative form and metaphors are created through a haunting and fetishised scientific and technological language that mirrors the rhetoric of many a modernist architectural manifesto. As if mimicking Le Corbusier, the engineer D-503 arrives at the grand mechanical ballet of the magical Integral that he finds utterly beautiful. Why? Because of its 'non-free movement, because all the fundamental significance of the dance lies precisely in its aesthetic subjugation, its ideal non-freedom' (Zamyatin 1993: 5). What is particularly remarkable about this short, highly influential novel is that long before the Frankfurt school, Zamyatin had alerted us to the dangers of the type of instrumental rationalism that was to plague concepts of both urban planning and social progress during the course of the twentieth century in both east and west.[25]

But it is not just in individual novels that we find this chronotopic fusion. There are whole genres that are predicated on the pre-existence of particular building typologies that frame, determine and spatially lock the narrative. The modern carceral novel that would include canonical texts such as Genet's *Miracle of the Rose* (1946), Koestler's *Darkness at Noon* (1940), Nabakov's *Invitation to a Beheading* (1936) and Kafka's *Trial* (1925) owe their origins not only to the invention of self-reproducing modern bureaucracies but to the architectural legacy of Jeremy Bentham's plan for the ideal Panoptican and Ledoux's scheme for a perfect surveillance city.[26] Equally the modern twentieth-century crime thriller is unimaginable without the modern city's socially heterotopic estates, slums, mansions, alleys, bars and clubs – the subterranean passages and labyrinths of streets and buildings that make up the 'noir' city and that are naturally predisposed to a 'literary genre concerned with revealing secrets' (Frisby 2007: 99). In fact not only does the city 'always remain to be detected', but a city only really becomes a city in the popular imagination when it has its own dedicated crime novel and private detective, such that the identity of the former is entirely wrapped up with the other. Imperial London is as unimaginable without Sherlock Holmes as post-war Los Angeles would be without James Elroy and Walter Mosley, Chicago without Paretsky's V.I. Warshawski, Barcelona without Montalban's Pepe Carvalho, and Edinburgh without Rankin's D.I. Rebus.

Optimistic architects and despairing novelists

This brings us to one of the most interesting features of the discussion about architecture, literature and modernity in the twentieth century, which is the often-striking disjuncture between the ways the architect and the writer depict the modern city. The architect, if he or she is to escape the prison of representation, is faced with the task of trying to mend, ameliorate or transcend the contradictions of the capitalist city. Whereas the writer, unencumbered by the practical tasks of physically altering material reality, is free to depict, represent and play with the contradictions thrown up by the instrumental acts of architect, urban designer, developer and politician. This dialectic has produced at times quite extraordinary urban and anti-urban visions, and some of the most powerful literary evocations of architecture and the city are historically and thematically linked to utopian and dystopian literature. For

FIGURE 1.5 'The collapsing solution to the modern city', Glasgow

example, two of the great utopian texts, More's *Utopia* (1516) and Bacon's *New Atlantis* (1627), are meaningless without the concretisation of their social vision in their respective cities, whose organisation and architectural ambition prefigure many of the recurring themes of contemporary urban life.

In fact it is a feature of most dystopian and utopian literature that it uses technology and architecture as a narrative device to reinforce the political critique of social progress that all such novels share. In the machinery of orthogonal grid and gleaming tower, the architect sees the prospect of civilisation emerging from the ashes of the old city. The writer however gazes out with suspicion and trepidation and sees a world bereft of adjectives inhabited by numbered individuals in precarious technological landscapes. There was an historical inevitability about this apparent paradox. Architects confronted with resolving the environmental and physical consequences of war, revolution, poverty and urban migration naturally sought radical solutions and projected ideal cities in which socio-spatial order and its technological organisation was largely seen as benign and benevolent. It reflects the enduring belief amongst many architects, urban planners and politicians, that has continued unabated from the urban improvement acts of the nineteenth century, that it is possible through the rational ordering of space to eliminate social disorder and indeed crime. It is a narrative that connects Fourier's Phalanstery of the eighteenth century to Hilbersheimer's project for Berlin (1928), and on to Bruce's Plan for Glasgow (1945). But it doesn't stop there. It is a project that continued through the 1960s and '70s with the industrialisation of building production and the radical restructuring of cities, and it finds a new home in the contemporary privatisation of urban space and the flight of the 'concerned' citizen to softly militarised condominiums and estates 'where safety is assured'.

As if in a mirror reflection, this working out of architectural reason was paralleled within literature with markedly different results. In the dystopian novel the development of the modern city is represented more as a 'journey into fear' (Jameson 2005). The city is panoptic, planned around wide, brilliantly illuminated streets with no dark corners and passages, and saturated with invasive forms of surveillance and control. Technology has not led to the liberation of human beings from need as dreamt of by the architect but has become an instrument of domination. It is a literary journey that starts with the sparkling metal and glass crystal palace of Wells' *The Sleeper Awakes* (1910), passes through the adjective-free One-State of Zamyatin, marches down the 'vitrified streets' of Huxley's *Brave New World* (1932), hides in the slums and glittering pyramids of Orwell's *1984* (1949), traverses the hauntingly familiar city of Padukgrad in Nabokov's *Bend Sinister* (1947), before arriving at the deeply unsettling, 'end of time' urban nightmares of Ferenc Karinthy's *Metropole* (1970), Ballard's *High Rise* (1975) and Saramago's *Blindness* (1995). It is a literary voyage that begins with scientific delight and ends in stifling claustrophobia. As in debates about science fiction, the literary representation of uncanny, strange and disturbing cities is as much about the political and social critique of everyday life as our transportation to future and imaginary worlds. In this sense such novels can be understood both as a warning about the dangers of dictatorship and bureaucracy and more generally as a critique of the form and socio-spatial organisation of the modern City.

In all of this it is tempting to see the spatial imagination of the writer and the architect as mutually exclusive and antagonistic, as if one of the novelist's roles is to function as a corrective to the contradictions thrown up by modern urbanisation and to critique the dangerous fantasies of architects. After all, Ludwig Hilbersheimer believed that 'calculation and measurement must impose itself as the master. In this way "chaos is forced to take form: logic, clarity, mathematics, law", that is the future'.[27] To which Zamyatin with a parodic swipe replied: 'Some day, an exact formula for the law of revolution will be established. And in this formula, nations, classes, stars – and books – will be expressed as numerical qualities' (Zamyatin 1991: 108). This meeting never took place. But when I imagine a television chat show where iconic dystopian novelists and utopian urban planners sit face to face in conversation, it normally becomes hostile. However, a more productive way of understanding the relationship between the imagination of the novelist and the architect–urbanist is to see them as indispensable to each other, such that when viewed together they enrich and deepen our understanding of the development of the twentieth-century city.

Notes

1 See also Marshall Berman's *All that is Solid Melts into Air* (1982), an inspirational book that is probably one of the best explorations of the relationship between the experience of urban modernity and literature.

2 Simmel commented that: 'The psychological foundation, upon which the metropolitan individuality is erected, is the intensification of emotional life due to the swift and continuous shift of external and internal stimuli' (Simmel 1997: 70)

3 Bakhtin suggests in his essay *Forms of Time and of the Chronotope* that it is not only through the space-time organisation of the novel that a narrative unfolds, but also that it is through chronotopic differences that we can distinguish between literary genres. 'Time, as it were, thickens, takes on flesh, becomes artistically visible; likewise, space becomes charged and responsive to the movements of time, plot and history' (Bakhtin 1981: 83). Another way of understanding this is in terms of the geographical focus of a novel. If for example the aim of classical nineteenth-century realism was in the words of Lukacs to 'portray the total context of social life', then it was inevitable at some point that narratives would shift from rural to urban locations. See for example Lukacs (1989: 242).

4 Alongside Lefebvre, David Harvey has been instrumental in injecting a spatial and geographical narrative to history. See for instance, *Consciousness and the Urban Experience* (1985), *Spaces of Hope* (2000), *The Condition of Post-modernity* (1989) and *Paris; City of Modernity* (2006).

5 The practice of measure and value was replaced by a new system where prices were agreed in advance. Coupled with the professionalisation of both surveying and architecture, the building industry was soon unrecognisable, dominated on one side by a new class of contractors and master builders, and on the other by what was in the first half of the nineteenth century the largest and most militant section of the new industrial working class. Such changes represented a wholesale transformation in the social and technological basis of building production, a process that was famously described at the end of the century in Robert Tressell's *Ragged Trousered Philanthropists* (1914). For three histories of the nineteenth-century construction industry, see Price (1980), Postgate (1923) and Powell (1982).

6 Such as the Peabody Trust housing schemes and company towns like Saltaire and Port Sunlight.

7 This reached its zenith in the work of the Soviet avant-garde, which was encapsulated in the concepts of the Social Condenser and New Way of Life (Noviye Beat). For a survey and analysis of early Soviet architecture see Khan-Magomedov (1983) and Cooke (1995).

8 Lukacs (1989: 203 and 334). Lukacs argued that the novel had retreated from any engagement with the broad sweep of history – turning history instead into 'private' narratives about the deeds of great men and social elites. Although his notion of 'mirroring objective reality' was according to Adorno and Bakhtin impossible, it does not negate the crucial role that this particular brand of literary social realism was to play, not least in the suggestion that it was instrumental in the development of sociology and the social sciences in the twentieth century.

9 For two important books on the relationship between history, nationalism, literature and culture in general, see Anderson (2006) and Hobsbawm and Ranger (2010).

10 One of the central themes in Said's work is the idea of a reflexive relationship between coloniser and colonised, such that cultural ideas and for instance architectural motifs and details from the colonised country feed back into the building language of the coloniser. He commented that 'Without Empire … there is no European novel as we know it, and indeed if we study the impulses giving rise to it, we shall see the far from accidental convergence between the patterns of narrative authority constitutive of the novel on one hand, and, on the other, a complex ideological configuration underlying the tendency to imperialism' (Said 1994: 82).

11 That was first described by Hegel in *Phenomenology of Spirit* (1977), and Marx, in the *Philosophical and Economic Manuscripts* (1981).
12 See for instance classic texts from the 1960s such as Debord (1999) and Marcuse (1964).
13 'Here precisely is what has become a fatality for Europe – together with the fear of man we have also lost our love of him, our reverence for him, our hopes for him, even the will to him. The sight of man now makes us weary – what is nihilism today if it is not *that*? – We are weary *of man*' (Nietzsche 2000: 480).
14 As Bakhtin put it: 'The novel orchestrates all its themes, the totality of the world of objects and ideas depicted and expressed in it, by means of the social diversity of speech types (*raznorechiye*) and by the differing individual voices that flourish under such conditions' (Bakhtin 1981: 263).
15 For an exploration of the concept of the *novum* and the idea of 'cognitive estrangement' in relation to forms of literary representation, see Suvin (1979).
16 It was a thesis reiterated by Adorno in the classic debate between Adorno, Benjamin, Bloch *et al.*, *Aesthetics and Politics in German Marxism* (1986: 159).
17 That continues 'nor confuse the listener or reader of multiple periods, recreating and renewing the text, with the passive listener or reader of one's own time (which leads to dogmatism in interpretation and evaluation)'.
18 Architectural and literary representation can reflect the world, anticipate, ignore, predict and act upon it, but they are inescapably in Bakhtin's words 'ideologically saturated'. See Bakhtin, M. M., *Speech Genres and Other Late Essays* (1986). For introductions to the debate about the nature of ideology see Marx and Engels (1985), Eagleton (1992) and Zizek (1994). For an earlier work by Eagleton in which he sketches out a theory of the 'science of the text', see Eagleton (1988).
19 Lukacs, Georg, *Realism in the balance,* in Adorno *et al.* (1986: 43–8).
20 It is worth remembering that Lukacs was not alone in his hostility to the 'conscious subjectivism' of the avant-garde. Lenin found Dada largely incomprehensible, and Trotsky not only attacked Futurism but also described one of the greats of Russian modernist literature Andre Bely as a corpse. See for instance Trotsky (1972: 55).
21 With the defeat and exile of the avant-garde in the USSR, art, literature and architecture were required to reflect the objective 'reality' of history and the everyday lives of peasants and workers, whilst somehow patriotically representing the ideological worldview of the Party. See Charley (1996: 19–37).
22 Bakhtin tells us: 'Time and space merge here into an inseparable unity, both in the plot itself and in its individual images. In the majority of cases, a definite and absolutely concrete locality serves as the starting point form the creative imagination. But this is not an abstract landscape, imbued with the mood of the contemplator – no, this is a piece of human history, historical time condensed in space. Therefore, the plot (the sum of depicted events) and the characters do not enter it from the outside, are not invented to fit the landscape, but are unfolded in it as though they were present from the very beginning' Bakhtin (1986: 49). See also Moretti (2009: 35ff).
23 Harding comments that: 'The modern cities of developing western nations were now figured as dynamic and kaleidoscopic environments, radically new and shifting signs of discontinuity that evoked disassociation in the midst of community: Eliot's fragmented London; Bely's mysterious Petersburg; Sue's surrealistic Paris; Dos Passos' protean Manhattan; and Joyce's transhistorical Dublin' (Harding 2003: 11).
24 'The sidewalks conversed in whispers and shuffled beneath the gang of stone giants – the houses. Prospect after prospect flew to meet them. And the spherical surface of the planet seemed embraced, as in serpent coils, by blackish gray cubes of houses. And the network of parallel prospects expanded into the abysses of the universe, in surfaces of squares and cubes: one square per solid citizen.' It is an anthropomorphism that is similar to the merging of buildings and bodies that Raymond Williams suggests is a characteristic feature of Dickens's novels.

25 A tendency that Adorno and Horkheimer would later explore in *The Dialectic of the Enlightenment* (1989).

26 Not forgetting the seminal essay by Foucault, *Discipline and Punish* (1987).

27 See for instance, Hilbersheimer, L. (1927) *Großstadtarchitektur*, Stuttgart: Julius Hoffman and (1925) *Großstadtbauten*, Hannover: Aposs.

References

Adorno, B. *et al.*, (1986), *Aesthetics and Politics in German Marxism,* London: Verso.

Adorno, T. and Horkheimer, M. (1989), *The Dialectic of the Enlightenment*, London: Verso.

Anderson, B. (2006), *Imagined Communities – Reflections on the Origin and Spread of Nationalism*, London: Verso.

Bakhtin, M. M. (1981) *The Dialogic Imagination*, Austin: University of Texas.

Bakhtin, M. M. (1986), *Speech Genres and Other Late Essays*, Austin: University of Texas.

Baudelaire, C. (2006), 'The Painter of Modern Life', in *Selected Writings on Art and Literature*, London: Penguin.

Bely, A. (1983), *Petersburg*, London: Penguin.

Berman, M. (1982), *All that is Solid Melts into Air*, London: Verso.

Charley, J. (1996), 'The Making of an Imperial City', *Journal of Architecture*, Volume 1, No 1, R.I.B.A, London: Chapman and Hall.

Cooke, C. (1995), *Russian Avant-Garde: Theories of Art, Architecture and the City*, London: Academy Editions.

Debord, G. (1999), *Society of the Spectacle*, London: Verso.

Dostoevsky, F. (1989), *Crime and Punishment,* Moscow: Raduga Publishers.

Eagleton, T. (1988), *Criticism and Ideology, a Study in Marxist literary theory*, London: Verso.

Eagleton, T. (1992), *Ideology. An Introduction*, London: Verso.

Foucault, M. (1987) *Discipline and Punish*, London: Penguin.

Frisby, D. (2007), *Cityscapes of Modernity*, Cambridge: Polity Press.

Harding, D. (2003), *Writing the City – Urban Visions and Literary Modernism*, London: Routledge.

Harvey, D. (1985), *Consciousness and the Urban Experience*, Baltimore: Johns Hopkins University Press.

Harvey, D. (1989), *The Condition of Post-modernity*, Oxford: Blackwell.

Harvey, D. (2000), *Spaces of Hope*, Edinburgh: Edinburgh University Press.

Harvey, D. (2006), *Paris; City of Modernity*, London: Routledge.

Hegel, G. W. F. (1977), *Phenomenology of Spirit*, Oxford: Oxford University Press.

Hobsbawm, E. and Ranger, T. (eds) (2010), *The Invention of Tradition*, Cambridge: Canto Press.

Karinthy, F. (2008), *Metropole*, London: Telegram.

Khan-Magomedov, S. (1983), *Pioneers of Soviet Architecture*, London: Thames and Hudson.

Lefebvre, H. (1991), *The Production of Space*, Oxford: Blackwell.

Lefebvre, H. (1997), *Writings on Cities*, Oxford: Blackwell.

Lefebvre, H. (2003), *The Urban Revolution*, Minneapolis: University of Minnesota Press.

Lukacs, G. (1986) 'Realism in the balance', in Adorno *et al. Aesthetics and Politics*, London: Verso.

Lukacs, G. (1983), *History and Class Consciousness*, London: Merlin Press.

Lukacs, G. (1989), *The Historical Novel*, London: Merlin Press.

Marcuse, H. (1964), *One Dimensional Man*, London: Ark.

Marx, K. and Engels, F. (1980), *The Communist Manifesto*, London: Penguin Classics.

Marx, K. and Engels, F. (1985), *The German Ideology*, London: Lawrence and Wishart.

Marx, K. (1990), *Capital Volume I*, London: Penguin Classics.

Marx, K. (1981), *Philosophical and Economic Manuscripts*, Moscow: Progress Publishers.

Moretti, F. (2009), *Atlas of the European Novel 1800–1900*, London: Verso.

Nietzsche, F. (2000), 'The Genealogy of Morals', in *Basic Writings of Nietzsche*, Kaufmann, W. (ed.), New York: Modern Library.

Postgate, R. W. (1923), *The Builders' History*, London: The National Federation of Building Trade Operatives.

Powell, C. G. (1982), *An Economic History of the British Building Industry, 1815–1979*, London: Methuen.

Price, R. (1980), *Masters, Unions and Men*, Cambridge: Cambridge University Press.

Said, E. (1994), *Culture and Imperialism*, London: Vintage.

Saramago, J. (2003), *The Cave*, London: Vintage Classics.

Simmel, G. (1997), 'The metropolis and mental life', 1903, republished in Leach, N. (ed.) *Rethinking Architecture – A Reader in Cultural Theory*, London: Routledge.

Suvin, D. (1979), *Metamorphoses of Science Fiction*, New Haven: Yale University Press.

Tressell, R. (1997), *Ragged Trousered Philanthropists*, London: Flamingo.

Trotsky, L. (1972), *Literature and Revolution*, Ann Arbor: University of Michigan Press.

Williams, R. (1985), *The Country and the City*, London: Hogarth Press.

Zamyatin, Y. (1991), 'Literature, Revolution, Entropy', in *Soviet Heretic*, London: Quartet Books.

Zamyatin, Y. (1993), *We*, London: Penguin.

Zizek, S. (ed.), (1994), *Mapping Ideology*, London: Verso.

All photos by the author.

PART I

Memory, nation, identity

2

REMEMBERING AND FORGETTING

Private and public lives in the imagined nation

Sarah Edwards

The essays in the first section of this volume re-visit the evocative and contentious themes of memory, nation and identity to explore the inter-connections between literary and architectural narratives of the modern city during the earlier twentieth century. They consider how maps, guidebooks and treatises have employed literary discourses to shape architectural visions of the nation; and how fictional works have drawn on theories of interior design and civic planning to represent both the colonisation of a foreign land and individual attempts to preserve an 'authentic' national identity within it. These essays, then, examine a range of individual and collective constructions of national identity and the ways in which these are inflected by familial, gendered, classed and civic identities: the roles of daughter, town planner and novelist. The authors consider how political and cultural ideas – from mesmerism to school reform, from Hindu nationalism to the practice of tramping – informed concepts of nationhood and nation-building in the aftermath of the Great War and the dismantling of empire. Furthermore, they also re-visit the suburban home and examine how conceptions of public and private have been constructed through transmissions between – as well as exclusions from – other national cultures and literatures. All of the essays trace the retrospective construction of memory in texts and spaces – the material traces of the past and the traces of past selves in the novel, the autobiography and the diary – and the roles of remembering and forgetting in the constitution of identity.

Many theorists who have analysed the role of memory in the development of identities over time have emphasised the visual, spatial and material dimensions of human recollections. For example, Aristotle's *On Memory and Recollection* suggested that each memory was composed of a visual image, modified by an emotional response; John Locke's *An Essay Concerning Human Understanding* (1690) suggested

FIGURE 2.1 Multi-culturalism?

Source: J. Charley

that memory could be defined as the 'Storehouse' of our ideas; while Sigmund Freud's model for the human mind, whose repressed unconscious memories were exhibited in dreams that must be translated into everyday language, also suggested that the mind was comparable to a text with its own internal structures.[1] This imagery of layers also suggests the multiple and unstable nature of human identity. Famously, in Marcel Proust's *Remembrance of Things Past* (1913–27), the narrator distinguishes between 'involuntary memory' (habitual learned movements, such as eating) and 'voluntary memory' (personal memories buried in the unconscious mind and linked to places). This work, then, is notable for its self-conscious use of literary devices like metaphor and metonymy, which highlight visual and material stimuli, such as the narrator's blissful, synaesthetic recollection of a summer's day which is characterised by sunshine and insects.[2]

During the final decades of the twentieth century, memory studies emerged as an important field of academic enquiry across a number of disciplines, including literature, architecture, cognitive science, urban studies, geography and social psychology.[3] This scholarly interest was paralleled by the 'memory boom' outside the academy, in the form of the heritage industry, which has also been well-documented by scholars.[4] While the stated reasons for this memory work are always clear, and range from commemoration and the re-building of communities following major cultural traumas such as the Holocaust and 9/11, the preservation of local communities through living museums in the face of unwelcome re-development, or the re-discovery and exploration of neglected working-class or ethnic histories, some questions persistently remain. Who is remembering, why, and why now? What form does this remembrance take – a monument, a memoir? In the narrative of remembrance, which events have been included and which have been forgotten or erased? In this section, Victoria Rosner's essay describes how the novelist Doris Lessing re-visits her childhood home in colonial Rhodesia to witness both the erasure of the house and a local black man's denial that the house ever existed, which in turn repeats the colonial erasure of native architecture. This example illustrates, then, how architectural, oral and literary narratives intersect to produce memories. The material traces of the house, and of the man's voice, are joined with Lessing's perspective as a white colonial woman to produce an autobiography where the structures of the house are ambivalently represented as a site of female freedom and of colonial oppression. When Lessing later experiments with the voices of her parents, however, these material symbols come to represent a different chain of associations.

Benedict Anderson's seminal work *Imagined Communities* (1983) provided a foundation for considering how groups nationalise themselves as communities, while later work on collective memory is often centred on 'memory places' or 'sites of memory' which bear witness to the conflicts of the twentieth century, such as the Jewish Museum in Berlin or the Menin Gate Memorial to the Missing in Ypres. These monuments are erected by the state to materially embody collective memories, thus transforming them into officially sanctioned histories. As the recent outcry over the possible building of a mosque near Ground Zero demonstrates, monuments inevitably sanction versions of national identity, which are exclusionary. Furthermore, the meanings of memorials shift over time, as new generations develop new relationships, new rituals and new narratives about the site – as Lessing represents in her autobiographies, ordinary houses can become monumental in significance and can then be ignored or destroyed. Canonical literary works are also commemorative sites: writing in 1919 in the aftermath of the Great War, T. S. Eliot explicitly likened the great literary work to a monument whose existence altered the inter-textual relationships between other works (Eliot 2001). Eliot's idea has an 'inter-generic' resonance, if we consider how narratives shape the meanings of buildings. However, Eliot's concept of the 'great tradition' shores up official histories, in this case the dominant influence of the literary canon. Literary forms which have until recently been denied the status of literature – such as diaries and autobiographies – frequently relate alternative histories.

Indeed, much recent work on urban memory (for example, Mark Crinson's *Urban Memory: History and Amnesia in the Modern City*, 2005) examines literary texts which blur the generic boundaries between novel and autobiography. Life-writings (biographies, autobiographies, diaries, letters) are fundamentally inter-textual and foreground both the limitations and distortions of individual memory and the ways in which history is shaped into narratives which employ fictional devices. They have performed the function of monuments (the recording of exemplary lives in Victorian biography) and of eyewitness accounts to wartime experiences (Primo Levi, *Survival in Auschwitz*, 1947; Vera Brittain, *Testament of Youth*, 1933). More recently, postmodern writers have utilised the form of the fictional autobiography to indicate that individual memory is itself a text shaped by inter-textual references from numerous texts and eras and is seeking a coherent narrative which will reconstruct and attempt to resolve the conflicts and traumas of the earlier twentieth century. Hence, writers on the Holocaust (W. G. Sebald, *Austerlitz*, 2001), familial bereavement (Paul Auster, *The Invention of Solitude*, 1982) and amnesia (Douglas Cooper, *Amnesia*, 1992) wander in posturban cityscapes which, in their selective quoting of the past – the collage of village areas, historic interiors and loft conversions utilising the styles of many different eras – mirror their internal sense of instability, absence and disorientation. The autobiographical element of these works is, then, an important political act. It not only challenges the demarcations of history, memory and fiction but emphasises the vital role of writing in narrativising and easing traumatic pasts. Rosner's essay confronts this issue in its exploration of Doris Lessing's most recent work, *Alfred and Emily* (2008), which she describes as 'a generic hybrid, a blend of memoir and counterhistory'. By writing both the real and imagined histories of her parents' lives and houses, Lessing is able to narrate the untold private aspects of their characters that might have been realised in an alternate historical reality and through this act she partially resolves her own traumatic history as a daughter.

Marianne Hirsch's concept of 'postmemory' develops the relationship between individual and collective memory further, by suggesting that individuals may be haunted by a past they have not experienced but which has been transferred by family members and their objects, such as photographs. Hirsch's theory might be extended to include books, both as literary texts and as material objects attached to familiar places (Hirsch 2007). Life-writings, in particular, are often imagined in connection with their place of origin and acquire talismanic status: for example, *The Diary of Anne Frank* (1947) is displayed in Frank's hiding-place (now a museum) in Amsterdam. This diary, which draws strongly on images of spatial confinement in the Nazi-occupied city, is both a resonant symbol of Jewish trauma and resistance and a record of an adolescent's developing identi(ties). By choosing to write in a genre that requires continuous recording of daily experiences, Anne is able to reflect on her earlier entries and assess her changing sense of national identity, as the identities of German and Jew become mutually exclusive; but this awareness of her increasingly restricted existence is measured by her gradual imprisonment inside the annexe.

The role of literary influence and collective identity in the formation of urban memory is further explored in Brian Ward's essay, which engages with a contemporary vision of the early twentieth-century city, Raymond Unwin's *Town Planning in Practice* (1909). Anthony Vidler has claimed that memory traces in the modern city enabled citizens to identify with the city as a political, cultural and social entity and indeed Ward's essay considers how Unwin was inspired by similar discourses of national unity (Vidler 1994). However, he also demonstrates that Unwin's understanding of urban memory was influenced by the very different conception of space found in nineteenth-century mesmerism, whereby 'travelling clairvoyants' defeated time–space relationships by entering minds, private homes, past and future eras at will. Like the figure of the Romantic poet, Unwin's town planner was imagined as a 'democratic' prophet whose identity became fused with the will of the common man.

Ward's work is not centred, then, on a 'literary' text and thereby challenges the classification of texts as literary and non-literary, through his productive reading of the range of textual influences that informed Unwin's re-invention of English urban identity. Ward uncovers a literary lineage that spans the transcendental poetry of American Walt Whitman, the work of English socialist Edward Carpenter, contemporary journals and Unwin's own diaries. By tracing these influences, he examines the textual identity of the town planner at the turn of the century and considers how and why he became embodied in the figure of the tramp, which was itself shaped by literary depictions. In this case, the diary functions as a record of the ways in which Unwin's personal identity was bound up with his political and pro-fessional affiliations – when, for example, he conflates his desire for the addressee (his fiancée) with his passion for the English landscape. But, as this example indi-cates, Unwin's self-construction both as town planner and as diarist is informed by literary strategies which include Morrisian images of urban cleanliness and beauty.

Indeed, Unwin's idealistic vision of an urban community in which traumatic memories of the divided Victorian city would be forgotten and all classes would live peaceably together recalls many literary, rural and nostalgic elements of turn-of-the-century socialism. The Garden City movement, which Unwin influenced significantly, sought to re-conceptualise the relationship between urban and rural spaces by its use of greenbelts, pieces of nature that were strictly controlled through civic planning and design.[5] Such ideals are embodied in William Morris's uto-pian vision of the future city, *News from Nowhere* (1890), in which the Victorian first-person narrator similarly becomes a representative of social unease and subse-quently the vehicle for social revolution. These elements of nostalgic radicalism are also embodied in many figures from Edwardian literature and social commentary: Robert Blatchford, whose *Merrie England* (1893) aligned socialism with an 'authen-tic' rural Englishness, supported the rights of common people to 'tramp' across the land, while in Kenneth Grahame's *The Wind in the Willows* (1908), Mr Toad of Toad Hall is a rich property owner who nevertheless aligns himself with marginal figures in his pursuit of open-air freedom and escape, even disguising himself as a washer woman.[6]

The scholarly study of nostalgia has until recently been the poor relation of mem-ory studies, castigated as a sentimental, conservative and regressive emotion in contrast to the knowing, self-aware and ironic tone of academic scholarship (Wright 1985; Hewison 1987). However, more recent work by scholars such as Anthony Vidler (*The Architectural Uncanny*, 1992) and Svetlana Boym (*The Future of Nostalgia*, 2001) has re-focussed attention on its importance for narratives of urban memory. The word 'nostalgia' signifies the loss of home and it was during the later nineteenth century that the concept of nostalgia gradually shifted from spatial imaginings of a lost place to temporal imaginings of a lost era.[7] Yet, although the sentiment of nostalgia is often connected with a rural, pre-industrial Golden Age personified by the English country house in works including E. M. Forster's *Howards End* (1910) or Rebecca West's *The Return of the Soldier* (1918), much twentieth-century fiction explores nostalgia for urban landscapes. Elizabeth Bowen's *The Heat of the Day* (1948) utilises modernist techniques of stream-of-consciousness and everyday imagery of trains and disappearing landmarks to convey the transient yet exciting quality of wartime London, when women have greater freedom to wander the city for adventures and citizens experience a sense of collective purpose. Indeed, Fred Davis in *Yearning for Yesterday* (1979) theorised nostalgia as a restitutive link by which people can preserve their identities during periods of major social upheaval, such as accelerating urbanisation or wartime. Boym, who writes principally about post-Communist cityscapes, uses the imagery of war when she describes 'restorative nostalgia' which reconstructs 'rituals of ... homeland' to restore an exact likeness of the past and 'reflective nostalgia' which 'cherishes shattered fragments of memory' but accepts the necessity of social and technological change (Boym 2001: 49). Even the country-house novelists of the earlier twentieth century engage in this reflective nostalgia, since most of these novels debate the social and cultural impact of encroaching towns and incipient suburbanisation. Many novels, including *Howards End* and Virginia Woolf's *Orlando* (1928), feature scenes of restoration and house-cleaning to accommodate modern, unconventional families. *The Return of the Soldier*, published in the immediate aftermath of the Great War, portrays its shell-shocked title character refusing to make modern improvements to the estate. His amnesia, which leaves him mentally stranded in 1901, becomes a metaphor for the foolishness of disengaging from modernity.

The essays by Victoria Rosner and Mark Campbell both engage with modern re-workings of domestic space. Rosner shows how Lessing's mother desperately clings to her English middle-class identity in the African bush by re-creating the material and ideological features of the suburban house. Throughout the second half of the nineteenth century, suburbia came to dominate both the physical and imaginary landscapes of Britain, producing new configurations of space, new forms of community and new social stereotypes. A product of industrialisation and urbanisation, and the subsequent creation of public and private spheres, the development of suburban spaces has impacted strongly on a range of literary and cultural genres.[8] George and Weedon Grossmith's *Diary of a Nobody* (1892) utilised the diary form to proclaim its accessibility to the lower-middle-class hero and his fellow clerks, who were often viewed with alarm by more prosperous members of the middle class as they too purchased suburban homes and aped middle-class mores. Throughout this text, the comically mundane nature of suburban life is depicted through the interactions of the Pooters with their home, notably the recurring motif of tripping over the foot scraper which comes to symbolise their frequent social embarrassments. These themes of pretence, respectability and denial also structure Lessing's work but in her texts they convey darker themes of exclusion, claustrophobia and mental illness.

Many texts that focus on domestic space, then, expose anxieties regarding the diverse and fractured state of middle-class identity. However, as the site of the nuclear family, and a location for nostalgic reminiscence, the private home is also a feminised space, bound up with anxieties about parental separation, the constraining effects of domesticity and the role of women in national culture. Anthony Vidler has claimed that for the modern subject, feeling homeless after the uprooting of cultural landmarks and identities following the world wars, and residing in urban apartments, the 'house of dreams' is at 'the center of his nostalgic vision'. However, this dream house represents a 'never-experienced space' and is merely an instrument of 'generalized nostalgia' (Vidler 1994: 64–5). In Rosner's and Campbell's essays, reconciling these cultural ideas of home with personal memories is vital for the attainment of an individuated adult identity.

Rosner's previous work on modernist literature and interior design (*Modernism and the Architecture of Private Life*, 2005) draws attention to the ways in which living spaces both reflect and shape ideals of family life and how literary texts employ a conceptual vocabulary to enact the shift away from Victorian ideals of class and gender. In this context, the notion of interiority comes to connote not only the modernist notion of psychic interiority; rather, the house becomes an exteriorisation of the subject's body in the text. In Lessing's *Under My Skin*, Rosner observes that the image of skin refers both literally and metaphorically to the younger Lessing and the walls of the house. Lessing details her struggle to differentiate herself from her mother, whose middle-class English identity is exteriorised in the house's decoration – as Rosner says, 'mother and daughter stage the struggle for individuation in architectural terms; the house structures their understanding of how they differ from one another.' Charles Rice observes in *The Emergence of the Interior* (2007) that 'the interior framed domesticity in its modern form' and that the private sphere of the home allowed for individual subjectivity to be marked in the city.[9] Through the collection of objects that link private activities to older traditions, we also create nostalgia for an idealised past. For Lessing's mother, then, decorating the interior of her Rhodesian bush house enables the maintenance of her English identity and heritage in an alien land.

Both Rosner's and Campbell's essays identify the home as an important site for colonial identity politics, in British Rhodesia and India respectively. Both authors show how British domestic designs were imposed on the colonial landscapes, leading to the erasure of native architecture and memory. Both also demonstrate, however, that this erasure could never be complete, leading to the inevitable development of hybrid identities. In 1893, in *Evolution and Ethics*, T. H. Huxley had compared the colony to a garden, which required careful tending if it were not to revert to a state of nature. Rosner shows how Lessing also employs natural metaphors, but to indicate her longing for a hybrid, rather than a dominating colonial, identity. The house is made out of the bush and needs similarly attentive maintenance to avoid merging with it. Unlike her mother, though, Lessing occupies both house and bush, private and public spaces. In so doing, she claims her right as a woman to occupy the public sphere.

Campbell's essay draws on the work of postcolonial critics such as Homi Bhabha and Gayatri Spivak, to investigate 'unhomely desire' and how in the encounter between different communities 'the borders between home and the world become confused; and uncannily, the private and the public become part of each other'. In contrast to Rosner, he demonstrates how the feminised private sphere is identified with cultural authenticity, and with the retention of traditional dress and practices, in the face of colonial occupation (an identification which is evident in other texts, such as Mehboob Khan's 1957 film, *Mother India*, in which woman, land and Hindu custom are conflated to represent a mythical village India in the wake of Partition). However, Campbell illustrates the different conception, and architectural realisation, of the private sphere within orthodox Hindu society where caste and gender restrictions are equally important. He shows how these architectonic devices (screens, separate living quarters, the idea of the fortress) determine both family structures, and the plots and literary structures in Tagore's *Gora* (1909) and in Bengali and Indian literature more generally from the turn of the last century. (For example, Mahatma Gandhi's *Autobiography: Or The Story of my Experiments with Truth* (1927) and Kamala Das, *My Story* (1976) are similarly patterned by Hindu beliefs and structures.) Ultimately, national unity or 'universalism' is envisioned through the transformation of the domestic sphere so that daughters (like Lessing) can undertake a political, as well as a maternal role in the new nation and through the development of a modern, palimpsestic architecture that reflects the hybrid nature of the nation's identity.

These essays foreground the connections between individual and collective identities, and Rosner's work again raises questions about the role of life-writing in this process. As she says, 'Lessing's meditations on the interplay of family, history, architecture and life-writing seem to assume a new dimension as she grapples with the ethics of her own role in the British colonization of southern Africa' as a white colonial woman. Traditionally, autobiographical forms have recounted the physical and emotional journey of the white male subject through a range of environments until he reaches maturity and autonomy in the public and/or colonial sphere (for example, Rudyard Kipling in *Something of Myself* (1937) or Raymond Unwin, tramping across, surveying and shaping the English landscape). By contrast, feminist critics have claimed that female autobiographers often write about themselves in relation to others, about their bodily experiences of public and private spheres and hence employ different formal structures (for example, *The Autobiography of Alice B. Toklas*, (1933) constructs a lesbian 'we' in its account of the couple's life in 1920s Paris).[10] In general, though, critics of life-writing have paid most attention to figurative, rather than literal, space. However, postcolonial critics have recently debated whether unique strategies to recount the construction of self, memory and environment can be found in the life stories of subjects who have lived under colonial regimes, while also questioning the political usefulness of such works.[11] When life-writing is explicitly linked to identity politics, does it represent the recovery of an individual voice, foreground diverse experiences, make theoretical debates about colonialism more accessible? Or are such accounts compromised by their personal and anecdotal nature and their 'unreliable' memories which may be mistaken for 'truth'?

Travel writing is often an important influence on such works, although the trope of the journey often diverges from the pattern of the Western autobiography or *Bildungsroman*. When colonial white women such as Lessing, or Olive Schreiner in *The Story of an African Farm* (1883), travel further into the bush or to metropolitan cities, these environments present different configurations of feminine vulnerability and colonial privilege, such as the fear of rape in the bush or a stifling marriage in a London townhouse. For colonial female subjects, journeys often represent individual agency, but this is defined by spatial transgression. In Campbell's essay, he describes how both lengthy travels abroad and brief journeys on ferryboats are equally associated with the adoption of secular values and the abandonment of caste restrictions and traditional Hindu femininity. Such journeys, then, involve a complicated process of rebellion and regret, and are marked by a series of choices about which identities should be remembered, forgotten or 're-membered' only in writing.

Postcolonial life-writing has flourished in the later twentieth century and has often been practised by critics who similarly attempt to mesh personal experience with critical reflection and often emphasise both the political importance of location and the spatial dimensions of consciousness (for example, Edward Said, *Reflections on Exile* and *Out of Place*; Henry Louis Gates, *In Search of Our Roots*; V. S. Naipaul, *Two Worlds*).[12] Maxine Hong Kingston's *The Woman Warrior: Memoirs of a Girlhood Among Ghosts* (1975) is an account of a second-generation Chinese-American woman growing up in San Francisco at mid-century. The memoirs encompass the lives of her female relations, who are an inextricable part of her story, as the alphabetical Chinese 'I' has several strokes, symbolising multiplicity. While her parents relate nostalgic myths of the homeland, Maxine's sense of trauma and cultural dislocation is symbolised by the loss of her voice and by the ghosts that populate her home and city, which represent both the lost past and the hostile anonymity of American urban space. The essays in this section similarly demonstrate how socio-spatial location has been crucial in the development of local and national identities, the concept of home and the 'haunting' legacies of modernity, such as colonialism and war.

Notes

1 For an historical overview of memory studies, and an account of contemporary debates, see Rossington and Whitehead (2007) and Eril and Nunning (2010).
2 See Paul de Man's reading of this passage in 'Semiology and Rhetoric' (1973) in Leitch (2001).
3 See, for example, Avishai Margalit (2002) *The Ethics of Memory*, Harvard University Press; Paul Ricoeur (2004) *Memory, History, Forgetting*, University of Chicago Press.
4 See Lowenthal (1985); Wright (1985); Hewison (1987); Samuel (1994).
5 For an account of the Garden City movement, see Ebenezer Howard (1902), *Garden Cities of Tomorrow*, Swan Sonnenschen and Co Ltd.
6 See Wright (1990) on Blatchford's influence on socialism and Bonnett (2010) on the concept of nostalgic radicalism.
7 The term originated in a medical thesis by Joseph Hofer in 1688 and is derived from the Greek *nostos*, which means to return home to one's native land, and *algos* which refers to pain, suffering or grief. See also Wilson (2001) on urban nostalgia.
8 For a history of suburban space, see Fishman (1987); Thompson (1982).
9 See chapter one in Rice (2007) on Walter Benjamin's Arcades Project. See also Stewart, (1993) on collecting.
10 See Estelle C. Jelinek (1986) *Traditions of Women's Autobiography*, New York: Twayne Publishers; Nancy Chodorow (1987) *The Reproduction of Mothering*, San Diego: University of California Press, on the concept of the 'relational self'.
11 For recent scholarship on postcolonialism and life-writing, see Huddart (2008); Moore-Gilbert (2009); Whitlock (2000); Smith and Watson (1992).
12 Other examples include Frantz Fanon, *Black Skin, White Masks*; Chinua Achebe, *Things Fall Apart*; Emily Eden, *Up the Country: Letters from India*; Mary Seacole, *Between Worlds*.

References

Bonnett, A. (2010) *Left in the Past: Radicalism and the Politics of Nostalgia*, London: Continuum.
Boym, S. (2001) *The Future of Nostalgia*, London: Basic Books.
Crinson, M. (2005) *Urban Memory: History and Amnesia in the Modern City*, London: Routledge.
Davis, F. (1979) *Yearning for Yesterday: A Sociology of Nostalgia*, London: Free Press.
Eliot, T. S. (2001) 'Tradition and the Individual Talent', in V. B. Leitch (ed.) *The Norton Anthology of Theory and Criticism*, New York and London: W. W. Norton and Company.
Eril, A. and Nunning, A. (eds) (2010) *A Companion to Cultural Memory Studies*, Berlin and New York: Walter de Gruyter.
Fishman, R. (1987) *Bourgeois Utopias: The Rise and Fall of Suburbia*, New York: Basic Books.
Hewison, R. (1987) *The Heritage Industry: Britain in a Climate of Decline*, London: Methuen.
Hirsch, M. (2007) *Family Frames: Photography, Narrative and Postmemory*, Harvard: Harvard University Press.
Huddart, D. (2008) *Postcolonial Theory and Autobiography*, London: Routledge.
Huxley, T. H. (2006) 'Evolution and Ethics', in S. Greenblatt and M. H. Abrams (eds) *The Norton Anthology of English Literature: Eighth Edition, Volume E, The Victorian Age*, New York: W. W. Norton and Company.
Lowenthal, D. (1985) *The Past is a Foreign Country*, Cambridge: Cambridge University Press.
de Man, P. (2001) 'Semiology and Rhetoric', in V. B. Leitch (ed.) *The Norton Anthology of Theory and Criticism* (New York and London: W. W. Norton and Company.
Moore-Gilbert, B. (2009) *Postcolonial Life-Writing: Culture, Politics and Self-Representation*, London: Routledge.

Rice, C. (2007) *The Emergence of the Interior: Architecture, Modernity, Domesticity*, London; Routledge.

Rosner, V. (2005) *Modernism and the Architecture of Private Life*, New York: Columbia University Press.

Rossington, M. and Whitehead, A. (eds) (2007) *Theories of Memory: A Reader*, Edinburgh: Edinburgh University Press.

Samuel, R. (1994) *Theatres of Memory: Past and Present in Contemporary Culture*, London: Verso.

Smith, S. and Watson, J. (eds) (1992) *De-Colonizing the Subject: The Politics of Gender in Women's Autobiography*, Minneapolis: University of Minnesota Press.

Stewart, S. (1993) *On Longing: Narratives of the Miniature, the Gigantic, the Souvenir, the Collection*, Durham: Duke University Press.

Thompson, F. M. L. (ed.) (1982) *The Rise of Suburbia*, Leicester: Leicester University Press.

Vidler, A. (1992) *The Architectural Uncanny: Essays in the Modern Unhomely*, Cambridge: MIT Press.

Whitlock, G. (2000) *The Intimate Empire: Reading Women's Autobiography*, London: Continuum.

Wilson, Elizabeth (2001) *The Contradictions of Culture: Cities, Culture, Women*, London: Sage.

Wright, M. (1990) 'Robert Blatchford, The Clarion Movement and the Crucial Years of British Socialism, 1891–1900', in T. Brown and T. N. Corns (eds) *Edward Carpenter and Late Victorian Radicalism,* London: Routledge.

Wright, P. (2009) *On Living in an Old Country: The National Past in Contemporary Britain*, Oxford: Oxford University Press.

3

POETS, TRAMPS AND A TOWN PLANNER

A survey of Raymond Unwin's on-site persona

Brian Ward

> As he tramps along there will arise in his imagination a picture of the future community …
>
> Unwin 1909: 149–50

In a critical sentence from Raymond Unwin's 1909 publication *Town Planning in Practice*, the image of a mobile, homeless vagrant is evoked. To the modern reader, it is an unlikely image in a book which is held to be instrumental, first in the creation of the town planner as a respectable figure embedded in the political structures of twentieth-century Britain and, second, in the design of large swathes of residential landscapes. To his contemporary readers, Unwin's usage of the term would have been understood within a wider discourse. The Edwardian tramp was a character that sustained two distinct bodies of writing – an official literature devoted to his control, and a romantic literature casting him as a figure of escape. Dovetailing with this discourse was the practice of 'tramping', the particular iteration of walking to which *Town Planning in Practice* refers. It was an activity which drew upon the duality of the Edwardian perception of the vagrant. Practitioners of tramping laid claim to the supposed innocent world-view of the vagrant, whilst simultaneously using an association with a figure on the margins of society to overlay their hiking with a political intent.

While Unwin's invoking of the tramp in *Town Planning in Practice* can therefore be understood within the general context of British Edwardian culture, this essay seeks primarily to situate his usage of the term within the particularities of his intellectual formation. In doing so, it identifies the figure of the tramp as a key determinant in Unwin's conception of the relationship between the town planner and the society in which he operated. The emulation of a vagrant, through the activity of tramping, involved a construction of identity that Unwin exploited to present the planner as a representative of those on the edge of civil society. This essay examines how Unwin employed tramping to democratise the design process of Arts and Crafts architecture so that it could be useful at the scale required by the new activity of municipal planning. The expansion of the self that he proposed and its democratic aspirations are best understood within an intellectual genealogy that runs from Walt Whitman through Edward Carpenter to the Ethical Socialist milieu in which Unwin matured. Unwin's construction of his town planner relied on tactics which Whitman had deployed in his creation of the poet. Our survey of the town planner's on-site persona will therefore begin with an examination of the manner in which a radical vision of democracy was brought from America to England through Carpenter's re-writing of Whitman. The nomadism of Whitman's figure of the 'great poet' will be identified as one of the prime reasons his work could be widely disseminated in this way, but the essay will question whether Unwin's subsequent use of the tramp in his construction of the town planner mitigated against the role he had identified for it – namely the expression in built form of the common life of local populations.

Many of these tensions between the global and the local and the peripatetic and the static were identified in early discussions about the reception of Whitman's poetry. In the preface to *Leaves of Grass* in 1855, Whitman had famously positioned himself as the object of the mid-nineteenth-century search for an American poet who would express the qualities of the burgeoning nation. The irony that his poetry, consciously linked to America in this way, had its greatest early impact in England was one that caught the attention of the American essayist, John Jay Chapman. In his 1899 essay, 'The Soul of a Tramp', Chapman suggested that a substantial component of the poetry's transatlantic appeal lay in the figure that Whitman presented to the English. He felt that the 'uncouth and insulting' figure that emanated from *Leaves of Grass* 'corresponded to the English' desire for 'everything in America' to be 'unpleasant and [rampantly] wild' (Chapman 1960: 68). Whitman used an engraving of himself in worker's clothes as the frontispiece to the first edition of *Leaves of Grass*, asserting the poet as 'the equalizer of his age and land' (Whitman 1959: 8). During a period when gulfs between the rich and poor and the North and South were calling into question the viability of the United States, Whitman attempted to invent an everyman character expansive enough to contain and solve the contradictions of his nation.[1] Constructed from the language he heard on the streets, *Leaves of Grass* presents the poet as an amalgam of the individuals he encountered in the teeming crowds of his daily life. '[T]he book arose out of my life in Brooklyn and New York from 1838 to 1853,' Whitman declared, 'absorbing a million people … with an intimacy, an eagerness, an abandon, probably never equalled' (Reynolds 1996: 82–3).

Romantic and transcendentalist conceptions of the poet/prophet had found renewed expression in Whitman, but for Chapman, the figure who stared at him

FIGURE 3.1 'There are, in every country, individuals who, after a sincere attempt to take a place in organized society, revolt from the drudgery of it, content themselves with the simplest satisfactions of the grossest need of nature …' (Chapman 1960: 69)

from the frontispiece was particularly redolent of a tramp (Chapman 1960: 70). In depicting Whitman in this way, Chapman utilised a term endowed with similar ambiguities in America as in Britain, the essential difference being that the tramp was seen as a relatively new figure on the American landscape.[2] Dating from the Civil War, when large numbers of men 'had been removed from their normal contexts and introduced to the possibilities of extended mobility', America's tramp population had been bolstered by the boom and bust cycles of the economy in the ensuing decades (Cresswell 2001: 34). By the late nineteenth century tramps were associated in the mainstream press with a moral panic – the 'tramp scare' or 'tramp evil' – and were frequently the recipients of beatings as they were chased out of town. Attempting to counter this vilification was a less voluminous literature of romanticisation. In poetry, dime novels and labour newspapers, the tramp was cast as a figure of liberation from the social mores of the Gilded Age. America's ambivalent attitude towards this modern nomadic figure finds expression in Chapman's essay. The tramp is criticised for his laziness and moral baseness while the attractions of his vagrant life are also described – 'the infinite pleasures of life in the open air … [with] the joy of being disreputable' (Chapman 1960: 69).

In attempting to unite a vast nation into a single whole, Whitman had described his 'great poet' pacing bodily across the country. Chapman believed that Whitman was giving utterance to a person enjoying an innocent freedom not afforded to those engaged in the responsible relationships of society. He contended that the way in which the poetry ranged across, rather than grounding itself in, America created placeless literature likely to appeal wherever the life of a tramp engaged the public's imagination. Any man on a holiday in the open air, 'sure of ten day's release from the cares of business and housekeeping', could gain access to the direct relationship with the universe that Whitman described (Chapman 1960: 72). Chapman proposed that Whitman's claims to patriotism were therefore disingenuous:

> Does all the patriotic talk ... about the United States ... poetically represent the state of any ... American citizen towards the country? Or would you find the nearest equivalent to this emotion in the breasts of the educated tramp of France, or Germany, or England? ... [H]is metaphors and catchwords are apparently American, but the emotional content is cosmic. He put off patriotism when he took to the road.
>
> *Chapman 1960: 70–1*

For Chapman, the cosmic aspect to his poetry decouples it from the America that Whitman hoped to absorb. In the act of assimilation involved in his creation of a democratic everyman, Whitman relied, amongst other things, upon the 'travelling clairvoyance' of mesmerism – the ability to travel mentally in a trance state to distant times and places. Based originally on Franz Mesmer's writings, mesmerism became, in mid-nineteenth-century America, a world-view which mediated between religion and science. Mesmerists believed in the existence of an electrical brain fluid which allowed one to roam through matter, seeing under the roofs of surrounding houses, delving into the thoughts of other individuals and even projecting one's mind 'backward into history and outward to the distant expanses of the heavens' (Reynolds 1996: 271). In Whitman's claim that 'I am afoot with my vision', he conflates descriptions of physical movement through territories with such cerebral time–space travel (Whitman 1959: 57).

'The Soul of a Tramp' was written more than thirty years after Whitman's vision had been brought to Britain with the publication of William Michael Rossetti's 1868 edition of *Leaves of Grass*. Explanations of the effusive English admiration for the poem at the turn of the century generally accord Edward Carpenter a central role in its propagation. Contrary to Chapman's assertion that Whitman's popularity rests on the way in which he explained America to educated Englishmen, a study of Carpenter's writings reveals instead the socialist writer and poet using Whitman's poetry to explain his own homosexuality and to situate himself within his own world. It also reveals that Chapman was only partially correct in his assertion that the cosmic nature of the poetry made it amenable to transference across the Atlantic.

The cosmic content had its biggest impact in allowing a re-casting of European ideas about democracy. In popular movements such as spiritualism and mesmerism, Americans had seen a complex interplay between religion and democracy that Whitman, in turn, absorbed into his poetry.[3] For Europeans such as George Santayana writing in 1901 it was notable that for Whitman 'democracy was not ... merely a constitutional device for the better government of given nations.' Instead, it became a social and moral aspiration that involved 'an actual equality among all men' (Santayana 1960: 80). For Carpenter, who situated Whitman's work amongst Hindu, Buddhist and Christian scriptures, the significance lay in how this new seer could equate his religious visions with the coming of a democratic society. He was less interested in how these visions arose out of nineteenth-century America and more interested in bringing them to bear on the social, political and cultural context in which he himself operated. Carpenter pointed out that Whitman was 'unique among the prophets' in that he gave 'the good tidings … a democratic scope and world-wide application unknown in the elder prophets' (Carpenter 1906: 78). In his opinion, this 'universality was the very key and centre' of Whitman's teachings, separating them from any particular 'race or nationality' (Carpenter 1906: 80–1). He records Whitman wondering in 1877 what impact his works could have in countries other that the United States:

> My original idea was that if I could bring men together by putting before them the heart of man … it would be a great thing; up to this time I have had America chiefly in view, but this appreciation in England makes me think I might perhaps do the same for the old world also.
>
> *Carpenter 1906: 14*

In Carpenter's writings Whitman is therefore extricated from the time and place from which he drew inspiration and associated solely with a content that is universally applicable. But this does not fully explain his role in fostering the English appreciation afforded to Whitman at the turn of the twentieth century. Noting the initial luke-warm reception of *Leaves of Grass* in Britain, Andrew Elfenbein draws attention to the way in which its popularity increased after the publication of Carpenter's 1883–1902 book of poetry, *Towards Democracy*. Proposing that it is central to the popularisation of Whitman in Britain, he highlights the manner in which enthusiastic reviewers in literary journals often twinned the two books. Elfenbein suggests that, contrary to traditional readings of *Towards Democracy* as a diluted imitation of *Leaves of Grass*, it is more usefully understood as an English translation of American poetry and the mechanism through which Carpenter 'reshaped Whitman to meet English desires' (Elfenbein 2001: 81).[4] The roughness of Whitman's language and rhythms is replaced with a smoother, slower-paced idiom more suited to the English palate, and it is bestowed with what Carpenter himself described as a 'milder radiance' (Carpenter 1918: 519). Even in his long catalogues, Whitman uses jarring imagery and rhythms that compel the reader to keep pace. This strategy is condensed in the short intro-duction he issues to his reader: 'Walt Whitman, an American, one of the roughs, a kosmos,/ Disorderly fleshy and sensual … eating, drinking and breeding' (Whitman: 1959). In contrast to this rushed series of staccato descriptions, Carpenter's pen-portrait of Whitman in *Towards Democracy* makes more concessions to its readers (as well as describing a more genial figure).[5] The slang is excised and the lengthy lines facilitate the slow progression from one thought to the next that is typical of the poem:

Grave and strong and untamed,
This is the clear-browed unconstrained tender face, with
full lips and bearded chin, this is the regardless defiant
face I love and trust;
Which I came out to see, and having seen do not forget

Carpenter 1918: 43

In translating Whitman in such a manner, Carpenter hoped to render his coun-
trymen more acquiescent to the American seer's democracy. By describing the
United States, Whitman was offering a vision of democracy.[6] America's landscape,
cities and people were all transposable with his conception of democracy in a manner that was manifestly not the case in the old world. In re-writing this vision for
England, Carpenter was compelled to relate it to an existing historical landscape
imbued with a contrary political system, a 'ground laden with the accumulated
wreck and rubbish of centuries' (Carpenter 1918: 29). Carpenter's descriptions of
England mention aristocratic estates and ecclesiastical monuments, but he focuses
on the ground between them. Moving through the country, 'aware of an imper-
ceptible change,' he is careful to cast democracy as something which is in the
process of emerging out of the relationship between the landscape and its common people rather than a foreign philosophy being imposed by external forces
(Carpenter 1918: 63). Cognisant of a general fear of 'the awful syllable Change,' he
assuages his readers that he 'hear[s] beyond' the usual connotations of that syllable
(Carpenter 1918: 62). *Towards Democracy* assures its readers that the democratic
England of the future is an evolution, 'a slow disentanglement' of its history rather
than a break with the past (Carpenter 1918: 64). The elements of the historic
English countryside that were suggestive of the loving labour of its people were
instilled, by Carpenter, with the values of the democratic England of the future:
'I see a great land waiting for its own people to come and take possession of it'
(Carpenter 1918: 58).[7]

Towards Democracy, paired with Leaves of Grass, presented democracy as an inspiring ideal, floating it above old world doubts about the expansion of the franchise.
It injected Whitman's idea of democracy into the emerging Socialist movement in
England, gaining most traction amongst the Ethical Socialists in the North.[8] For
some, like Katherine Bruce Glasier, the two poets provided the founding documents of their socialist beliefs:

It is no exaggeration for many of us inside and outside the political Socialist
movement to say that Walt Whitman's Leaves of Grass and Edward Carpenter's
Towards Democracy have become as a kind of Twentieth-Century Old and
New Testament.

Beith 1931: 86[9]

FIGURE 3.2 'I have sat with you long, and loved you well, unknown to/ You, but now I go otherwhere' (Carpenter 1918: 62)

It was within Ethical Socialist circles that the intellectual development of Raymond Unwin took place. A tireless worker for the Socialist movement, he was a close friend to central figures like the Glasiers, and was also in regular contact with Carpenter who is recognised as the formative influence on his politics.[10] Carpenter presented a 21-year-old Unwin with a copy of *Towards Democracy* in 1884. Recognising the debt his mentor owed to Whitman, Unwin later noted how 'some of the less civilized elements of the conceptions' had become, in Carpenter's work, 'more intimate and mature, [and] better balanced' (Beith 1931: 237). His primary memory of the 'bewildering revelation' that accompanied his first reading, though, was a 'sense of escape from an intolerable sheath of unreality and social superstition' (Beith 1931: 234–5). Unwin, self-confessedly grappling with 'the overwhelming complexity and urgency of the social problem', was the perfect constituency for Carpenter's book and its optimistic vision of social unity (Beith 1931: 234). Working as a draughtsman in the North of England, he felt keenly how the segregation of British society created a sense of division within himself. Recording a visit to a flower show in Chesterfield in his diary in July 1887, he dissected his contradictory feelings after being seen in the company of a working man whom he had befriended.

> I profess to believe nothing in rank … but I could not help feeling that I did not like all the foremen and so on at the works … to see me with … a working man and his family. I tried to shake off the feeling and couldn't and … I do despise myself for it … It seems rather queer that we should have feelings of that sort that we really hate but can't help feeling.
>
> *Unwin 1887*

His diary documents how he would alleviate such despair by reading *Towards Democracy*: 'it makes one in a way satisfied with one's position careless as to what people think' (Unwin 1887). Written between May and September 1887, the diary takes the form of letters to 'Ettie', or Ethel Parker, his future wife. His writing is suffused with his desire for her, so much so that it is sometimes difficult to distinguish between this desire and his yearning for the seductive, feminised landscape in *Towards Democracy*.

Whitman and Carpenter offered Unwin's generation a porous relationship between their selves and the world around them, or as D. H. Lawrence described it, a conception of the self as 'a pipe open at both ends' (Lawrence 1971: 156).[11] *Towards Democracy* conflated all of their emotions towards individuals, society and the landscape into one amorphous outpouring and promised them that England would be re-organised such that it would reflect their desires back to them. It offered comfort that any divisions among them were created by the divisions within society and predicted that these would melt away as the new democratic order emerged.

It is only part of a misty idea that comes over me at times of a better land altogether where life would be freer and happier more natural everything made
pure and clear clean food, clean lines, clean bodies and all open and above
board. Of course it is the idea of *Towards Democracy*.

Unwin 1887

Carpenter had positioned within English society Whitman's presumption that in a
democracy there would be an equalisation between bodily desires and the society
in which that body is situated; that everyone would, in Chapman's phrase, share
the tramp's 'joy of being ... unashamed' (Chapman 1960: 69).

Carpenter's vision, which had been almost a palpable reality for Unwin, served as
an aspiration against which to measure contemporary Britain as he entered increasingly into public life, first as an architect in partnership with Barry Parker, and then
as a town planner.[12] As he did so, he maintained a distinction between Carpenter's
'real democracy' and the 'electoral democracy' of Britain in which existing political
institutions were given a representative gloss only partly obscuring their background
in feudalism (Unwin nd 2). Yet his career involved an engagement with these institutions that brought into relief their absence from the Whitmanian tradition of
democracy. Writing about *Towards Democracy* in 1931 after many years of government service, Unwin notes that while Carpenter had been able 'to give body to the
fresh sense of freedom and equality of place and partnership in the universe' he had
not been able to articulate successfully how a society based on such equality should
be structured 'in political or other institutions' (Beith 1931: 236). Unwin was of
a generation that invented the town planner as an expert moulded to the needs
of 'electoral democracy'.[13] Yet, in Unwin's life there was a continuous interplay
between the two types of democracies, and the optimism of one intersected with the
pragmatic realities of the other. This, as we shall see, is evident in his construction of
the town planner, a figure whose absence began to be felt in the search for a solution
to the complex problems presented by the late nineteenth-century city.

Following his success with Letchworth Garden City and Hampstead Garden
Suburb, the 1909 publication of *Town Planning in Practice* located Unwin at the centre of discussions about this new figure. During a period when local authorities began
seriously to consider the construction of housing estates for the working classes, it
presented an authoritative figure, skilled in the creation of urban form. The range of
the town planner's knowledge is best exemplified by the last twenty pages where a
detailed analysis of the byelaws related to practical aspects such as construction and
drainage is followed by a bibliographic survey of contemporary international thinking on the emerging field of town planning. This breadth of knowledge was to be
put at the service of 'corporations and other governing bodies' (Unwin 1909: 1). The
town planner would be in a position to decipher the information from the objective
data-collecting exercises in which many corporations were engaged and to translate it
into built form. The figure that emerges from the book fits closely therefore with the

requirements of English 'electoral democracy' in which experts advise elected representatives, but running through the text there can also be found a line of thought which suggests that Unwin was simultaneously creating a town planner for the 'real democracy' that he continued to seek.

When Parker and Unwin wrote about democratic architecture it was architecture within this version of democracy to which they were referring. Carpenter's belief that a new democratic England would emerge from the people's work within the landscape finds its way into their writings on architecture and town planning.[14] The role for a town planner within this process of emergence was rife with contradictions. While hypothetically open to any form that democratic architecture would take, Unwin in *The Art of Building a Home* presumed it would work within the partnership's chosen language: 'the relationships of feudalism have gone, and democracy has yet to evolve some definite relationships of its own, which when they come will doubtless be as picturesque as the old forms' (Parker and Unwin 1901: 95). In Parker's 1912 article entitled 'Democracy's Influence on Architecture', he postulated that 'democratic architecture will only be fully realised when the mass of the people take an intelligent interest in [architectural] problems and insist upon their dwellings being the sincere expression of their own ideals.' However during an indeterminate transitional period, according to Parker, the people would rely on architects 'to infuse this spirit of democracy into their buildings' (Hawkes 1986: 153–4).

Unwin must have recognised the contradiction whereby architects with undue and undemocratic influence over the built environment attempted to imbue that environment with democracy. It was a contradiction which became particularly acute at the scale of town planning where one individual was invested with the power to organise vast residential landscapes.[15] Looking for a means to resolve the contradictions of his position as an expert within a 'real democracy', as well as an 'electoral democracy', it was to a Whitmanian line of thought that Unwin turned. His descriptions of the town planner suggest a figure constructed on a similar line of thought to that adopted by Whitman in his creation of the 'great poet'.

Whitman's poet relied on scientists to provide 'the structure of every perfect poem' much as Unwin's town planner sought authority for his designs through reference to sociological surveys (Whitman 1959: 14). But while professing a respect for science, both poet and town planner also claimed to be media through which they could channel the experiences of people around them. Whitman declared that '[t]he great poet absorbs the identity of others, and the experience of others ... but he presses them all through the powerful press of himself' (Reynolds 1996: 336), while Unwin described the town planner as a 'channel through which [common life] expresses itself – the brush with which [the community] paint[s]' (Unwin 1908). They both allowed this life flowing through them to find a form unhindered by any preconceived ideas. Whitman regarded the United States as 'the greatest poem' (Whitman 1959: 5) to be expressed with 'the most translucid clearness' (Carpenter 1906: 106), while Unwin's town planner described 'the requirements … of the town' as a song to be sung and asked: 'Is it not enough for the singer that he should finely voice the song of the poet? Must he also dictate what the poet shall say?' (Unwin 1909: 140).

If democracy bestowed equality on the populace this process of absorption and lucid channelling was surely possible. Whitman, the putative great poet, had pre-empted the paradoxical position that Unwin found himself in when inventing his town planner and addressed it head-on in the opening lines of *Leaves of Grass*, using an iteration of equality to excuse his dictatorial tone: 'what I assume you shall assume/ For every atom belonging to me as good belongs to you' (Whitman 1959: 25). Whitman therefore portrays the poet as a teacher, adopting a position of authority until he could make his fellow Americans see what he could perceive: 'the others are as good as [the great poet], only he sees it and they do not.' By giving utterance to that which he saw, Whitman proposed that he would usher the general populace into a new era of equal 'greatness' (Whitman 1959: 9). In *Town Planning in Practice* Unwin suggested that the town planner, given appropriate powers, could do the same through architecture and landscape design:

> [T]own planning powers will … for the first time make possible an adequate expression of such corporate life as exists. Here, as elsewhere, action and reaction will take place … [and] the outward forms of the town will both stimulate and give fresh scope to the co-operative spirit from which it has sprung.
>
> *Unwin 1909: 13*

The frontispiece of *Leaves of Grass* provides the reader with an image of the bodily presence of the medium that is described within its pages. Enunciating the knowledge that was to be associated with the town planner, the body of the new expert is, in contrast, conspicuously absent from *Town Planning in Practice*. The vast bulk of the book offers a compendium of urban typologies that its author had compiled. However, a revealing glimpse of the figure of the town planner emerges in the crucial passage from his description of the planning design process mentioned previously. This process was to begin with the gathering of an exhaustive list of information stretching from sociological surveys of a town's population to detailed geological data about the site identified for its extension. Having absorbed this data, Unwin sends the town planner walking through the landscape:

> As the designer walks over the ground to be planned, he will picture to himself what would be the natural growth of the town or district if left to spread over the area … As he tramps along there will arise in his imagination a picture of the future community, with its needs and its aims, which will determine for him the most important points; and the main lines of his plan should take shape in his mind before ever he comes to put them on paper.
>
> *Unwin 1909: 149–50*

FIGURE 3.3 'Shoulder your duds, and I will mine, and let us hasten forth;/ Wonderful
cities and free nations we shall fetch as we go' (Whitman 1959: 79–80)

While Whitman presents his medium as 'one of the roughs', the bodily presence
of Unwin's town-planning medium is represented by a 'designer' who walks the
site in the manner of a 'tramp' as he transforms a survey into a plan. In locating
the essential moments of the design process on the site Unwin drew the design

methodologies of town planning from the design strategies of the Arts and Crafts architectural tradition, appropriating their respect for the *genius loci*.[16] He insists upon the designer's embodied experience as a subjectivity to balance the objectivity of the scientific information that he has imbued before pacing the site. But by including the tramp in his description, Unwin complicates the identity of the town planner and indicates that his was a tactical rather than an invested subjectivity. Within the tramp rather than the designer lies a strand of thought suggestive of the town planner's status as a Whitmanian medium. The implications of Unwin's tactical use of the word 'tramps' can be understood through an examination of its potency both in the general context of Edwardian culture and within the particularities of Unwin's intellectual development.

Tramps is, at first glance, an incongruous word to use. Three years prior to the publication of *Town Planning in Practice,* the Parliamentary Report of the Departmental Committee on Vagrancy had recommended that labour camps be utilised to control the dangerous tramp population and its suggestions had been widely accepted.[17] Unwin's usage of the potentially toxic imagery of the tramp can be partially understood within the context of the Edwardian practice of 'tramping' or 'vagabonding' in which association with the objects of official disapproval was used to imbue hiking with a faint political focus.[18] Given that gentlemanly walking groups such as the 'Sunday Tramps' emerged alongside groups affiliated with the socialist newspaper, the *Clarion*, the practice cannot be said to have been associated exclusively with the left. However, tramping held particular attractions for socialists such as Unwin in that it asserted the poor's right to walk across private estates, and figures within socialist circles like Holbrook Jackson argued that tramping could be seen as 'practical politics' (Jackson 1912: 60).[19] By using tramping in the construction of the town planner as a municipal figure replacing the land agent of the feudal system, Unwin situated him within a tradition of romantic vagrancy which was historically interwoven with hostility towards the enclosures.[20]

As we saw, John Jay Chapman noticed the way in which an 'emotional content' could be gathered around the nomadic figure of the tramp, through which Whitman's message could be spread abroad. Whitman's cosmic vision enlivened a British literature of vagrancy when it crossed the Atlantic and served as a touchstone to much of the literature of tramping that arose to complement the practice of vagabonding.[21] Arthur Rickett's *The Vagabond in Literature* celebrated Whitman as 'the supreme example' of the type (Rickett 1906: 169) while the journal *The Tramp: An Open Air Magazine* which appeared monthly between March 1910 and March 1911 opened its first issue with a quote from his poem, 'Open Road'. Accounts of the vagrant life such as W. H. Davies' *The Autobiography of a Super-Tramp* were hungrily consumed by Edwardian society and prose renditions of tramping can also be found in such popular fictional works of the time as Kenneth Grahame's *The Wind in the Willows*. Providing a romantic counterpoint to official documents on vagrancy, what is striking about the figure of the tramp in such literature is the manner in which it

FIGURE 3.4 '… such poems as are good for him will come bubbling up of their own accord to the surface of the wanderer's mind' (Lady Margaret Sackville, cited in Howarth 2003: 166)

expresses an Edwardian desire for an innocent view of the landscape. He was created as a figure who responded to the world 'with a child's freshness' (Howarth 2003: 160) as one author noted, and who lay 'close to the essential facts, to the really significant things' as another opined (Southworth 2009: 40). Tramping was construed as a means through which people enjoying a civilised existence could temporarily access the perceived advantages of the tramp's life. It was described variously as 'a lapse from the upholstery of civilised life', and a 'tonic [which] puts us once more in tune with reality' (Jackson 1912: 35).

The literary journal, *The Tramp*, gives us some idea of how tramping could negotiate the apparent contradiction between the informed view of the middle classes and the innocent view of the vagrant population. The interaction between literature read in the upholstered domestic realm and the direct experience of nature enjoyed on a tramp was detailed by Lady Margaret Sackville in the first issue. She recommended that books be left behind when vagabonding as 'such poems as are good for him will come bubbling up of their own accord to the surface of the wanderer's mind' (Howarth 2003: 166). Unwin exploits this aspect of tramping in his usage of the term in *Town Planning in Practice*. As a young man, he had considered a similar interaction between a 'primitive' and a 'civilised' method of examining the world when he described how mature artists created pictures by combining 'the freedom of impulse and action' they had had as a child with the formal rules they learnt during their training (Unwin post 1887). The type of tramping described by Lady Sackville provided a vehicle for a system of perception familiar to Unwin, and one which can be deciphered in the particular role he assigns to tramping in town planning.[22] The planner was to tramp across the landscape on which he was working after studying a large body of information about the site and the community for which he was designing. Tramping is invoked at a point in the design process when an adherence to 'the essential facts' and a 'child's freshness' would be beneficial in coming to a decision about the built form that would best interpret the community's wishes. Unwin's town planner uses tramping to sift the information and allows the plan to emerge from the interaction between a received and an innocent view of the site.

A genteel activity with a problematic relationship to impoverished vagrants, tramping is perhaps best understood as a phenomenon of the Edwardian transition away from Victorian moral and social codes that justified the poverty of the lower classes as due recompense for sinful indolence. It offered itself as a practice that could temporarily transcend the class structures which those codes served to reinforce, and in doing so brought the foundations of those structures under question. In an 1889 article in *Commonweal* entitled 'A Tramp's Diary' Unwin presents a cutting from the *Pall Mall Gazette* which had published the contents of a diary that was found in a Tyneside tramp's pocket when he was arrested. Unwin asks any readers 'with the least feeling and imagination' to 'go through the [tramp's] eleven days' of hungry wandering (Unwin 1889: 132). He contextualises the tramp's experience within the 'present system of industry' and claims that there could be no 'happiness for [anyone] with any sympathy for their fellow men till the system is entirely swept away and something more human put in its place' (Unwin 1889: 132).

This call to replace the industrial capitalist system with one which somehow gave due recognition to feelings such as sympathy sits comfortably within John Ruskin's rhetoric. Unwin's 'early days were influenced by [his] musical voice …

vainly striving to stem the flood of … materialism' and his work as a designer can be placed within the second generation of architects to labour in Ruskin's slipstream (Unwin 1931: 9). However Ruskin had never been able to articulate a vision of society devoid of the hierarchical structures that had become problematic to socialists in the late nineteenth century. Even when arguing that love should be recognised as the primary bonding agent in society, he relied upon a master exercising a loving paternal authority in order to maintain a moral order.[23] Unwin came of age when Ruskin's moralising presence on English thought had become ponderous.[24] One of the reasons why *Leaves of Grass* and *Towards Democracy* were read with a sense of elation in England is that they provided a necessary bulwark against the more reactionary ideas of writers like Ruskin. In 'A Tramp's Diary', Unwin pointedly positions himself somewhere outside the Victorian ethical system before criticising the churchgoers that the tramp had described 'sailing past' as if he were invisible (Unwin 1889: 132). Unwin finishes the article by attempting to undermine any effort by his readers to use a religious or moralistic standpoint to deny the tramp his due sympathy.

By moving the town planner through space in the manner of a tramp Unwin dismantled old hierarchies and invoked a contentious contemporary figure in the decision-making process. In Ruskin's allusions to vagrancy, Marcus Waithe notes his frequent use of the medieval word 'wayfarer' (as opposed to 'vagrant' or 'tramp'), reading in his avoidance of contemporary language a deliberate attempt to demonstrate how figures peripheral to Victorian society had been dealt with more sympathetically during medieval times (Waithe 2006: 50).[25] The wayfarer could be sure of hospitality in a way that the modern tramp was not, and by restoring an 'obsolete' representation of the poor, Ruskin aimed to expose the alienation of industrialised society (Waithe 2006: 50). But, remote in time, the wayfarer could attract the reader's sympathy while that reader simultaneously avoided contemplation of contemporary homelessness. As Waithe points out Ruskin's 'strategy was not immune to the difficulties imposed by the revivalist's captivity within the present' and Ruskin could appear trapped within a static medievalism that sometimes had little relevancy to the problems of contemporary society (Waithe 2006: 50). While the twin agents mentioned in the town planner's shift from survey to plan – the act of walking and the use of the imagination – can be traced back to a Ruskinian tradition, his emulation of the tramp indicates a Whitmanian tactic.[26] To assign influences to the town planner's constituent subjects, it could be posited that while Ruskin informed the designer's imaginative picture-making, it was Whitman and Carpenter who modernised the tramp's walking.[27]

Whitman presents himself to his readers as a vagrant dressed in modern attire. He makes no apologies for his vagrancy, and beseeches them to join him, with their clothes bundled over their shoulders *et al.* Rather than bringing them into the past, they are to move across a vast continent where they will contribute to the construction of a free and democratic society:[28]

I tramp a perpetual journey.
My signs are a rain-proof coat and good shoes and a staff cut from
The woods; …
Shoulder your duds, and I will mine, and let us hasten forth;
Wonderful cities and free nations we shall fetch as we go.

Whitman 1959: 79–80

Carpenter appreciated Whitman's 'sense of nowness' and located his own iteration of Whitman's vagrant within the context of the tramp scares of the late nineteenth century (Carpenter 1906: 18–19). His vagabond, less well equipped than Whitman's, has to confront and dissipate the contemporary discomfort that vagrants presented to sedentary life:

I have been on tramp, and my boots are dusty and
hobnailed, and my clothes are torn: do not ask me into
your house; (God knows; I might spoon my food with
a knife!)
Give me a penny on the doorstep and let me pass on.
I have sat with you long, and loved you well, unknown to
You, but now I go otherwhere.

Carpenter 1918: 62

Interested in the universal rather than the local content of Whitman's work, Carpenter nevertheless was compelled to re-contextualise the figure that John Jay Chapman saw as a cosmic tramp.[29] Just as Whitman had attempted to root his everyman persona in the America through which he passed, part of Carpenter's success in *Towards Democracy* was his revision of this character for late nineteenth-century England. Diligently negotiating the prejudices of that society, his tramp persona was a benign presence that walked across England, careful not to disturb those he encountered as he brought Whitman's ideas to bear on the old world.

In *Towards Democracy* walking is nominated as an activity that transcends class divisions because, in a line admired by Unwin, it 'give[s] the sign of equality' (Carpenter 1918: 42).[30] The walking associated with Carpenter's tramp becomes endowed with democratic intent because it visibly asserts an equality with the outcasts in society:

If I am not level with the lowest I am nothing; and if I
did not know for a certainty that the craziest sot in the village
is my equal, and were not proud to have him walk with me
as my friend, I would not write another word – for in this is
my strength

Carpenter 1918: 6

FIGURE 3.5 'As the designer walks over the ground to be planned, he will picture to himself what would be the natural growth of the town or district if left to spread over the area ... As he tramps along there will arise in his imagination a picture of the future community ...' (Unwin 1909: 149–50)

Addressing a memorial event for Carpenter in 1939, Unwin quoted this and similar passages from *Towards Democracy* where the poet professed his equality with the 'scorned' (Carpenter 1918: 34).[31]

Declaring that '[t]he average man of a land at last only is important' (Whitman 1888: 33), Whitman had written as if a 'meridian' and 'average' of mankind could be almost mathematically formulated (Whitman 1888: 37). Part of the remit of the great poet, 'the arbiter of the diverse ... the equalizer of his age and land', was to construct this man (Whitman 1959: 8). Edward Carpenter's first biographer, Lewis, reads in his subject a similar attempt to attain the average, and sees in Carpenter's declaration of equality with the very lowest ranks, an attempt to counter his exalted position in society so that his experience was rendered more universal. This re-balancing of the median in favour of the overlooked, was for Lewis a deliberate tactic, akin to 'men of high rank ... [going] incognito to share the lives, and enter into the experience, of the average people'. Usually divorced from this experience, role-playing allowed such a man to 'mix easily with the crowd, he can go here, there, and everywhere, and enter into all kinds of experience, enjoy life with *naivete* and naturalness' (Lewis 1915: 216). According to Lewis, Carpenter found within his 'manhood' an equality which allowed him to penetrate into that common experience at a more fundamental level than would be achieved by role-playing (Lewis 1915: 217). By walking level with the most repellent sot, Carpenter gained not just the benefit of his companion's observations, but the perceptions of humanity in general.

In his reading of *Towards Democracy,* Unwin discovered this arena in which an understanding of bodily equality re-organised one's relationships with the world. Recalling his epiphanic first reading of the poem, it was the effect it had on his comprehension of the body that Unwin remembered:

> a new understanding, relation and union to be realized between the spirit of man and his body, the animal man no longer a beast to be ridden, but an equal friend to be loved, cherished and inspired.

> Growing out of this, made possible by it, there then emerges a new sense of equality and freedom in all human intercourse and relationships.

> Content, in happy unity with its body, the soul of man thus accepting equality of spiritual status, and enjoying free communion with its fellows, discovers a new relation to the universe, to nature, and to the Great Spirit which pervades it; a new faith, not of belief in this or that, but of trust.
>
> *Beith 1931: 235*

The body is posited as a medium (or 'a pipe open at both ends') through which disparate elements of life are funnelled and 'mingled' as they are brought into close concord with each other. The foregrounding of his physiology, which he shared with the sot or the tramp, allowed Unwin to become representative of his fellow men. It was as such an equaliser or arbiter that the tramp was enabled to interpret a community's needs and to determine the mapping of a town around his body as he walked across suburban fields.

Writing about Carpenter's proselytising, in a manner relevant to Unwin's town planning, Lewis perceptively identified the primary problem in this assumption of a universal acuity. He described a self which, having absorbed and overcome so many of the complexities of human relationships, feels little need to contextualise that which he emits on mankind's behalf:

> Carpenter has the casualness of the wayside sower of seed. Because he believes in himself, it does not seem to him to matter much where he casts himself; because he believes in the inherent vitality of his message it does not matter on what soil it may be flung …
>
> *Lewis 1915: 302*[32]

Whitman asserted that there was a profound connection between his work and the setting from which he drew inspiration and yet at the start of this chapter, John Jay Chapman questioned the rootedness of his peripatetic poetry in America. Carpenter re-orientated his mentor's 'prophecy' towards England and yet here

Edward Lewis queries whether his message was specific to the English ground he traversed. As their critics perceived, in the construction and representation of their selves, both poets relied on a universalism that complicated any connection with context. In the expansion of their selves, in their claims to encapsulate (at the least) the experiences of a whole nation, they forfeited associations with any particular locations. The cosmic emotional content of the poetry seemed to resist grounding, raising doubts about its efficacy to Unwin's project of creating town plans that responded to a site and its community.

Nevertheless, in *Democratic Vistas* Whitman had invited his readers to be 'gymnasts' with his texts, to construct their own works from the framework he had provided (Whitman 1888: 81). In this survey of readings, critiques and rewritings of his work, his readers have often wandered far from the original text. It is the body afoot with his vision of democracy that has remained constant. Unwin's appropriation of this body in his creation of the tramping town planner positioned a representative of the full spectrum of society at the key moment of the planning process. In the same year as *Town Planning in Practice* was published The Royal Commission of the Poor Laws described vagrants as the 'shifting and shiftless fringe of the population' (Vorspan 1977: 63). In his attempt to pull this fringe into the centre Unwin raises pertinent questions about how planning is to be conducted within a democratic society.

Notes

1 The process of eradicating divisions can be seen in Whitman's first idiomatic lines, dating from 1847: 'I am the poet of slaves and of the masters of slaves, […]/I go with the slaves of the earth equally with the masters/ And I will stand between the masters and the slaves,/ Entering into both so that both shall understand me alike' (Reynolds 1996: 119).
2 Whitman himself saw their poverty as an indictment of the American economic system. He observed the manifestation of tramps in America – 'vast crops of poor, desperate, dissatisfied, nomadic, miserably-waged populations' – as an example of an old world phenomenon arising in the new world because of its 'social and economic organization' (Whitman 1888: 161).
3 As one adherent of spiritualism announced: 'Spiritualism is democratic. It is addressed to the common people, and we are all common people' (Prothero 1993: 199).
4 Elfenbein is of the opinion that this translation mapped Whitman onto the 'affective power' of the English clerisy radicalising that tradition so that it became attractive to a new breed of self-made English professionals. Without an Oxbridge education, they needed an 'art of their own, radical enough to distinguish them from the bourgeoisie yet not radical enough to be incomprehensible; elevated enough to mark their superiority to the working-class yet not so elevated as to be antidemocratic; serious enough to be recognized as culture while daring enough to reject established institutions' (Elfenbein 2001: 101).
5 Although Whitman is not named in Section XXX of *Towards Democracy,* the central figure of the section is recognisable from *Days with Walt Whitman* in which Carpenter notes the rapport Whitman enjoyed with 'the common people' and children of Philadelphia.
6 'I shall use the words America and democracy as convertible terms …' (Whitman 1888: 3).

7 Unwin drew attention to this line in a speech at Carpenter's residence, Millthorpe, on 03.07.39 (Unwin 1939).

8 Stanley Pierson discusses the overlapping conceptions of socialism in its early years, distinguishing Ethical Socialism from Social Democratic and Fabian variants. See 'The "Divided Consciousness" and British Socialism' (Pierson 1979: 6–42).

9 For Mark Bevir, the representation of socialism as a religion in this way is a trait in Ethical Socialism which betrays its strong reliance on American as well as British Romanticism. See in particular 'British Socialism and American Romanticism' (Bevir 1995: 878–901).

10 See 'Raymond Unwin: The Education of an Urbanist' (Swenarton 1989: 126–66). On receiving the RIBA Gold medal in 1937, Unwin listed Ruskin, Morris, Carpenter and Hinton as the primary influences on his career (Unwin 1937: 582).

11 Lawrence was an adherent of Whitman as a young man. For a study of the probable influence of Carpenter on Lawrence see Delavaney (1971).

12 Tantalisingly imminent, but always slipping into the distance, Unwin resigned himself in 1887 to the realisation that his wait for the land described in *Towards Democracy* would extend to '7 [or] 10 or even 20 years' rather than the '3 or 4 years' he had originally estimated. See Unwin (1887).

13 A prescient note in his diary asserts that the potential of 'anarchy of opinion' in a democratic society would be circumvented if the populace had experts of quality – 'men whose … disinterestedness they can trust and whose ability is known' (Unwin: 1887).

14 For instance: '[Civic Art] works from within outward … [Beauty] results when life and the joy of life, working outwards, express themselves in the … perfection of all the forms which are created for the satisfaction of their needs' (Unwin 1909: 9).

15 The scale of town planning was identified by Unwin as a particularly modern aspect of the new activity (Unwin 1909: 13–14).

16 Unwin later reiterates the importance of the time spent on the site 'only when, on the ground, all [the] formative influences have been balanced, can the designer safely commence to draw out his design' (Unwin 1909: 153). For examples of similar sentiment within the Arts and Crafts tradition of architecture, see, for instance, Lethaby's account of how, after 'long working over the site' (Lethaby 1979: 101), Webb's buildings would be 'seen on the site' (Lethaby 1979: 93) they 'came to him' (Lethaby 1979: 129) on a site before he began to draw the plans.

17 In Britain, usage of the word 'tramp' can be traced back to the late seventeenth century. It was originally applied to men who travelled purposefully in search of employment, but by the early twentieth century it had become synonymous with the 'aimless wandering of the dispossessed'. A rise in the homeless population, caused by the vagaries of a capitalist economy and the return of ex-servicemen from the Boer Wars, had seen tramps become a repository of society's fears, suspected typically of 'terrorizing unprotected housewives, thieving … and … being the carriers of cholera and smallpox' (Crowther 1992: 97).

18 Unwin partook in the practice of tramping, mentioning in a lecture that in becoming a town planner he had replaced rural tramping holidays with urban tramps (Manchester University Archives, RUC Box 1/2: Personal Papers Folder 1). In 'Gladdening v. Shortening the Hours of Labour' he endorsed the practice of hiking as a worthy use of leisure time prior to a 'complete socialist system [being] established' (Unwin 1897).

19 The historian, Raphael Samuel, claims that tramping or hiking became 'a major if unofficial, component' of the socialist religion (quoted in Solnit 2001: 164).

20 'general control could be best secured by giving to some architect … powers similar to those usually possessed by the agent of a large ground landlord' (Parker and Unwin 1901: 100). For a study of romantic vagrancy and land ownership see Langan (1995).

21 Leslie Stephen, the founder of the Sunday Tramps and the author of the essay 'In Praise of Walking', being a notable exception to the practice of invoking Whitman. He disapproved of the American poet (Blodgett 1934: 186).

22 Unwin reassured the town planner that the study of information prior to a site visit would not constrain his creativity (Unwin 1909: 140).
23 See 'Political Economy of Art' (Ruskin 1907: 205–334).
24 'Ruskin made an onslaught on democracy, especially in *Fors Clavigera*.' Unwin, R. (nd) Handwritten notes for lecture, Manchester University Archives, RUC Box 1/4: Personal Papers Folder 3.
25 Unwin's partner, Barry Parker, used the term 'wayfarer' in one of his essays for *The Craftsman* in 1910–12 (Hawkes 1986: 127–8).
26 Personal notes in the RIBA archive mention Ruskin in terms of site planning (Unwin nd 3). They evoke Ruskin's theories of the Imagination which are most legible within *Modern Painters* (Ruskin 2000: 269). Ruskin encouraged architects to commune directly with nature. See for instance Ruskin 1989: 117–18. The Wordsworthian practice of walking as a means of achieving this was appropriated by Ruskin. Admitting that he 'used Wordsworth as a daily text-book,' Ruskin deferentially prefaced each volume of *Modern Painters* with an extensive quotation from *The Excursion* (Birch 1999: 343).
27 For an argument in favour of tramping being seen as a modernist activity see Southworth (2009).
28 Whitman observed that 'Ruskin seems to think himself constituted to protest against all modern conveniences' (Blodgett 1934: 162).
29 Early English critics were happy to identify Whitman with the United States and deployed American terminology to describe the poet staring at them from the frontispiece. The London *Examiner* saw a 'New York rowdy ... a Brooklyn boy' (Unauthored 1860: 46) while the *Leader* observed a 'Yankee-doodle ... [a] roystering blade' (Unauthored 1860: 48).
30 Unwin drew attention to this line in a speech at Carpenter's residence, Millthorpe, on 03.07.39 (Unwin 1939).
31 See also 'Gold is not finer than lead ...' (Carpenter 1918: 41) and 'Are you laughed at? ...' (Carpenter 1918: 34). Manchester University Archives, RUC Box 1/4: Personal Papers Folder 3.
32 Rowbotham sees in this description of Carpenter, 'a Bergsonian super-tramp' (Rowbotham 2008: 340).

References

Beith, G. (ed.) (1931) *Edward Carpenter in Appreciation*, London: George Allen and Unwin Ltd.
Bevir, M. (1995) 'British Socialism and American Romanticism', *The English Historical Review*, 110, 438: 878–901.
Birch, D. (1999) 'Elegaic Voices Wordsworth, Turner and Ruskin', *The Review of English Studies*, 50, 199: 332–44.
Blodgett, H. (1934) *Walt Whitman in England*, New York: Cornell University Press.
Carpenter, E. (1906) *Days With Walt Whitman, With some Notes on his Life and Work*, London: George Allen and Unwin Ltd.
—— (1918) *Towards Democracy*, London: George Allen and Unwin Ltd.
Chapman, J. (1960) 'The Soul of the Tramp', in L. Marx (ed.) *The Americanness of Walt Whitman*, Boston: DC Heath and Company.
Cresswell, T. (2001) *The Tramp in America*, London: Reaktion Books.
Crowther, M. A. (1992) 'The Tramp', in R. Porter (ed.) *Myths of the English*, Cambridge: Polity Press.
Delavaney, E. (1971) *D. H. Lawrence and Edward Carpenter, A Study in Edwardian Transition*, London: William Heinemann Ltd.

Elfenbein, A. (2001) 'Whitman, Democracy, and the English Clerisy', *Nineteenth-Century Literature* 56, 1: 76–104.

Hawkes, D. (ed.) (1986) *Modern Country Homes in England, The Arts and Crafts Architecture of Barry Parker*, Cambridge: Cambridge University Press.

Howarth, P. (2003) 'The Simplicity of W. H. Davies', *English Literature in Transition 1880–1920*, 46, 2: 154–74.

Jackson, H. (1912) *All Manner of Folk, Interpretations and Studies*, London: Grant Richards Ltd.

Langan C. (1995) *Romantic Vagrancy, Wordsworth and the Simulation of Freedom*, Cambridge: Cambridge University Press.

Lewis, E. (1915) *Edward Carpenter, An Exposition and an Appreciation*, London: Methuen.

Lawrence, D. H. (1971) *Studies in Classic American Literature*, London: William Heinemann Ltd.

Lethaby, W. R. (1979) *Philip Webb and his Work*, London: Raven Oak Press.

Parker, B. and Unwin, R. (1901) *The Art of Building a Home. A Collection of Lectures and Illustrations*, London, New York and Bombay: Longmans, Green & Co.

Pierson, S. (1979) *British Socialists, The Journey from Fantasy to Politics*, Cambridge, Massachusetts and London, England: Harvard University Press.

Prothero, S. (1993) 'From Spiritualism to Theosophy: "Uplifting" a Democratic Tradition', *Religion and American Culture: A Journal of Interpretation*, 3, 2: 197–216.

Reynolds, D. (1996) *Walt Whitman's America, A Cultural Biography*, New York: Alfred A. Knopf.

Rickett, A. (1906) *The Vagabond in Literature*, London: J. M. Dent & Co.

Rowbotham, S. (2008) *Edward Carpenter, A Life of Liberty and Love*, London: Verso.

Ruskin, J. (1907) '*Sesame*', '*Unto this Last*' *and* '*Political Economy of Art*', London: Cassell and Company.

—— (1989) *The Seven Lamps of Architecture*, New York: Dover Publications.

—— (ed. and abridged by Barrie, D.) (2000) *Modern Painters*, London: Pilkington Press.

Santayana, G. (1960) 'The Poetry of Barbarism', in L. Marx (ed.) *The Americanness of Walt Whitman*, Boston: D. C. Heath and Company.

Solnit, R. (2001) *Wanderlust, A History of Walking*, London: Verso.

Southworth, H. (2009) 'Douglas Goldring's The Tramp: An Open Air Magazine (1910–1911) and Modernist Geographies', *Literature & History*: 18, 1: 35–53.

Swenarton, M. (1989) *Artisans and Architects, The Ruskinian Tradition in Architectural Thought*, New York: St Martin's Press.

Unauthored (1860) *Leaves of Grass Imprints, American and European Criticisms on Leaves of Grass*, Boston: Thayer and Eldridge.

Unwin, R. (1887) *Diary for the Year*, RUC Box 1/6, Manchester University Archives.

—— (post 1887) 'James Hinton's Ethical Word', papers relating to Unwin's research on James Hinton, RUC Box 1/7, Manchester University archives.

—— (1889) 'A Tramp's Diary', *Commonweal*, April 27: 132.

—— (1897) 'Gladdening v. Shortening the Hours or Labour', UnR/2/3, RIBA archives, London.

—— (1908) 'Notes of lecture on town planning given at Essex Hall, 28 February 1908', UnR/1/2, RIBA archives, London.

—— (1909) *Town Planning in Practice, An Introduction to the Art of Designing Cities and Suburbs*, London: T. Fisher Unwin.

—— (1931) 'The Inaugural Address by the President, Dr Raymond Unwin, read before the RIBA on Monday 2 November 1931' *RIBA Journal*, 39, 1: 5–12.

—— (1937) 'The Royal Gold Medal presentation to Sir Raymond Unwin, Monday 12 April 1937', *Journal of the Royal Institute of British Architects*: 144, 12: 581–7.

—— (1939) 'Notes on Edward Carpenter, Millthorpe', RUC Box 1/4, personal papers folder 3, Manchester University archives.

—— (nd 1) 'Notes for Lecture in Belfast', RUC Box 1/2, personal papers folder 1, Manchester University archives.

—— (nd 2) 'Notes for Lecture on Aristocracy and Democracy', RUC Box 1/4, personal papers folder 3, Manchester University archives.

—— (nd 3) 'Notes for Lecture on Pleasant Living', UnR/1/7, RIBA archives, London.

Vorspan, R. (1977) 'Vagrancy and the New Poor Law in late-Victorian and Edwardian England', *The English Historical Review*, 92, 362: 59–81.

Waithe, M. (2006) *William Morris's Utopia of Strangers, Victorian Medievalism and the Ideal of Hospitality*, Cambridge: D. S. Brewer.

Whitman, W. (1888) *Democratic Vistas, And Other Papers,* London: Walter Scott.

—— (1959) *Leaves of Grass*, New York: Penguin.

All photos, Hampstead Garden Suburb, 30 July 2010, Paul Tierney.

4

UNHOMELY DESIRE

Dismantling the walls of difference in Gora's Kolkata

Mark Mukherjee Campbell

Introduction

Rabindranath Tagore (1870–1940), Nobel Laureate and erstwhile Knight, was a central figure of the Bengal Renaissance, a broad-based cultural, literary and social movement that originated in the early decades of the nineteenth century.[1] Emerging out of the collision between East and West, and with its epicentre in Kolkata, the capital of colonial India and 'the second city of Empire', it drew upon ideas from both European and indigenous intellectual traditions.[2]

With the subordination of the Bengali population in the colonial public sphere, both politically and spatially, Partha Chatterjee argues that early nationalist thought divided the arena of culture conceptually into 'material' and 'spiritual' spheres. The former related to the 'outer' colonial public sphere, where the superiority of the European was recognised in areas such as science, the economy and administration and where the Bengali was subordinate. The latter referred to the superiority of India in spiritual matters and relates to the 'inner' domestic realm, which assumed a central position in nationalist thought, since it was discursively produced as a space where the Bengali maintained sovereign power and represented the locus of an authentic cultural identity to be guarded against colonial interference.[3]

As Partha Chatterjee has asserted, 'the home' was 'the original site on which the hegemonic project of nationalism was launched' (Chatterjee 1993: 147). Bengali imaginative literature therefore took the domestic world as its chief object, exploring alternatives to colonial modernity's dominant discourse, by reflecting on, and reimagining, notions of identity, domesticity, community and nation.[4] Such issues became central to the development of nationalist ideology before its entry into the public sphere towards the turn of the twentieth century.[5] Ideological shifts were instrumental in redefining domestic socio-spatial relations, where the role and position of women came to occupy an important and contested site for nationalist assertions of difference and superiority, not least in response to colonial representations of native ill-treatment of women as a justification for their 'civilising' mission. With the new centrality accorded to the domestic realm, women were elevated to a central position, as maternal figures responsible for the cultivation and protection of cultural identity.

Rabindranath Tagore's *Gora* (1910), meaning 'white man', has been described by his biographer Kripalani as 'the epic of India in transition' (Kripalani 1962: 207).[6] Set during an era where nationalism began to enter the public sphere, it breaks with many of the ideas established by earlier nationalist discourse, particularly in relation to the role of women, and those 'Others' outside the Hindu community.[7] This essay explores the ways in which identity, difference and modernity are imagined and developed in *Gora*, and how the new social relations that emerged in the context of colonial rule were manifested spatially.[8]

The architecture of orthodox identity

The novel is set in the late 1870s, when the legacy of the Indian Mutiny of 1857 had led to increasingly racist constructions of native inferiority in colonial discourse, markedly increasing the gulf between coloniser and colonised. The main character Gora was adopted by a high-caste Indian couple after his Irish mother died during his birth, having taken refuge in their house during the mutiny, and is subsequently raised as a Bengali, unaware of his European identity.[9]

The novel opens with Gora, who having recently converted from Brahmoism to strict Hindu orthodoxy, becomes chairman of the 'Hindu Patriots' Society', a nationalist party of which his childhood friend Binoy is secretary. Brahmoism was a religious movement which aimed to create a reformed monotheistic Hinduism, either through its purification or by drawing upon other religious traditions including Christianity. In the face of colonial oppression and the transformative impact of colonial modernity on traditional culture, Gora's revivalist Hindu nationalism attempts to combat westernisation through firm adherence to tradition and the strictures of caste, which he propounds as essential for the preservation of indigenous culture.[10] As such, Gora's nationalism no longer recognises the superiority of the West in the 'material' domain as earlier nationalist formulations had done. He rejects European culture entirely, and embarks on a struggle against its oppressive effects, particularly in regard to the assumed superiority of westernised Bengalis through their imitation of colonial culture, and the attendant disintegration of Hindu cultural identity.

The complex relations between the Hindu and Brahmo communities are explored in the novel through everyday interactions and occasionally polemical exchanges between characters that represent a range of positions within both communities. These exchanges are played out predominantly within the domestic sphere. Circumstances lead Gora and Binoy to become involved with the Brahmo household of Paresh Babu and Baroda, where their four daughters, the adopted Sucharita, Lolita, Labonya and Lila, are, in accordance with Brahmo culture, free to mix with men, and it is through the subsequent interaction with the daughters that the story unfolds.

Initially, Gora tries to prevent Binoy from visiting the house on the pretext that mixing with an 'other' culture may compromise his cultural identity. On Gora's initial visit to the house, his appearance and behaviour are openly aggressive: 'He came in like an incarnate image of revolt against Modernity. Even Binoy had never before seen him in such martial guise' (p. 52). In accordance with Hindu orthodoxy, he does not acknowledge the presence of Baroda or her daughters and due to caste observances refuses the offer of tea.[11]

This conflict between religious tradition and cultural and political modernity is a recurrent theme. For example, Anandamayi, Gora's unorthodox mother, describes the difficulty of movement and interaction within domestic space, a consequence of the divisive spatial practices associated with orthodox Hindu notions of purity and contamination: 'What happiness can it be for me, at every step I take, to come into collision with husband and child?' (p. 17). Her husband Krishnadayal, who occupies a separate portion of the house, is perpetually engaged in ascetic practices and is visited regularly only by priests. He shows little interest in the everyday lives of his family, and doesn't allow the outside world, even in the form of newspapers, to contaminate his private self and quest 'for some hidden short cut to salvation' (p. 29). He visits the other parts of the house to interact with his family only when compelled to do so.[12] In relation to such division, Tagore writes elsewhere, that India had 'set up boundaries of immutable walls', a 'magnificent cage of countless compartments' (Tagore quoted in Sarkar, S. 2002: 129).

These socio-spatial rules are explored throughout the novel, for example when Sucharita's Hindu aunt Harimohini, together with Sucharita and her younger brother, move to a house close to Paresh Babu's home. There, despite her aunt's own tragic experience of the oppressive effects of Hindu patriarchy, which culminated in the death of her daughter and banishment from the house of her deceased husband, she attempts to impose Hindu orthodoxy upon Sucharita by restricting her movement and preventing her 'corruption' by mixing with individuals who are located 'outside' Hinduism – including her own family. To avoid such contamination, and with the selfish goal of moving back into her dead husband's house, she tries to arrange Sucharita's marriage to one of her brothers-in-law, in order to 'transfer her to the safe fortress of her father-in-law's house' (p. 491).

The position of women is a dominant theme within the novel, and ideologically Gora's orthodoxy is in keeping with the tenets of earlier nationalist discourse, and its emplacement of women within the home.[13] He states that, ' ... The altar at which Woman may be truly worshipped is her place as Mother, the seat of the pure, right-minded Lady of the House ... ' (p. 12), which he contrasts to the nationalist image of the European woman as an object of male desire. Binoy, who serves as a counterpoint to Gora and his orthodox views, challenges the scriptural authority that Gora draws upon and its positioning of women, by asking, 'Would you contemptuously dismiss a great idea because it occasionally gets clouded over?' (p. 11). Furthermore, he claims that Gora's idea of India is 'womanless', dismissing his rhetoric on their 'proper' place at home as 'delusion', and whilst remaining unsure of the extent to which women should 'show themselves in public' argues ' ... that so long as our women remain hidden behind the *purdah*, our country will be a half-truth to us ... ' (p. 114).

Gora's nationalist orthodoxy, with its object of protecting cultural identity and indigenous space from the eradicating power of colonial territorialisation, emphasises its difference and superiority to the coloniser's culture through the creation of an oppositional nationalist identity and domestic culture.[14] Under the exceptional circumstances of colonial rule, the dominant socio-spatial thematic of conservative orthodoxy entails physical separation through self-enclosed configurations of space, immobility and rigid boundaries within and in relation to the outside world, where Others, particularly the European, are denied entry.[15] It connotes the traditional multiple courtyard house, which expresses a large patriarchal world with a complex spatial hierarchy and separate compartments for women, where gender separation is further articulated through the use of architectonic devices such as venetians, screens and other socio-spatial boundaries and rules.

Such elements are highlighted in Tagore's *The Broken Nest* (1901), which Satyajit Ray later adapted for his film entitled *Charulata* (*The Lonely Wife*, 1964). In the novella, the wife Charulata is depicted observing the arrival of her brother-in-law through 'the peephole of the inner rooms' (Tagore 1901: 36) and clapping her hands at its 'boundary' to attract his attention in the male domain. Ray's film opens with her moving around the side of a space in the *andarmahal* (women's compartment) and using a pair of opera glasses to peer through the venetians at the outside world and later eavesdropping at the threshold of the male domain. Similarly, in Bankimchandra Chattopadhyay's novel *Bishabriksha* (*The Poison Tree*, 1873), the lady of the house, Suryamukhi, communicates through her servant from behind a screen adjacent to the veranda, where the visitor remains located.

The *andarmahal* assumed a new prominence in nationalist ideology both as a refuge and as a fortress, since it is a site where difference with the coloniser is emphasised, where cultural identity is protected and developed, and where the woman finds expression as '*grihalakshmi* [bounteous goddess of the home]' (Tagore quoted in Sarkar, S. 2002: 112). Although gender divisions persist within the home, the *andarmahal* as a specific female space vanishes in the late nineteenth-century single courtyard house and modern house types of the twentieth century.

The fortress is a recurring metaphor for domestic space and cultural orthodoxy. For example, Binoy, reiterating Gora's rhetoric, tells us that, ' ... when the enemy attacks a fortress from all sides it shows no lack of a liberal mind to guard with your

FIGURE 4.1 A 'magnificent cage of countless compartments' (Tagore quoted in Sarkar,
          S. 2002: 129)

very life every road, lane, door, window, and even crack leading into the fortress'
(p. 20). The same spatial metaphor is also used to refer to Gora's appearance: 'His
face seemed needlessly large and excessively strong, the bones of his jaws and chin
being like the massive bolts of a fortress' (p. 8). The 'fortress' of orthodoxy charac-
terising nationalist ideology thus provides protection from the aggressive expansion
of colonial modernity. And in the same way as Gora's identity and strict adherence to tradition serves to protect culture, the notion of domestic space-as-fortress
constitutes the response to the alien circumstances of colonial domination, where
the boundaries and walls of domestic space become stronger than those typical of
precolonial spatial arrangements. But it is also suggestive of his European identity
since the fort was a central architectural feature of the 'white town' where the
majority of Europeans resided in the early days of the East India Company.

The construction of the fort represented the first stage in the development of
colonial space and imperial territorialisation characterised by the erasure of indigenous culture. This erasure incorporated the gradual eradication of the original
group of villages, and the relocation of the native population from Gobindapur
to Sutanuti following the 'Sack of Calcutta' (1756), in which large numbers of
European settlements within the original fort were destroyed.[16] Subsequently,
European settlement spread out into surrounding areas encroaching on native
space. The result over a hundred years later was a town with marked European
features, celebrated in Rudyard Kipling's depiction of Calcutta as a translocation of

London and an important node in the nexus of imperial space: 'We have left India behind us at Howrah station, and now we enter foreign parts. No, not wholly foreign. Say rather too familiar … "Why, this is London!"' adding that it would be, ' … a criminal thing to allow the natives to have any voice in the control of such a city … ' (Kipling 1899: 7–10). Kipling's proclamation constituted a form of the colonial uncanny, a theme to which I will return.

For Gora, the European construction of Calcutta was nothing less than a cultural invasion and provided one of the justifications for his desire to reconstruct an authentic identity and future, free from the fetters of European influence:

> Is there nothing but this falsehood on every side! This Calcutta of yours, with its offices, its High Court … because we call this falsehood of some evil genie India, is that any reason why 350 millions of people should honour what is false and go about intoxicated with the idea that this world of falsity is a real world?
>
> (pp. 23–4)

The anxiety of the colonial authorities in the face of such increased resentment, made explicit in Gora's hostility to British rule, resulted in a marked intensification of socio-spatial divisions in the city. This was manifested both in increased residential segregation and in the continued construction of walled residential complexes.[17] These complexes were built as ornamentally gated, classically inspired mansions in large grounds, often set far back from the street with quarters for exorbitant numbers of servants: an architectural symbol of the colonial desire for separation.

The extension of colonial modernity can also be seen in the operations of the Calcutta Improvement Trust (CIT), formed in 1911. Headed by E. P. Richards, an English engineer, a report was prepared based on a comparison with London that broadly ignored the specific history and cultural logic of Kolkata, and proposed a large number of new thoroughfares that involved the large-scale demolition of 'native' parts of the city and their replacement with wide Haussmann-style avenues typical of European urban modernity.[18]

Such a phallocentric approach to urban space is mirrored in the violent masculinity and aggressively polemical identity represented by Gora in his assertion of an image of India which others must accept, and finds a parallel in the imperialist project with its 'civilizing mission' and forceful insistence on the supremacy of western culture, as well as in the violent means by which it imposes its will.[19] Sucharita, for example, observes,

> How violent to Gora was his own will! And how ruthlessly he would push aside others and overwhelm them when he once applied that will with full force! Anyone who wanted to agree with Gora on any subject had to humble himself completely to Gora's will.[20]
>
> (p. 444)

As Ashis Nandy comments, the Hindu nationalist's desire to reject Europe as embodied by Gora, in his adoption of the European idea of a modern nation, has as its outcome an aspiration 'that Hindus should become a single homogenous nation' (Nandy 1994: 39).[21] Hence, Gora's image of nation and identity becomes an 'internalisation' of European discourse. This articulation of monolithic categories of identity and their association with territory, marks, as Joya Chatterjee has shown, a stage in the development of communalism culminating in India's partition, its huge population transfers, and the subsequent transformation of urban space and notions of home (Chatterjee, J. 1994: 150–90).

Gora is engaged in a search for identity and the articulation of a utopian future reality, which supersedes and supplants the 'illusion' of colonial modernity. This is illustrated when he says,

> The whole quest of man is the vision of the New as it appears in all its beauty on the flaming crest of the Old as it is destroyed. On the background of this blood-red sky I can see a radiant Future, freed from its bonds, – I can see it in to-day's approaching dawn.

(pp. 97–8)

FIGURE 4.2 'His tiny home and the ugly city that surrounded it suddenly seemed to him an abode of illusion' (p. 4)

His vision, liberated from the anomalous circumstances of colonialism, implies a new architectural modernity that presupposes the destruction of the colonial world. This modernity, and the suggested re-territorialisation, can be seen to mimic the 'violent' imperial extension of European space, which it seeks to replace.

However, although Gora's nationalist orthodoxy involves adherence to tradition, it differs from the conservative orthodoxy of his father and Harimohini since it entails a desire to generate cultural unity. This aim presupposes an openness and mobility that takes Gora to the street and to the village with the aim of creating unity across divisions of caste and class through social work and political action, while also attempting to transcend the elite basis of nationalism.[22] He therefore mixes with the subaltern masses, which he believes to embody his revivalist idea of traditional Hinduism. Every day he visits 'the poor people of his neighbourhood' stating that, 'he was hardly so intimate with his circle of educated friends' (p. 107), and he decides to travel through a number of the villages surrounding Kolkata, in this, his first journey beyond urban society. But his image of identity, constructed within the confines of upper-caste urban society, is challenged by the reality of traditional rural social life, which is bound by the tradition he propounds. His orthodox friends believe the impoverished condition of the poor to be natural, but Gora, in his devotion to India's well-being and search for radical equality and unity, finds 'this terrible load of ignorance, apathy and suffering' a 'constant agony' (p. 182).

Gora's image of orthodoxy is further challenged in Ghosepara where he comes to a realisation of the injustice associated with caste contamination. These customs prohibit him from accepting water from a Hindu barber who has adopted a Muslim boy and risks being outcaste to stay with the oppressed Muslim villagers, whilst permitting him to accept it from the Bengali collector who has colluded with the colonial authorities in their oppression. Finally, his cognisance of the conflict between his anti-colonial project of unity formation and the divisive practices of caste tradition, lead him to disregard caste and eat with the barber.[23]

Gora's desire for inclusion of the subaltern, his revivalist Hindu orthodoxy and his idea of an unrealised architectural modernity resonates with Mahatma Gandhi's 'anti-colonial "anarcho-communitarianism"' (Khilnani quoted in Ranjan 2011: 248), imagined as a non-statist decentralised 'system of self-sufficient village republics' (Chatterjee, P. 1986: 121). Although in Gandhi's vision 'Towns will not disappear completely' (Chatterjee, P. 1986: 121), Gora's utopia seeks to replace the city with an architectural modernity based on traditional rural typologies: a return to the original village paradigm that existed prior to colonial territorialisation.

Parallels to this erasure of colonial urban memory can be observed in the demolitions of colonial mansions, removals of statues and renaming of streets, which accompanied independence. For example, the majority of colonial mansions in the former European town were subsequently replaced by an architecture of global capitalist modernity, expressed by multi-storey apartment blocks, commercial and

FIGURE 4.3 'In those days the Ganges and its banks had not been invaded by the ugliness which commercial greed has since brought in its train. There was no railway beside it, and no bridge across it, and the sky on a winter evening was not obscured by the soot-laden breath of the crowded city. The river used then to bring its message of peace from the stainless peaks of the distant Himalayas into the midst of Calcutta's dusty bustle' (p. 146)

financial institutions. This theme is highlighted in Satyajit Ray's *The Middleman* (1976), where capitalist speculators corrupted by greed are depicted purchasing a colonial house in order to demolish it and construct a more profitable multi-storey apartment block in its place.

Monstrous hybridism

The source of much of Gora's anger can be traced to the native internalisation of colonial ideas of racial inferiority and the consequent class-based divisions within Indian society. He argues that not only English Magistrates but now ' … the Deputy Magistrates [Indian] of the present time are gradually coming to look upon their fellow-countrymen as little better than dogs' (p. 140). This was representative of Macaulayan colonial ideology, rooted in the belief in the inferiority of indigenous culture that advocated a type of colonial hybridisation to create a class of Anglicised Indians, described in his infamous minute of 1835 as 'Indian in blood and colour, but English in taste, in opinions, in morals, and in intellect' (Lees 1871: 102). It was a prejudice reinforced in his claim that ' ... single shelf of a good European library was worth the whole native literature of India and Arabia' (Lees 1871: 91), a view shared by a number of Victorian architectural scholars such as James Fergusson (Metcalfe 2002: 33–5). Kipling, on the other hand, who believed in fixed racial differences and who remained hostile to ideas of cultural mixing, referred to the mimicry of the westernised native as 'the monstrous hybridism of East and West' (Kipling 1994: 318).[24]

These racial tensions come to the fore in one of the important parts of the book, which deals not only with gendered, but with racial socio-spatial transgressions. The wife of a magistrate, formerly acquainted with Paresh Babu, asks Baroda whether her daughters could perform an English play at the magistrate's annual birthday celebrations. Such a performance of a western drama to a European audience symbolises the success of the Macaulayan project of cultural hybridisation. But when it comes to light that Gora has been sentenced to a month's imprisonment for his part in aiding a group of students from Calcutta in resisting police oppression, the rebellious Lolita refuses to participate. Furthermore, in an act of defiance, she transgresses the limits of propriety in relation to women's presence in public space, by returning alone with Binoy on a ferry to Calcutta.

Haran later expresses his outrage to Paresh Babu and blames him for 'bringing outsiders into the family circle, who are seeking to drag it away from its traditions' (p. 310), criticising the daughters' behaviour and trying to reconstruct barriers to their movement, which Paresh Babu had removed from domestic space. Such disciplinary power, as embodied by Haran, is also highlighted when rumours about the family are propagated by him in community publications. This incident illustrates the ways in which print culture, by revealing the inner life of the home to the public gaze, is instrumental in the maintenance of patriarchal society, due to its role in defining and regulating notions of identity and domesticity.[25]

Similarly, Baroda assumes a westernised identity that displays 'an anxiety to keep pace with advanced society' (p. 48), reflected in her desire to maintain a clear distinction between 'things that were Brahmo and things that were not' (p. 48). This distinction is illustrated in the hostility shown by her and her Brahmo friends to Sucharita's Hindu aunt, Harimohini, who stays with her Hindu idol in 'the lonely room at the top of the house' (p. 266) in order that she can adhere to caste restrictions. One of the friends disregards these restrictions when she attempts to enter the room with her shoes on.[26] Whilst they treat her as if she belonged to 'some different species' (p. 282), Harimohini is equally unsure 'How far one could safely associate with them' (p. 292). Sucharita and her young brother Satish thus 'form a separate little family in one corner of Paresh Babu's home' (pp. 270–1), with Lolita as 'the only bridge between the two divisions' (p. 271). Due to her adoption of Hindu habits, Baroda pressurises Paresh Babu to marry Sucharita to Haran in order that she may leave the house, while threatening to take her daughters elsewhere if he does not agree. This aspect of the novel resonates with the historical reality of the Tagore house where Rabindranath was raised, and which was amicably divided between the two sections of the extended family – one Brahmo and the other Hindu.[27]

Baroda performs her colonial mimicry through the wearing of 'high-heeled shoes', the consumption of 'tea and cakes', and the adornment of her daughters in western apparel and make-up. She proudly presents Labonya's album of English poems, has Lila recite 'Twinkle Twinkle, little star' to Binoy and on her adoption of Sucharita, changes her name from Radharani, due to its Hindu associations. In Paresh Babu's house, there are other elements of European material culture, for example, a 'picture of Christ', a number of European books and artefacts specific to Brahmoism. However, in keeping with his syncretic sense of self, that 'drew no line between Brahmo and non-Brahmo' (p. 103) in relation to religious texts, he also keeps the *Bhagavadgita* and the *Mahabharata,* in contrast to Haran who 'wanted to banish all such books from Brahmo households' and for whom, 'Amongst the scriptures of the world-religions his only support was the Bible' (p. 103).[28]

An equally problematic issue for Indian national identity was the dissemination of western architectural languages that could be interpreted as signifying an acceptance of colonial superiority and the Macaulayan project of colonial hybridisation. This contributed to the erasure of indigenous space, and its replacement by 'the colourless vagueness of cosmopolitanism' (Tagore, quoted in Nandy 1994: 42) intrinsic to colonial mimicry as personified by Haran and Baroda, with its denial of the specificity of Indian history and cultural pluralism. Such a mode of being modern is summarised by Tagore:

> Modernism is not in the dress of the European; or in the hideous structures where their children are interned when they take their lessons; or in the square houses with flat, straight-walled surfaces, pierced with parallel lines of windows where these people are caged in their lifetime; certainly modernism is not in their ladies' bonnets carrying on them loads of incongruities. These are not modern but merely European. True modernism is freedom of mind, not slavery of taste. It is independence of thought and action, not tutelage under European schoolmasters.
>
> *Quoted in Kopf 2011: 305–6*

This notion of mimicry is reflected in a number of houses of the Bengali elite which exhibit typical European features. Several of these houses are located in the 'white town', and are comprised of formal organisations typical of colonial house types, for example incorporating drawing rooms, billiard rooms and European-style facades. Such characteristics express a desire for the power and culture of the coloniser. In *The Tiger's Daughter* (1971), Bharati Mukherjee makes reference to such a house on Camac Street, emphasising its exclusionary and inward-looking character, ' ... in a house that filtered sunlight and unwelcome guests through an elaborate system of coir blinds, rose-water sprays, *durwans* [watchmen], bearers, heavy doors, locks, chains and hooks. She was home in a class that lived by Victorian rules, changed decisively by the exuberance of the Hindu imagination' (Mukherjee 1987: 34).

Similarly, 'the popularization of the European notion of a façade' (Chattopadhyay, S. 2005: 157) and the subsequent proliferation of the neoclassical style, which became the dominant architectural language of the city in the nineteenth-century residences of the elite in the 'black town', demonstrates a similar hybridisation. This is exemplified further by the influence of European material culture, in the adoption of objects that ranged from Victorian furniture to European art prints and literature.

However, the effect of colonial mimicry on urban and architectural space, although implying the spread of European archetypes at the expense of indigenous paradigms, is a more complex process, which does not result in simple homogenisation, since cultural translation of the architectural object produces a new set of meanings.[29] The same process of western mimicry can be traced in modern domestic architecture, which arose in the early decades of the twentieth century, incorporating influences from international modernism and Art Deco. The

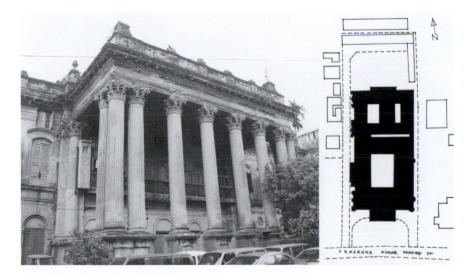

FIGURE 4.4 '... a child gradually grows up to become a man, but man does not suddenly become a cat or dog. I want the changes in India to be along the path of India's development, for if you suddenly begin to follow the path of England's history then everything from first to last will be a useless failure.' (p. 461)

Site plan based on a drawing in the archive of the Kolkata Municipal Corporation.

majority of such domestic architecture was built in the south of the city, on the new roads constructed by the CIT. The Bengali population that moved there considered themselves to be modern, secular and cosmopolitan and so produced house types that reflected the increasing adoption of the nuclear, rather than the extended family. This led in turn to the dissolution of the traditional courtyard house type and other spaces associated with traditional domesticity. Following independence, the westernised Bengali upper class moved into the former European enclaves of the centre, and the garden houses of the south, whilst the production of modern domestic space continued to increase throughout the south of the city.

The resulting residential patterns can be understood as neocolonial in character. The western-educated *nouveaux riches* occupied former colonial locations, and a fuzzy class-based dualism gradually replaced the racial divisions between European and native in the colonial city, with the north becoming associated with Hindu orthodoxy and the south with western secular values. Many modern house forms consist of organisations that reflect this mimetic modernity. Hence, neocolonial gated houses and apartment complexes employ a western syntax, in a similar manner as the earlier houses of the Bengali elite in the white town had, incorporating 'modern' spaces

FIGURE 4.5 'True modernism is freedom of mind, not slavery of taste. It is independence of thought and action, not tutelage under European schoolmasters' (Tagore quoted in Kopf 2011: 305–6)

such as drawing and dining rooms. Such spaces replaced indigenous forms and utilised new western domestic technologies, reflecting the newly adopted lifestyles.

Such an architectural modernity is reflected in Satyajit Ray's Calcutta trilogy,
where the capitalist class is depicted as inhabiting spacious, modern and often gated
dwellings in the postcolonial south. Ray draws upon Tagorean themes relating to
loss of cultural identity, patriarchal subordination of women and their transformation under modernity. He also portrays pre-industrial rural utopias as an image of a
counter-modernity, figured as the lost home and locus of authentic cultural identity and morality. Similar themes are explored in a more starkly political fashion in
Mrinal Sen's Calcutta trilogy. For example, in *Calcutta 71* (1972) members of the
urban elite are shown getting drunk in a 'club', an exclusive space of European
sociability in colonial times, which Sen juxtaposes with disturbing images of urban
poverty. In his trilogy, spaces of global capitalist modernity are depicted as symbols
of neocolonial exploitation and become targets of revolutionary activity.

The architecture of the universal self

The idea of universalism is presented as an alternative to the exclusionary constructions
of difference relating to race, caste and class, which were enshrined in both Hindu
and Brahmo notions of community.[30] Paresh Babu is eventually outcaste from both
communities. Indeed, a number of characters aligned to the general good are outcastes
– Paresh Babu, Anandaymoi, Gora, Lolita and Binoy – which would seem to indicate
a privileging of the 'outsider', and a desire to escape the category of community.

The universal self, embodied by Paresh Babu, has 'no place in any society'
(p. 569), and although his sense of self is located within Brahmoism, he doesn't
perceive this faith to be divorced from Hinduism. Instead, he distances himself
from its present form, since he rejects its divisive character both within (caste hierarchy), and without (one has to be born into the religion).

Paresh Babu's hospitality to the Other, and his enlightened attitude to gender
equality, is explored through the narrative surrounding his daughters, for whom
he promotes free movement at home (a feature of Bramho culture). This differs
radically from Haran's and Baroda's discriminatory elitism, since by increasing the
level of access to the world beyond the household, it creates greater possibilities
for social mixing. In contrast to the self-enclosed complex of boundaries that char-
acterise orthodox Hindu domesticity, Paresh Babu's daughters are free to appear
in front of, and to converse with, male 'outsiders' to their community. This leads
to their transformation through contact with the Hindu Other as represented by
Gora and Binoy. Paresh Babu believes, ' … that girls ought to mix with people of
all shades of opinion, otherwise they will simply remain narrow-minded' (p. 64).

As a consequence of the absence of gendered spatial divisions, his daughters are
involved in discussions relating to identity and culture which are normally the preserve
of men, and they are therefore included in the development of modernity. Since,

as he states, 'I too once came out from my home in revolt' (p. 433), Paresh Babu is the only member of the household to support the 'rebellious' Lolita in her transgression of social prohibitions – both in relation to the ferry incident and her subsequent marriage to Binoy – since he believes that through the challenges performed by individual 'revolt', 'society ought to become more liberal out of regard for the individual' (p. 443). He refers to her dissent and singularity as leaving an 'accustomed path' into a 'vast unknown' (p. 443); an uncertain modernity that she and the other central characters, caught as they are in its formation, are all involved in articulating. The manner in which he nurtures his daughters suggests their future presence and free agency in public space. Indeed, Lolita's rebellion and entry into a marriage with the 'outsider', Binoy, is at odds with Brahmo patriarchy, as are her attempts to open a school that has as its goal the emancipation of women. In several instances, her youthful radicalism surpasses that of Paresh Babu; she challenges her subordination as a woman, and asserts that, ' … I am determined to be free from this society of Haran Babu and his set!' (p. 344). Furthermore when Paresh Babu explains the difference between societies, she has difficulty comprehending, since she considered 'the differences between different societies' to be 'negligible' (p. 433). In relation to Sucharita's attraction towards Hinduism, resulting from both Harimohini's and Gora's influence, Paresh Babu arranges for Sucharita, Satish and her aunt to move to a nearby house, providing his daughter with freedom 'to find her own true relations with the outside world' (p. 301).

Homi Bhabha has explored the central position of domestic space in the development of modernity. He writes that the 'unhomely' prevents the 'fixity and fetishism of identities' (Bhabha 2008: 13) and is brought about through 'the intervention of the "beyond" that establishes a boundary: a bridge, where "presencing" begins … that is the condition of extra-territorial and cross-cultural initiations … ' (Bhabha 2008: 13). In the context of the novel, this condition of the unhomely, and its transformation of domestic space and identity, is brought about by Paresh Babu's hospitality to the Hindu Other and the domestic culture he has created. As Bhabha comments, 'The recesses of the domestic space become sites for history's most intricate invasions. In that displacement, the borders between home and the world become confused; and uncannily, the private and the public become part of each other … ' (Bhabha 2008: 13) Furthermore, in reference to Tagore's next political novel *The Home and the World* (1919), Bhabha writes of Bimala – who embodies the logical progression of female subjectivity – that she is 'drawn forever from the zenana, the secluded women's quarters, as she crosses that fated verandah into the world of public affairs' (Bhabha 2008: 14).

Since the trope of women in public was '*the* central problematic of the Bengali discourse on modernity' (Chattopadhyay, S. 2005: 227), it is explored in much of the significant literature embodied by the nationalist corpus and beyond. For example, Bankimchandra Chattopadhyay, Tagore's predecessor and key progenitor in the formulation of nationalist discourse,[31] depicts in *Bishabriksha*, women who are caught up in the socio-spatial transgression of defined moral boundaries of domesticity, which leads to their actual or ritual death (for example, through their exile from home and their pilgrimage to a holy site).[32] Bankim represents women as crucial to the well-being of the family. However, their sexuality requires disciplining, since any transgressive behaviour could lead to the departure of *Lakshmi*, the goddess of domestic well-being and the subsequent ruin of the household. It is a theme that recurs in the novels of the second half of the twentieth century, due to the gradual consolidation of women's presence in the public realm, bringing to the fore new tensions between tradition and modernity. In Narendranath Mitra's *Mahanagar* (The Big City, 1967), set in the immediate post-Independence period, the main character Aroti, an East Bengali refugee, is compelled to enter the public sphere to take up employment alongside a young Anglo-Indian woman named Edith.[33] Her subsequent journeys into the public spaces of the city result in a new sense of discovery and liberation, whilst her encounters with men provoke her husband's anxiety. This theme is also taken up in Amitav Ghosh's *The Shadow Lines* (1988), where the diasporic Ila, a young Bengali woman resident in London, is referred to by her grandmother's sister as 'wearing tight trousers like a Free School Street whore' (Ghosh 2005: 79). Then, in the following year during a visit, her

FIGURE 4.6 'Women have been enfolded into the stereotypes of mother and housewife … Then came an earthquake in the West which has shaken up this age-old structure of discrimination … We will have to recognise the common humanity of women as well as men, beyond all differences … ' (Tagore quoted in Sarkar, S. 2002: 148)

young and cosmopolitan uncle forbids and removes her from the dance floor when she defiantly dances with a businessman at a hotel nightclub. Afterwards, he insists that such behaviour transgresses the cultural norms of Calcutta, to which she responds by declaring her preference for life in London: to be 'Free of your bloody culture and free of all of you' (Ghosh 2005: 87). This theme is also explored in Swati Chattopadhyay's discussion of Dipesh Chakrabarty, which highlights the new possibilities opened up for women in public space, with 'the proliferating public spaces of colleges, coffee-houses, and bookshops in the early twentieth century' (Chattopadhyay, S. 2005: 19).

The desire for a social life free from strict codes of moral conduct is also fundamental to Gora's concept of universalism. At the end of the novel he renounces his rigid orthodoxy, observing of the subaltern that, 'every act … in every home, was under the vigilant eyes of society … it seemed as if their whole natures had become entangled from head to foot in a network of various penalties for transgressing against rules forbidding them to do this or that at every step … ' (pp. 510–11). He recognises that this system, and the colonial structure framing it, has led to a complete lack of unity.

Gora's search for an appropriate form of self and for an enlightened modernity finds resolution at the end of the novel when his Irish origin is revealed to him. He immediately senses the dissolution of his identity. However, this sense of 'negation' turns quickly to one of emancipation, since his radical sense of non-belonging and singularity dissolves the sense of difference associated with his orthodox identity and the fact of belonging to a particular community, which had formed a barrier to his ability to engage with Others.

He realises that 'To-day I am free … I need no longer fear being contaminated or becoming an outcaste … ' (p. 567). Conversely, then, his sense of homelessness leads to the lifting of his psycho-social signs of difference, thus unveiling his vision of a universalist Indian identity and modernity which transcends distinctions, and accommodates 'unity in diversity'.[34] He proclaims, 'To-day I am really an Indian! In me there is no longer any opposition between Hindu, Mussulman, and Christian. To-day every caste in India is my caste … ' (p. 568). His universalist image of India also exposes the inadequacy of his adopted European idea of the modern nation and its coupling of territory with ethnic identity, showing it to be another form of closed community on a larger scale. With the erosion of his orthodox identity, Gora unites with Sucharita signifying the union of East and West. Gora's doubled identity, as both European and Indian, serves as a challenge to late Victorian colonial discourse, by demonstrating that a European can be completely acculturated. The novel therefore disrupts assertions of immutable difference to disclose the fundamental equivalence of coloniser and colonised.[35]

Universalism thus provides a way of being modern, which transcends the local, the home and the fortress-like barriers of Hindu orthodoxy, without negating cultural identity through the imitation of the West. Instead, universalism proposes an alternative modernity, which looks beyond difference, and requires a mode of being in space that involves mobility and an open, tolerant acceptance of the Other.[36]

FIGURE 4.7 'on the shore of this vast sea of humanity that is India … No one knows
whence and at whose call came pouring endless inundations of men …
Aryans and non-Aryans, Dravidians and Chinese, Scythians, Huns, Pathans
and Moghuls – all are mixed, merged and lost in one body. Now the door
has opened to the West … they will give and take, meet and bring together,
none shall be turned away …' (Text extract of hymn by Tagore quoted in
Kripalani 1962: 209–10)

This vision of a universalist modernity, with its ideal of 'unity in diversity' delin-
eates a palimpsestic architecture and literature that incorporate a multiplicity of
'different' cultures.[37] It indicates the translation of 'other' forms as they are absorbed
into their new context, bestowing upon them new meanings. The transformations
that have accompanied the colonial encounter, liberation struggles and multicul-
turalism, have cultural syncreticism as their natural consequence. Such a modernity
implies an evolution 'rooted' in multiple cultural traditions, where difference and
identity are maintained in a hybrid culture that assimilates 'other' influences, without blindly imitating them.[38]

Notes

1 Tagore, the first Asian recipient of the accolade, received the Nobel Prize for Literature
in 1913 for his collection of poems entitled *Gitanjali* (Kripalani 1962: 225–9). Tagore
resigned his knighthood following the Amritsar massacre of 1919 (*ibid.* 265–6).
2 The movement arose in a context of mutual transcultural exchange between the early
orientalists and the indigenous intelligentsia. Its beginnings have been associated with

Rammohun Roy (Dasgupta 2007: 5), 'the progenitor of all modern reform movements in India' (Kopf 1969: 3) and founder of Brahmoism, who sought the abolition of *sati* and idol worship. Tagore belongs to the late renaissance period, and was also preoccupied with social reform and the principles of universalism. He is recognised as an important figure 'in shaping the modern consciousness in India' and was acknowledged by Jawaharlal Nehru as his intellectual guru (Nandy 1994: 4). See Dasgupta (2007: 1–20) and Kopf (1969: 1–9) for a short introduction to the movement.

3 For greater detail see Partha Chatterjee (1986: 66–79; 1993: 6–9, 119–21, 126; 1999: 237–40).

4 Tanika Sarkar has observed that the new products of modernity such as 'railways, electricity, telegraph, urban growth, city crowds, street scenes' do not feature centrally in literature, 'except in a tangential and negative sense' (Sarkar 2001: 29).

5 For an analysis of the relationship between domesticity and literature in this context see Tanika Sarkar (2001: 23–52).

6 The definition of *Gora* has a class association denoting the ordinary white man and can refer to a British soldier (Yule and Burnell 1886: 297). Also see Spivak (2002: 53–4).

7 As in the novels of Bankimchandra Chattopadhyay, one of which, *Bishabriksha*, is referred to below.

8 All page references refer to the 2002 edition of the novel.

9 Ashis Nandy has stated that Gora's character is based on the nationalist revolutionary Brahmabandhab Upadhyay and Sister Nividita, both of whom changed their names. The former, originally Hindu, converted to Brahmoism then to Catholicism, later returning to Hinduism (Nandy 1994: 51–67). The latter was an Irish Catholic who converted to Hinduism, becoming the disciple of prominent Hindu revivalist, Swami Vivekananda (Nandy 1994: 36). Pandit has also noted that Gora contains traces of the Vivekananda, Tagore and Gandhi (Pandit 1995: 219).

10 According to Nandy the revivalist strand of nationalism embodied by Gora did not exist as a political force during the time that the novel is set but arose later. 'Originally inspired by the "nativism" of Bankimchandra Chattopadhyay and Swami Vivekananda, this strain only became a significant political movement after the partition of Bengal in 1905' (Nandy 1994: 36).

11 Brahmo culture permits that girls may appear in front of men and as Lalita Pandit highlights, novels by other authors such as Saratchandra Chattopadhyay have depicted Brahmo households as 'socio-sexual spaces that provide free access to women' (Pandit 1995: 224).

12 In Tagore's memoirs he describes a servant who exhibits a similarly obsessive concern to avoid all possibility of contamination (Tagore 2005: 15).

13 For extended discussions on the 'women's question' and domesticity in nationalist thought see for example Partha Chatterjee (1999: 233–53; 1993: 116–57) and Tanika Sarkar (2001: 23–52).

14 Benita Parry comments in relation to such an oppositional identity, that it leads to 'the construction of a politically conscious unified revolutionary self, standing in unmitigated opposition to the oppressor' (Parry 1987: 32). See Gandhi's discussion on the complication of such oppositional positions in postcolonial theory (Gandhi 1998: 9–22). See also Gayatri Spivak's discussion of 'strategic essentialism' (Spivak 1993: 1–23).

15 Patrick C. Hogan has explained that according to Hindu philosophy, history is divided into different ages, with the last, which includes the period of colonialism being known as *Kaliyuga*, 'the age of ill fortune', where under alien domination, regulations relating to caste and other aspects of tradition become exaggerated (Hogan 2000: 216–21).

16 Prior to the arrival of the British, what is now Kolkata consisted of three villages: Sutanuti, Gobindapur and Kalikata.

17 The more radical type of such spatial distancing is expressed in the expansion of hill-station settlements, as for example those in the lower Himalaya, including Simla, which became the summer residence of the colonial government (Metcalfe 1995: 160–85).

18 Improvement programmes began in the early nineteenth century with the Lottery Committee, followed later by the Fever Hospital committee, both of which undertook changes to the urban form of the city based on theories that disease was transmitted through the air and derived from the native quarters due to the lax morals of its population (Beattie 2004).

19 The novel reflects Tagore's shifting views on nationalism. Previously a keen supporter of the Swadeshi movement, the activities of which included the boycotting of foreign goods and schools, he became increasingly disillusioned with the increasingly violent 'imperialistic' methods and the Hindu revivalist modes that it employed, see Nandy (1994: 1–9) and Sarkar, S. (2002: 118–19).

20 This parallel with European imperialism is also developed through his physical appearance and behaviour, for example ' … Professors used to call him the Snow Mountain, for he was outrageously white … nearly six feet tall, with big bones and fists like the paws of a tiger' (Tagore, R. 2002: 8).

21 See Chakrabarty's project of 'Provincialising Europe', that seeks to 'provincialise' the hegemonic, universalist claims of western knowledge and assert the importance of 'other' knowledges and 'life-worlds' in the creation of an 'original' narrative rather than the mimetic adoption of the historical trajectory of Europe (Chakrabarty 2000: 27–46).

22 Sumit Sarkar has noted that, in line with Gandhi's politics, Tagore recognised the elitism of nationalism, and the need to unite with the masses (Sarkar 2002: 122–3).

23 In Abanindranath Tagore's *Apon Katha: My Story* the translator states that in his memoirs Abanindranath recounts that during a festival in which 'siblings tie silken cords around each other's wrists to protect them with the bonds of love' Rabindranath went to the Nakodah Mosque to do so with the local Muslims, expressing his desire to forge unity with the Other in reality (Tagore, A. 2004: 13).

24 Gora expresses a similar view in relation to mimetic hybridity, commenting that 'by mere imitation we shall eventually be neither one thing or the other' (Tagore, R. 2002: 141).

25 See Tanika Sarkar for more detail on how the new public sphere and the development of print culture addressed matters relating to domestic life (Sarkar 2001: 25–30).

26 The religio-spatial transgression would be created by entering the room with shoes on, since it is considered sacrilegious in Hindu custom.

27 See Abanindranath Tagore (2004: 34) for greater detail.

28 See Hogan (2000: 223–4, 227, 235) on the cultural resonances in the context of colonialism of the specific literature referred to in the novel.

29 See Homi Bhabha's discussion of colonial mimicry in the context of colonial identity formation for insight into such cultural complexity (2008: 121–31).

30 For further discussion of universalism in the novel see Hogan (2000: 216, 220, 224–5, 243–8, 251–4), Nandy (1994: vii, 39–42, 46, 81) and Pandit (1995: 207–8, 217–18, 220, 231–2). See Saranindranath Tagore (2008) and Laura B. Williams (2007) for a discussion of cosmopolitanism in the context of Rabindranath's thought. Nandy highlights that 'the ultimate civilizational ambition of India' was 'to be the cultural epitome of the world … and to redefine or convert all passionate self-other debates into self–self debates' (Nandy 1994: 82). This resonates with Julia Kristeva's notion of 'uncanny strangeness' that recognises the presence of the other in the self (Kristeva 1991: 191–2).

31 See Partha Chatterjee for a detailed elaboration of the relevance of Bankim for the development of nationalist discourse (1986: 54–81).

32 For an in-depth discussion see Chattopadhyay (2005: 239–48).

33 The novel is based on his short story *Abataranika* (1955), which he extended following Satyajit Ray's film adaptation also entitled *Mahanagar* (1963).

34 Nandy has observed that Tagore saw that it was 'this solution – unity through acknowledgment of differences – that India has to offer the world' (Nandy 1994: 6).

35 On the comparison of the universalism of *Gora* with the imperialist reinforcement of colonial difference as explored in Kipling's *Kim* (1901), which explores the same idea

of a European 'resident alien' brought up in India, see Pandit (1995: 209–15), Nandy (1994: 42–50) and Spivak (2002: 47–61).
36 Williams asserts that Tagore's ideas hold 'hope for a new cosmopolitanism, which respects cultural differences while insisting on some fundamental universal values', (2007: 99–100).
37 Nirmal K. Bose in his 1964 study characterises the city as a mosaic of different cultures inhabiting separate ethnic enclaves (1968: 27–85), but this view is challenged by Biswas *et al.* (1976) and their interpretation of census data for 1961, finding that almost all areas of the city are in fact ethnically mixed, with some wards having high concentrations of all ethnicities that inhabit the city.
38 Anthony K. Appiah comments that movement and mixing does not lead to homogenisation (1998: 92) and promotes the notion of the 'rooted' cosmopolitan, attached to the home or the nation but embracing a wider sense of belonging, potentially to multiple sites (91–114).

References

Appiah, K. A. (1998) 'Cosmopolitan patriots', in P. Cheah and B. Robbins (eds) *Cosmopolitics: thinking and feeling beyond the nation*, Minneapolis: University of Minnesota Press.

Beattie, M. (2004) 'Sir Patrick Geddes and Barra Bazaar: competing visions, ambivalence and contradiction', *The Journal of Architecture*, 9: 131–50.

Bhabha, H. (1994; 2008) *The Location of Culture*, London: Routledge.

Biswas, A., Chatterjee, P. and Chaube, S. (1976) 'The ethnic composition of Calcutta and the residential pattern of minorities', *Geographical Review of India*, 38: 140–66.

Bose, N.K. (1968) *Calcutta 1964: a social survey*, Bombay: Lalvani Publishing House.

Chakrabarty, D. (2000) *Provincializing Europe: postcolonial thought and historical difference*, Princeton N.J.: Princeton University Press.

Chatterjee, J. (1994) *Bengal Divided: Hindu Communalism and Partition, 1932–1947*, Cambridge: Cambridge University Press.

Chatterjee, P. (1986) *Nationalist Thought and the Colonial World*, London: Zed Books for United Nations University.

—— (1993) *The Nation and its Fragments*, Princeton, N.J.: Princeton University Press.

—— (1999) 'The nationalist resolution of the women's question', in K. Sangari and S. Vaid (eds) *Recasting Women: Essays in colonial history*, New Delhi: Kali for Women.

Chattopadhyay, B. (1872) *Bishabriksha* (*The Poison Tree*); trans. M. Maddern, in *The Bankimchandra Omnibus: volume 1* (2005) New Delhi: Penguin Books.

Chattopadhyay, S. (2005) *Representing Calcutta: modernity, nationalism and the colonial uncanny*, London and New York: Routledge.

Dasgupta, S. (2007) *The Bengal Renaissance: identity and creativity from Rammohun Roy to Rabindranath Tagore*, New Delhi: Orient Longman.

Gandhi, L. (1998) *Postcolonial Theory: a critical introduction*, Edinburgh: Edinburgh University Press.

Ghosh, A. (1988; 2005) *The Shadow Lines*, New York: Houghton Mifflin Company.

Hogan, P.C. (2000) *Colonialism and Cultural Identity: crises of tradition in the Anglophone literatures of India, Africa and the Caribbean*, Albany: State University of New York Press.

Kipling, R. (1891; 1899) *The City of Dreadful Night*, New York: H. M Caldwell Company Publishers.

—— (1901; 1994) *Kim*, London: Penguin.

Kopf, D. (1969) *British Orientalism and the Bengal Renaissance: the dynamics of Indian modernization 1773–1835,* California: University of California Press.

—— (1979; 2011) *The Brahmo Samaj and the Shaping of the Modern Indian Mind*, New Delhi: Atlantic Publishers and Distributors.

Kripalani, K. (1962) *Rabindranath Tagore: a biography*, London: Oxford University Press.

Kristeva, J. (1991) *Strangers to Ourselves*, trans. L. Roudiez, New York: Columbia University Press.

Lees, W. N. (1871) *Indian Musalman's Being Three Letters, Reprinted From the 'Times': with an article on the prince consort* [&c.], London: Williams and Norgate.

Metcalfe, T. R. (1995) *Ideologies of the Raj*, Cambridge: Cambridge University Press.

—— (2002) *An Imperial Vision: Indian architecture and Britain's Raj*, Delhi: Oxford University Press.

Mitra, N. (1968) *Mahanagar*, trans. S. K. Chatterjee and M. F. Franda, Bombay: Jaico Publishing House.

Mukherjee, B. (1971; 1987) *The Tiger's Daughter*, New York: Penguin Books.

Nandy, A. (1994) *The Illegitimacy of Nationalism: Rabindranath Tagore and the politics of self*, New Delhi: Oxford University Press.

Pandit, L. (1995) 'Caste, race and nation: history and dialectic in Rabindranath Tagore's Gora', in P. C. Hogan and L. Pandit (eds) *Literary India: comparative studies in aesthetics, colonialism, and culture*, Albany: State University of New York Press.

Parry, B. (1987) 'Problems in current theories of colonial discourse', *Oxford Literary Review*, 9: 27–58.

Ranjan, R. S. (2011) 'Postcolonial relations: Gandhi, Nehru and the ethical imperatives of the national-popular', in E. Boehmer and R. Chaudhuri (eds) *The Indian Postcolonial: a critical reader*, London: Routledge.

Sarkar, S. (2002) *Beyond Nationalist Frames: relocating postmodernism, Hindutva, history*, Delhi: Permanent Black.

Sarkar, T. (2001) *Hindu Wife, Hindu Nation: community, religion, and cultural nationalism*, New Delhi: Permanent Black.

Spivak, G. C. (1993) *Outside in the Teaching Machine*, London: Routledge.

—— (2002) 'Resident alien' in D. T. Goldberg and A. Quayson (eds) *Relocating Postcolonialism*, Oxford: Blackwell.

Tagore, R. (1901) *The Broken Nest: (nashtanir)*, trans. M. M. Lago and S. Bari (1973), Madras: Macmillan.

—— (1910; 2002) *Gora*, New Delhi: Rupa & Co.

—— (1917; 1991) *My Reminiscences*, London: Papermac.

—— (1919) *The Home and The World*, trans. S. Tagore, London: Macmillan.

—— (1940; 2005) *My Boyhood Days*, New Delhi: Rupa & Co.

Tagore, A. (1946; 2004) *Apon Katha: My Story*, trans. R. B. Chatterjee, Chennai: Tara Publishing.

Tagore, S. (2008) 'Tagore's conception of cosmopolitanism: a reconstruction', *University of Toronto Quarterly*, 77: 1070–84.

Williams, L. B. (2007) 'Overcoming the "contagion of mimicry": the cosmopolitan nationalism and modernist history of Rabindranath Tagore and W. B. Yeats', *The American Historical Review*, 112: 69–100.

Yule, H. and Burnell, A. C. (1886) *Hobson-Jobson: being a glossary of Anglo-Indian colloquial words and phrases and of kindred terms*, London: John Murray.

All photos by the author.

5

'THE PAST FORSWORN'

Colonialism and counterhistory in the work of Doris Lessing

Victoria Rosner

In a 1980 interview, Doris Lessing speculated about 'the effect the proportions of buildings have on the people who live in them', insisting, 'this is not a metaphorical thought at all. This is a practical thought, which I think about more and more' (Lessing 1994a: 61). The building most crucial to Lessing's own self-construction was the rickety old settler's farmhouse her family built and lived in for years in the Lomagundi district of Southern Rhodesia (modern-day Zimbabwe). 'No house,' Lessing writes, 'could ever have for me the intimate charm of that one' (Lessing 1994b: 54). That first house was simply a thatch-topped homestead, rapidly constructed in the local style, with linoleum laid over floors of dung, mud and blood, and earthen walls in which hornets would occasionally nest. From the day it was built, that house began to erode, and only attentive maintenance kept it from merging back into the bush that spawned it.

The ephemeral nature of Lessing's childhood home should not be taken as a measure of its influence or importance. It is a topic Lessing returns to repeatedly, almost compulsively: it figures prominently in her first book, the novel *The Grass is Singing* (1950), in one of her most recent works, *Alfred and Emily* (2008) and in many others in between. The house is a touchstone for Lessing, an anchor for a writer whose unusually diverse works have ranged across space, time and genre. The cultural practices associated with the building and maintenance of this house provide an interesting view into a British settler culture rooted in a set of contradictions about the form and meaning of domestic space, contradictions that have played themselves out throughout Lessing's body of work. Insecure in both form and status, the house where Lessing grew up becomes, in her work, part of the larger historical and personal problem of her family's unhappy relocation to Southern Rhodesia.

Reading Doris Lessing's autobiographical writing about Southern Rhodesia across the arc of her career, I show how the construction of domestic space for Southern Rhodesian settlers was infused with ideas about motherhood and the maternal body. For Lessing, this spatial association creates the grounds for the psychological and territorial contest of a daughter's rejection of her mother. Lessing writes, 'I was in nervous flight from [my mother] ever since I can remember anything, and from the age of fourteen I set myself obdurately against her in a kind of inner emigration from everything she represented' (Lessing 1994b: 15). Lessing's 'inner emigration' cuts across the concentric circles of mother and daughter, home and exile, domestic and foreign, and imagines her separation from her mother as a form of international migration. If the mother sends her daughter into flight, the house pulls Lessing back, playing out an ambivalence that has powered Lessing's work for the last half-century and that, in her latest work, seems to have taken a new turn.

In 1924, on home leave in England from the Imperial Bank of Persia, Alfred Tayler and his wife Emily, Lessing's parents, went to the British Empire Exhibition at Wembley. There, at the Southern Rhodesia stand, they saw giant maize cobs, and posters and pamphlets proclaiming that for a man with a bit of capital, there were fortunes to be made in farming. Alfred Tayler had 1,000 pounds and a pension because of a leg lost in the war. He was still suffering from shell shock, and wanted to feel some space around him. At his urging, Emily packed up their two young children, and within weeks the family had shipped out for Cape Town. It is hard to imagine what Alfred Tayler was thinking: that somehow a man with no farming experience and only one leg would make a success of homesteading in Southern Rhodesia. It is equally difficult to imagine what Emily, caring for two children under five years old, thought about how she would raise her children on a remote and unfamiliar African farm.

The Taylers learned about Southern Rhodesia from the extensive pamphlet literature produced first to lure British citizens to emigrate, and then to educate settlers about their new homes. These pamphlets were generally published through government offices, and sought to advise the prospective settler on a wide variety of practical matters related to emigration. Most guidebooks included a section on local housing practices. For example, one early guidebook for settlers in Southern Rhodesia explained to the prospective farmer that:

> While the land is being broken up, the farmer will erect temporary accommodation; at least, he will supervise whilst a few natives will quickly put up two or three huts – a bedroom, a sitting room, and a kitchen. If the farmer would like his dining room to be rectangular, he must mark it out himself, because, though a native can build in a perfect circle, he cannot draw a straight line.
>
> *British South Africa Company 1915: 57*

The basic arrangement of multiple huts to form a single family dwelling is a traditional nineteenth-century indigenous form. Round sleeping, cooking and storage huts were typically built in a circle around a cleared outside area, where many domestic activities took place. The outside space was considered part of the dwelling place; as Peter Jackson writes, this was 'a complete spatial system, with the enclosed structures forming only a part of a homestead' (Jackson 1986: 13). Because the material of the huts came directly from the area being settled, the distinction between inside and outside was relatively unimportant.

Although newly arrived English colonists might initially live in these kinds of huts, their preferred approach to dwelling was quite different: for the colonists the distinction between inside and outside was paramount. The guidebooks advised that the house should provide a solid barrier between the family and the unfamiliar landscape. As another settler guide advised: 'A house or dwelling in Southern Rhodesia should form a protection from the sun's rays, excessive heat, wind, rain, and the mosquito ... The space immediately around the house should be kept free of bush and undergrowth' (Southern Rhodesia 1924: 54). But while it was recommended that the house be kept as separate as possible from the land in which it was located, to save money, the first house was nevertheless built with local labour, and in the local style.

The straight line signified a markedly different approach to building from what was indigenous to Southern Rhodesia, where circular forms dominated. The circle of the hut was only the first in a series of circles: the one-roomed huts circled a cleared area, and the entire village was laid out on a circular plan. By contrast, settler towns were composed of rectangular houses laid out in rectangular grids.[1] The streets of the town closest to the Taylers' farm, Salisbury (modern-day Harare), settled by Cecil Rhodes, were at first adapted to the huts of the pioneers. One of these early settlers recalls how:

> The Company ... weakly consented to lay out the plots to fit the straggled huts. It was a fatal mistake and one that took years to overcome ... [Salisbury] suffered a long time from the disadvantage of having some of its streets adapted to the irregular lines of the scattered pioneer shanties, instead of being planned in rectangular blocks.
>
> *Hole 1928: 76*

That the town planners might have wanted to eradicate traces of native settlement seems understandable, both as an intimidation tactic and because an essential aspect of the coloniser's mentality was the fantasy of the 'waste place', the idea that what was being colonised was essentially empty space. Of course, this was not at all the case in Southern Rhodesia, where the land was emptied through the forced dislocation of the people living there. But even the homes of the first wave of settlers had to give way in order that the straight lines of rectangular grids might be found everywhere that English civilisation had reached. Conversely, these rectangles, beginning from the dining-room table where the family gathered to eat and spanning outward, represented strength and power that the colonisers wanted to believe was uniquely English.

The Taylers' new home in Southern Rhodesia was a long, rectangular construction, sliced across to create rooms, and built by Tayler's newly hired native servants. Normally, when a settler began to turn a profit, this house was torn down and a brick, rectangular structure replaced it. As a 1924 pamphlet for settlers instructed,

> Temporary homesteads are quickly erected by natives using pole and thatch, the interstices of the walls being filled with mud. These buildings should be regarded as temporary quarters only for good housing is conducive to good health.
>
> Guide to Rhodesia 1924: 209

Housing in the local style was, by definition, not 'good housing'.

In describing the building of her family's house, Lessing accentuates its organic qualities. This particular settler house had even more organic elements than was typical, for white bone meal from buried tribal chiefs was found in the earth used to make the walls. But Lessing sees a living element even in the plant life used to construct the house. She writes, 'from the trunk of living trees in the bush fibre is torn; for under the thick rough bark of a certain variety of tree is a thick layer of smooth flesh' (Lessing 1996: 38). A live creature is being flayed, the description suggests, and the walls of the house are to be constructed from its flesh. The skin of the house is a recurrent image in Lessing's descriptions; she refers to 'the grass of the roof flattened like old flesh' and 'the walls ... covered with a thick, dark mud-skin' (Lessing 1994b: 41, 40). A link is established between the walls of the house, and the skin of the body, the centrality of which is reaffirmed in the title *Under My Skin*. For Lessing, the house models the experience of living in a skin.

If Lessing loved the house for its connections to the bush, her mother's view of the house was the opposite. Lessing's love of the bush enabled her to thrive in it, but she recognises that her mother's feelings were closer to the typical white female settler's story of depression and eventual nervous breakdown. For Emily Tayler, the house marked a crucial division between inside and outside that the guidebooks advocated. Although Emily Tayler could not provide her family with brick walls, she did her best to keep the outside out, and the inside in. Emily's fantasy was that she could bring England with her to the Southern Rhodesian bush, filling the thatched house with the contents of Liberty's and Harrods. Outside was Southern Rhodesia, but inside remained an enclave of the white English middle class — at least as far as she could keep it so. As an adult, reading memoirs of other English women who emigrated to Africa, Lessing reflects:

> The … memoirs reminded me of what was worst for my mother. Hard to believe that the first thought in the minds of the … memoir writers, with everything they were being tested by wildness and hardship, was this: were they still middle-class people, 'nice people'?
>
> *Lessing 1994b: 58*

This was more of a woman's worry. Women settlers were more likely to remain involved with life back in England, perhaps because colonial life in the bush offered them so little; as Lessing remembers, for her mother, 'real life' was in England.

Settler women in the Taylers' time were advised or ordered to remain inside or close to the house, fulfilling their role as signifiers of home, and of whiteness, of 'white values'. The bush was considered to present a special threat for women. As one 1924 guidebook stated, 'occupation of land, either in the country or near town by unprotected women is distinctly undesirable' (*Guide to Rhodesia* 1924: 199). Lessing indicates that a relatively groundless fear of rape was the basis for most of these precautions. Known as the 'black peril', black male rape of white women was highly legislated and punishable by death. John Pape has shown how the 'peril' served to unify and perpetuate whites' racist stereotyping (Pape 1990: 720).[2] While staying with family friends, Lessing explores the surrounding bush and stumbles across a spring. When she shares her discovery with her hostess, Lessing remembers,

> [S]he sighed and said, 'Are you sure you ought to be … ?' This meant, as it did when my mother remembered to say it, 'Are you sure a white girl should be risking rape by a kaffir by running around though the bush by herself?' I took no notice. No one was ever raped, I believe.
>
> *Lessing 1994b: 143*

Still, fear of rape kept girls and women close to or inside the house. A guidebook mentioned by Lessing in *Going Home* stipulated, 'you must never leave your daughter with an African male, nor allow her to wander alone in sparsely populated areas' (Federal Information Department 1954: 20). The fear of rape – whether or not rape was likely – had its own ends.

In addition to the threat of rape, settler women were thought to be especially vulnerable to the health risks the bush supposedly presented. English men were considered able to remain in the bush for ten years without significant risk; women, on the other hand, were advised to journey at least as far as the coast every four years (FID 1954: 18). The male settler's relation to the spaces of his new home is purportedly one of penetration and possession; as one British historian of Rhodesia expressed it in 1930: ' … here, at last, out under the open sky with his own land beneath him a man is his own master. He possesses himself' (Macmillan 1930: 465). Standing confidently bestride the land he has conquered, the male settler is defined through the act of possession, both of himself and of his land.[3]

In spite of the warnings in the guidebooks that good housing was conducive to good health, the Taylers never had the economic security to rebuild. Lessing remembers her parents telling her that the house 'had been built to last four years', but it lasted far longer (Lessing 2008: 221). The family remained in those 'temporary quarters' for upwards of twenty years, making repairs as needed. The pole-and-thatch house was a vernacular architectural form, and like other such forms in the early twentieth century, systematically denigrated; it was the devalued form in the modernist aesthetic division between high and low, progressive and traditional, art and craft, elite and popular (Upton 2002). This aesthetic division also had evident social dimensions, since the vernacular character in this case carried racial and nationalist associations. For colonisers like the Lessings, vernacular forms were utilised for the sake of convenience and economy, but were to be cast off as quickly as possible in favour of imported styles.

'Good housing', by contrast, was understood to be English housing – housing not made of local materials, housing that created a strict division between the interior and the exterior of the house, and between England and Southern Rhodesia. These second-stage houses were no closer to architecture with a capital 'A' than the pole-and-thatch; the significant distinction here was not between craft and art but rather between native and foreign. Inside the house, the health-producing illusion of the English climate might be maintained. So although Emily Tayler could not provide her family with brick walls, she did her best to keep the outside out, and the inside in. Lessing speaks of the 'solid brick, ceilinged houses that announced success' – these second-stage houses that eluded the Taylers were desirable because they were 'solid', providing a stronger barrier between the occupants and the bush (Lessing 1994b: 57). Thus, though she and her family lived in a mud hut, Lessing's mother was deeply committed to maintaining the structural integrity of the house, preserving a barrier against the bush. In *Going Home,* it is her mother whom Lessing recalls routinely calling the 'thatching-boy' (likely not a 'boy' at all) to repair leaks in the roof (Lessing 1996: 49).

An insistence on the separation of house and bush is so important to Lessing's mother that the clash between these spaces contributes to her physical collapse. Lessing explains her mother's nervous breakdown (not uncommon among settler wives) as resulting from an inability to reconcile the inside of their house with the outside.

> All around her [Lessing's mother] were the signs and symbols of the respectable life she had believed was her right, her future, silver tea trays, English watercolours, Persian rugs, the classics in their red leather editions, the Liberty curtains. But she was living in what amounted to a mud hut, and all she could see from her high bed was the African bush.
>
> *Lessing 1994b: 64*

Placing the future in a parallel category with possessions from home, Lessing underscores the way her mother considered English objects to be talismans both of Home (always capitalised by her mother) and of social class. But these objects didn't accord with the unfamiliar African landscape seen from her window. Her mother's breakdown, in this sense, is seen to be caused by an intolerable geographical assimilation, a crumbling of the barriers that separated England from Africa. More specifically, the artifacts Lessing's mother treasures stand for culture: literature and art. They stand for rarefied experience and a taste for 'finer' things as opposed to the Taylers' subsistence lifestyle. That dangerous view may also explain why settlers' handbooks recommended that 'newcomers wishing to build houses in country districts should not do so without consulting the local Government Medical Officer' (FID 1954: 15). The doctor's role in assimilating settlers not just medically but patriotically should not be overlooked; after all, when the doctor is called for Lessing's mother's breakdown, the prescription is for a heavy dose of English interiors, otherwise known as 'bed rest', further limiting the world to the space of a bed, where Emily Tayler remained for almost a year.

Like her mother, Lessing also experiences the house as an extension of her own body, referring to the house as her 'other skin'. But Lessing's identification with the house is filtered through the material connections already in place between the house and her mother's body. This identification is formed on a maternal basis; her sense of a bodily link to the house coincides with her own maternal instincts. Lessing relates how when she was seventeen, her father fell ill and her parents had to make an emergency trip into Salisbury, leaving her alone on the farm to tend an incubator of eggs. Alone in the house, she strongly feels her bodily connection to it: 'I was full of triumph alone in my house that was like my other skin' (Lessing 1994b: 195). Describing herself as part of the bush, Lessing's sense of bodily integrity expands to merge with the walls of the house so that her skin and the 'skin' of the house are one. This house–body merger during her parents' absence produces maternal behaviour. Lessing writes of tending the eggs as though she had laid them: 'I turned the eggs as a hen might, making sure those great feet of hers did not miss a single egg, and I brooded over those eggs as if the future depended on seventy-two chicks' (Lessing 1994b: 196). Lessing's anxieties about the role of reproduction in securing the future can be contextualised in terms of a common local fallacy. Fears about the ability of white settlers to propagate and thus assure continuing settlement were active in settler culture; many feared that the East African climate would cause sterility in the third generation of settlers (Kennedy 1987: 127).[4]

Lessing's rebellions against her mother are generally staged by creating breaks in the structural integrity of the house. Emily Tayler struggles to preserve the interior of the house as a sealed relic of England; to enact her separation from her mother, Lessing effaces the house/bush distinction upon which her mother's fragile psychic security depends. Conversely, her mother's efforts to preserve this distinction can be read as attempts to mould her daughter in her own image. Mother and daughter stage the struggle for individuation in architectural terms; the house structures their understanding of how they differ from one another. For instance, Lessing tells us that she liked to keep the door of her room propped open with a stone at all times so she could view directly the activity in the bush a few yards away. Lessing writes, 'I fought with my mother to have this door open. "Snakes", she cried, "scorpions … mosquitoes … I won't have it!" But I kept the door open knowing I was safe inside the mosquito net' (Lessing 1994b: 70). As with the imagined threat of the African rapist, Lessing's mother most fears threats that will penetrate her daughter's body, things that can go under the skin, as with the mosquito's bite. If the skin her mother imagines is as solid as the walls of the house, and somehow the more vulnerable to intruders, Lessing's image of her skin is more like the mosquito net, porous, and somehow safe. These competing ideas of the function of skin resonate strongly in a society where skin colour organises every aspect of life.

The mother–daughter battle reaches its peak when Lessing is fourteen, at the onset of puberty, when her body's maternal capabilities emerge. If her mother sees her daughter's sexuality as a source of new vulnerability, her daughter experiences it as a strength, one that will give her the power to separate from her mother. Lessing's first striking experience of her body as sexual takes place in the bush.

> In a corner of the bush near the big land, I stood with my rifle loose in my hand, and suddenly saw my legs as if for the first time, and thought, They are beautiful. Brown slim well-shaped legs. I pulled up my dress and looked at myself as far up as my panties and was filled with pride of body. There is no exultation like it, the moment when a girl knows that *this* is her body, *these* her fine smooth shapely limbs.
>
> *Lessing 1994b: 173*

This is a feeling she cannot have in the house; the gun in her hand signals that the feeling will be a kind of weapon that she can use both to push her mother away and to assert her dominion over the land. Lessing's body is a weapon that can transport her back and forth across purity markers separating bush and house. Her escape, however, takes place within assumptions about English domination. As the child of white settlers, her very presence in the bush is the result of conquest and forced dislocation of the original inhabitants, as Lessing knows. As Kevin Magarey points out, at the time Lessing lived in Southern Rhodesia, 54 per cent of the land belonged to the five per cent of the population who were white (Magarey 1986: 50). The ability to impose one's identity on this landscape was largely a white male prerogative. Her bodily self-confidence defies cultural efforts to force her into a house that denies the bush, but sends her into a colonial paradigm of conquest and control, a conqueror of the bush, not a creature of it.

Lessing's antagonism toward the house, and by extension, toward her mother, is expressed more pointedly in her fantasies, where she often dreams of the destruction of the house, playing out a displaced aggression toward her mother. In *Going Home* she imagines the death of the house in detail, how it would have taken place.

> It was the ants, of course, who finally conquered, for when we left that house empty in the bush, it was only a season before the ant-hills sprouted in the rooms themselves, among the quickly sprouting trees, and the red galleries must have covered all the walls and the floor. The rains were heavy that year, beating the house to its knees.
>
> *Lessing 1996: 55*

Similarly, in *Under My Skin,*

> the house I had been brought up in was crumbling in my sleep, demolished by white ants and borers, the thatch sliding off the old rafters to lie in dirty heaps on earth blackened by a recent bush fire. Dreams have always been my friend ...
>
> *Lessing 1994b: 297*

Ants are the next wave of colonisers, rebuilding the house as the Taylers could not afford to do, and the bush reclaims its property. These dramatic images of the house, debased and overrun, are never actually seen by Lessing, only fantasised. Lessing's image of the house not merely destroyed but humbled, affirmed by repeated description of the house 'on its knees', is also a fantasy of Lessing's triumph over her mother.

At one point, the young Lessing actually does set fire to the house. Admonished not to play with matches, she nevertheless decides to burn down the dog house. The flames spread to the adjacent structures and the entire property is threatened: 'I thought our house would be burnt down and that would be the end of our family' (Lessing 1994b: 108). She associates the destruction of the house with the dissolution of her family as though the family unit can only exist in relation to the house. Her description of setting fire to the house is immediately preceded by her account of a failed attempt by Lessing and her brother to run away from home. When the attempt fails Lessing remembers herself 'burning with shame' (Lessing 1994b: 107). Lessing's own burning, sparked by her furious desire to get away, becomes a real burning that could accomplish precisely that. Lessing's desire to destroy the house, or, more precisely, to break down the house/bush division her mother depends on, is a product of her drive to separate from her mother.

In fact it is fire that does eventually obliterate the house, a bush fire occurring some months after the Taylers moved out. Though she didn't witness the fire, thoughts of it occupy Lessing's mind for many years. As she recalls: 'For a long time I used to dream of the collapse and decay of that house, and of the fire sweeping over it, and then I set myself to dream the other way. It was urgently necessary to recover every detail of that house' (Lessing 1994b: 55). Having 'recovered' the house from its actual death by reconstituting it in her memory, Lessing is unwilling to revisit the site of the house on a return trip to Rhodesia. Her reason for not actually going home (or at least to the site of the house) is strange – she fears to find the house still standing. '[S]upposing then that the house was still there after all?' (Lessing 1994b: 55). Writing long after the house has disappeared, Lessing rebuilds it on her own, textual terms, refusing to cede the authority of the interior to her mother. Lessing's autobiographical identity as a writer is expressed through the reconstruction of the house from which her mother has been dispossessed. She has surpassed her parents, rebuilding the house as they never could.

Yet in her recent work *Alfred and Emily*, Lessing does return to the site of the house. Her latest account of her life in Southern Rhodesia is a generic hybrid, a blend of memoir and counterhistory and it seems to mark a shift in Lessing's representation of the mother–daughter relationship. Telling the story of her childhood yet again, Lessing clearly feels compelled to return to her memories by some unfinished business. In place of the antipathy, rejection and rage we saw in Lessing's earlier autobiographical writings, Lessing now gives us moments of identification, generosity and forgiveness. The burning of the house, staged once more, becomes not a symbol of the daughter's destructive anger but a necessary, if tragic, loss that clears the ground for future inhabitants. Lessing's meditations on the interplay of family, history, architecture and life-writing seem to assume a new dimension as she grapples with the ethics of her own role in the British colonisation of southern Africa.

Alfred and Emily has a split structure that bears witness to Lessing's complex feelings about her parents and her own sense of origins: half the book describes an imaginary history while the other half depicts actual events. In the first half of the book ('Alfred and Emily: A Novella'), Lessing, acknowledging that her parents' lives were marked by frustration, deprivation and trauma, writes a counterhistory in which her parents never marry each other and lead the lives they originally wanted for themselves. To accomplish this feat, Lessing must eliminate the First World War; without it, Alfred Tayler keeps his leg and becomes an English farmer with a loving wife and children. Emily marries a wealthy physician and is widowed young. Unlike Alfred, she has no children, but does discover that she has a great gift for telling stories to children, a gift that leads her to found a series of successful progressive schools. 'Alfred and Emily: A Novella' is notably generous to its subjects in its attempt to fulfil their wishes even at the cost of obviating the author's own existence.

In the first half of *Alfred and Emily*, the title characters never emigrate and live out their lives within the borders of England. The role of architecture in this counterhistory is much diminished, perhaps because home is so unequivocally identified with family, stability and domesticity – and everyone agrees about what these things mean. A few pointed echoes of real events can be discerned in this invented story, as when Alfred Tayler discusses with his employer and patron the building of a separate house on the farm for Alfred and his new wife (who is, of course, not

Emily). "'Are you going to want thatch or slates for the roof?" said Mr. Redway. "Slates," said Alfred. "Better for fire'" (Lessing 2008: 30). This counterhistory is careful to avoid any turn of events that might produce the unfortunate outcomes that eventuated in real life. The fire that constantly threatens and eventually consumes the Taylers' thatched Rhodesian farmhouse never has the chance to be kindled in Alfred's slate-topped English homestead. He settles down with his new wife, Betsy, in this cosy home and follows the life of a farmer.

For her part, Emily works as a nurse at the Royal Free Hospital in London and marries the well-to-do Dr William Martin-White. She moves into his large London home and the frustrated decorative impulses that the real Emily Tayler experienced in the Rhodesian bush are able to be given the fullest expression. Yet this desire, given rein, fails distinctly to provide anything like real satisfaction. Emily submerges herself, as if in a dream, in transforming her home, but in the end, she feels she has accomplished very little.

> Emily suddenly understood that she had not thought about anything but her house, or rather William's house, for months — years? Curtains, wallpapers, the cover for a chair, a new dining-table, carpets, rugs had filled her mind, day and night … This realization had come to her when she was visiting Daisy, where she had not been for some time, being too busy with soft furnishing … It seemed as if she had been under a spell. The swatches of fabric now seemed like a comment on the absurdity of her, Sister McVeagh. This was not what she was.
>
> *Lessing 2008: 47–8*

Emily finds herself at odds with the life she has chosen — the house loses its allure in an instant; she does not become pregnant; her husband is diffident and cold; her economic status bars her from undertaking any paid work that might satisfy her more deeply. She falls into a neurasthenic depression that only comes to an end when her husband dies unexpectedly and she is eventually able to turn her energies to philanthropic work with children. In fact, she discovers this path through telling stories she invents to children, who gobble up her tales. The vocation of writer, Lessing seems rather pointedly to suggest, is far more vital than that of housewife.

Whereas Alfred is able to find happiness in the fulfilment of his ambitions, Emily is revealed to have had the wrong dream, a dream that is empty and self-centered. Lessing may have a feminist viewpoint at the back of this contrast, since the fantasy of perfected domesticity is not just Emily's but one commonly dangled before women. The home, in 'Alfred and Emily: A Novella', is at its best a place of embracing shelter, a support for the growth and life of a family, and a refuge from the vicissitudes of human existence. At its worst, it is an empty shell of vanity, used to flaunt financial surplus and to impress others. Emily eventually cedes her grand home to her nephew by marriage and his wife; they fill the place with children and thrive there.

The second half of the book, 'Alfred and Emily: Two Lives', returns us to the by-now familiar story of the lives that Alfred and Emily Tayler really did lead, out in the Southern Rhodesian bush on their failing farm. But rather than representing her parents, and her mother in particular, as foils for their daughter's frustration and rebellion, Alfred and Emily appear as the leading characters. They are seen as victims of the war, her father crushed by physical and mental illness caused by his experiences as a soldier and her mother forced to give up her ambitions and resign herself to a life of isolation and deprivation. Lessing is not without sympathy for her mother in *Under My Skin*, but in *Alfred and Emily* her sympathy expands into identification and a focus on her mother's strengths rather than her foibles. In *Alfred and Emily* she devotes a full chapter to the clinic her mother ran for local labourers from her kitchen, while in *Under My Skin* the clinic is never mentioned. In *Under My Skin*, when she describes her mother's emergence from an illness that kept her bedridden for months, Lessing writes, 'Then my mother got out of bed. She had to' (Lessing 1994b: 68). In *Alfred and Emily*, this memory becomes: 'she got up, and what that must have cost her I cannot begin to imagine', a formulation that both puts Lessing in her mother's place and acknowledges a suffering that deserves respect (Lessing 2008: 158).

The fantasised and actual destruction of the house in the bush that is central to Lessing's previous accounts is significant in *Alfred and Emily* as well. In earlier versions the burning of the house expresses a fantasy of escape. But in *Alfred and Emily* Lessing imagines the grief of the insects and animals that sheltered in the abandoned house: 'I could imagine a tiny screaming and protesting, but that did no good, the house burned' (Lessing 2008: 221–2). Now the burning house is not an image of escape but one of catastrophic loss.

Lessing argues through *Alfred and Emily* that her mother should have been a storyteller but was prevented by the war from expressing her gift. In a further gesture of identification, Lessing considers how the same fate could befall her as a writer, though in her case it is the war with her mother that has the capacity to silence. At the end of the book, Lessing recalls that she used to have the odd habit of making up brief narratives of mothers and daughters in conflict. Although she tried, Lessing was never able to expand any of these notes into full-fledged stories. She offers a sample:

> A mother and daughter did not 'get on'. Why did the girl not leave home? She stuck around, railing at her mother, but making use of any advantages, such as baby-sitting or handouts. Then her mother had a heart attack, was helpless. The girl said to her, 'Very well, you've got me where you want me. I'll look after you but I shall never, ever say a word to you again.' And that was what happened. The mother lasted twenty years, and the daughter refused to ever say a syllable.

> *Lessing 2008: 267*

Here, in a distilled form, is Lessing's fantasy of triumphing over her mother through the purest denial, of at last bringing her mother to her knees and holding her there until death parts them. The house provides the spatial confinement that keeps the daughter in a torturous lock with her mother. The daughter never leaves the battleground, the war never ends, and the result is that the daughter loses her voice; her belligerence keeps her silent. The angry daughter is the silent daughter for both the subject of this fantasy and for its author, since none of her mini-narratives ever became a full-fledged story. Hating your mother, this fantasy seems to assert, has the potential to hobble you as a writer. At the same time, there seems to be no possibility for both mother and daughter to survive and find their respective voices at the same time. In the first half of *Alfred and Emily*, the mother is the storyteller and the daughter is never born. In the second, the war silences the mother and the daughter becomes the storyteller.

The young Lessing's relationship with her mother in *Under My Skin* is most prominently one of repeated denial, simply saying 'no' to her mother over and over. She refuses acknowledgment or identification: 'I won't. I will not. I will not be like that' (Lessing 1994b: 120). In a suggestive scene from *Alfred and Emily*, Lessing becomes not the denier but the one who is denied. She recalls a trip back to the site of her family home in the 1980s. The house, of course, is gone but there instead is a very drunk black man who looks poor and angry. Lessing tells him, 'our old house used to be there' and explains further that the landscape has apparently been modified since. The man says no, nothing has changed. Lessing next recalls an old tree that used to be on the site and now is gone. '"There was no tree there," said the man, swaying and leaning. "There was never any tree."' She tells him they called it the *mawonga* tree. '"It is the wrong name"', the man replies (Lessing 2008: 229).[5] These denials, like Lessing's as a child, are a performance rather than a correction; the man's refusal of Lessing, like Lessing's of her mother, arises not from a disagreement over issues but from an anger that spawns denial.

The relation between Lessing and the man she encounters is in many ways parallel to the relationship between Lessing and her mother. In describing the burning of the house, Lessing wrote that for her mother the house was a fantasy or, as she characterises it later, 'a feat of the imagination' (Lessing 2008: 218). Lessing repudiates her mother's misguided fantasy about the house, the fantasy of realising in the interior a reproduction of middle-class English domesticity. And now the man Lessing encounters wants to skewer her fantasy: your idea about your old house is misguided, the man seems to say; you were never here; the house never existed. Denying Lessing's memories, he positions her family's occupation of the land as a historical mistake that he can erase. In the broadest sense, this man's gesture is a sequel to the long-ago eradication of the circular plans of the indigenous dwellings in favour of the rectangular grids that, to the English settlers, heralded the arrival of civilisation. Lessing's family home was made possible by the erasure of the previous occupants, a gesture that, many years later, is returned to her by the man she encounters at the site.

This gesture forces her to see herself not solely as the rebellious daughter but as the recipient of a colonial legacy, however unwanted. In representing herself as the recipient of angry denial, rather than its author, Lessing holds herself, to an extent, accountable for her role in defrauding this man's ancestors of their homeland. After describing her meeting with the Zimbabwean man, Lessing comments: 'Interesting, watching history being unmade, the past forsworn' (Lessing 2008: 229). The work of forswearing the past and unmaking history is, of course, also Lessing's work in *Alfred and Emily*, which performs an even greater feat of unmaking in cutting the First World War out of history in order to imagine different lives for Lessing's parents.

If the man's erasure of Lessing's past makes room for his own occupation, though, Lessing's acts of unmaking also unmake Lessing herself. She concedes that both the original inhabitants of the land of her childhood and her parents would have had better lives had she never existed. It is an uncanny observation for a writer to make, but in a sense it affirms her profound identification with that birdcage of a house on the bush: both hybrid creatures caught between worlds; both inadvertent participants in the work of empire; both forged on a hill in a former British colony. Throughout Lessing's childhood, the house on the bush was the arena that held Lessing and her mother in tension with each other. Lessing's new sympathy for her mother in *Alfred and Emily* seems to flow from the fantasised unmaking of history; from the imagined possibility that the war never happened, the English stayed at home, and the house was never built. What we can see from both Lessing and her angry hillside interlocutor is that unmaking history is rough work, requiring anger, denial, hopeless fantasy, and even suicidal instinct, insofar as erasing history means erasing your own past. Yet it is work that you can be driven to do, and in Lessing's terms there would seem to be two ways to go about it. Faced with an unacceptable situation, be it colonialism or a bad mother, you can lock yourself into a position of sheer denial. Or you can try to invent a story in which it all turns out differently.

Despite the unconvincing blanket refusal of the Zimbabwean man that Lessing encounters, we can see the emotional logic of his claim that the house was never there. The house, it might be said, is both there and not-there. It is there because it is part of the place where it once stood. The house has an organic tie to the land that neither Lessing nor her mother can claim. Because the materials for its construction were gathered from the area, even in its absence it is still in some way part of the landscape. Yet it is also the symbol of an illegitimate invasion and so should never have been built. Local and foreign at the same time, it was a settler's house, the interior of which stubbornly rejected the vernacular and any acknowledgment of its location. It belonged to a country, Southern Rhodesia, which no longer exists. The house, even in its absence, remains an overdetermined site of projection, fantasy and denial, its decomposition only another chapter in a long, palimpsestic story about the afterlife of colonisation.

Notes

Part of this chapter was published in a different form as 'Home Fires: Doris Lessing, Colonial Architecture, and the Reproduction of Mothering', in *Tulsa Studies in Women's Literature*, 18, no. 1 (Spring 1999), 59–89.

1 Bulawayo, for example, the second largest town in Southern Rhodesia, was sited on the *nativekraal*, or village, which was the last stronghold of Lobengula, chief of the Matabeles, in his effort to defend the Matabeles' land from Cecil Rhodes' colonising party. This site had no natural features to recommend it, but symbolically it represented Rhodes' victory, a victory he rooted in the soil by effacing the Matabele circular dwelling pattern and re-planning the town in a solid grid pattern.
2 See Pape (1990: 720). By comparison, white male rape of black women was much more widespread and barely reprimanded when discovered. Jenny Sharpe provides an insightful and nuanced analysis of the comparative case of interracial rape in imperial India in *Allegories of Empire* (1993). See also Susie Jacobs (1995).
3 Lessing's own father, struggling to tame the bush with only one leg, demonstrates how imperial mastery was neither automatic nor easily achieved. His inability to make a financial success of farming becomes a failure of masculinity; this process is dramatised by Lessing in the figure of Mary's husband Dick, in *The Grass is Singing*. Like Lessing's father, he was lured to emigrate by promises of masculine self-determination; as Mary describes it, '[O]n an impulse [he] had come to Southern Rhodesia to be a farmer, and to "live his own life". So here he was, this hopeless, decent man, standing on his "own" soil, which belonged to the last grain of sand to the Government, watching his natives work, while she sat in the shade and looked at him, knowing perfectly well that he was doomed: he never had a chance' (Lessing 1978: 158).
4 As Dane Kennedy has documented, solar radiation was thought by settlers to pose a serious threat to people with light skin, even causing sterilization in later generations. Another widespread belief was in the danger of the 'suicide months' (October and November), when settlers were supposedly most vulnerable to neurasthenic despair. Kennedy notes that the proposed remedies for these problems did not advocate permanent removal from the seemingly malignant environment; rather 'they advised the observance of functions intended to isolate the settler from the host environment, in both symbolic and physical terms'. See Kennedy (1987).
5 The man may have a linguistic point here, since *mawonga* is actually the Spanish name for this type of tree.

References

British South Africa Company (1911) *A Land of Sunshine, Southern Rhodesia, Unique Openings for Farmers*.
Federal Information Department for the Federation of Rhodesia and Nyasaland (FID) (1954) *A New Life in the Federation of Rhodesia & Nyasaland: Facts and Figures for the Immigrant*, Glasgow: Robert MacLehose and Company Limited.
Guide to Rhodesia for the Use of Tourists and Settlers (1924) 2nd ed. (Bulawayo: Pavis & Co., 1924).
Hole, Hugh Marshall (1976) *Old Rhodesian Days,* Bulawayo: Books of Rhodesia. Originally published 1928.
Jackson, Peter (1986) *Historic Buildings of Harare 1890–1940,* Harare: Quest Publishing.
Jacobs, Susie (1995) 'Gender Divisions and the Formation of Ethnicities in Zimbabwe', in Stasiulis, Daiva and Nira Yuval-Davis (eds.) *Unsettling Settler Societies: Articulations of Gender, Race, Ethnicity and Class*, London: Sage Publications.

Kennedy, Dane (1987) *Islands of White: Settler Society and Culture in Kenya and Southern Rhodesia, 1890–1939*, Durham: Duke University Press.

Lessing, Doris (1978) *The Grass is Singing*, New York: Plume Editions.

—— (1994a) 'Creating Your Own Demand' (interview with Minda Bikman), in Earl G. Ingersoll (ed.) *Doris Lessing: Conversations*, Princeton: Ontario University Press.

—— (1994b) *Under My Skin: Volume One of My Autobiography, to 1949*, New York: HarperCollins.

—— (1996) *Going Home*, London: HarperPerennial.

—— (2008) *Alfred and Emily*, New York: HarperCollins.

Macmillan, Allister (1930) *Eastern Africa and Rhodesia*, London: W. H. & L. Collingridge.

Magarey, Kevin (1986) 'The Sense of Place in Doris Lessing and Jean Rhys', in Peggy Nightingale (ed.) *A Sense of Place In the New Literatures in English*, St. Lucia: University of Queensland Press.

Pape, John (1990) 'Black and White: The "Perils of Sex" in Colonial Zimbabwe', *Journal of Southern African Studies* 16.4: 699–720.

Sharpe, Jenny (1993) *Allegories of Empire: The Figure of Woman in the Colonial Text*, Minneapolis: University of Minnesota Press.

Southern Rhodesia (1924) *Handbook for the Use of Prospective Settlers on the Land*, issued by Direction of the Hon. Minister for Agriculture and Lands.

Upton, Dell (2002) 'Architecture in Everyday Life', *New Literary History* 33.4: 707–23.

PART II

Movement, culture, genre

6

DRUGS, CRIME AND OTHER WORLDS

Jonathan Charley

Democratising the field of enquiry

Welcome to the marginal places that the obedient citizen rarely encounters. Welcome to the deviant places through which no god-fearing middle-class person would ever dare wander. And welcome to the parts of cities and towns where fearful prejudice forbid you to go. Enter the literary world of narcotics, theft, murder and weird technology, of back street alleys, cocktail penthouses and paranoid suburbs, of the lo-fi, the downbeat and the popular, of crime, sci-fi, sex and drugs. In all of this beware of the pushers, pimps and androids, who curl a beckoning finger and invite you to take a trip into the type of novels and buildings historically frowned upon by the great and good of the Academy. But be equally beware of the frock-coated sages who reside within and who ridicule the idea that pulp fiction and the garden shed have aesthetic and cultural value and who shake at the proposition that the pigeon racer's dovecot should sit alongside the Opera House or that the novels of Dashiell Hammett should be allocated space next to Hemingway.

Forty years ago the literary sub-genres of crime, sci-fi, sex and drugs, along with the architectural structures famously dismissed by Niklaus Pevsner as mere buildings, at best occupied the margins of literary and architectural scholarship. They were like 'guilty pleasures' wrapped in brown paper, something to be consumed surreptitiously.[1] Since then it is tempting to think that the battle against such intellectual conservatism has largely been won and to be sure there are now peer-reviewed journals and anthologies devoted to both science fiction and crime that nestle alongside critical works on Joyce, Mann and Woolf.[2] In a similar vein, architectural students are just as likely to hear discourses on prisons, bus stops and haunted houses as lectures on iconic modern masters like Gropius, Mies van de Rohe and Le Corbusier.

FIGURE 6.1 'Uncovering marginalised histories', alley wall, Glasgow

But this new-found status for the previously ignored did not occur overnight or without a struggle, and was very much part of a cultural revolution after the Second World War that sought to democratise the field of that deemed worthy of study. New narratives began to emerge that aimed to uncover the forgotten and marginalised histories of the disenfranchised and dispossessed, and to illustrate social history with the material and cultural phenomena that make up the fabric of actual real life.[3] 'The Making of the English Working Class' meant not only understanding the political subject in terms of class, but also gender and race and this was paralleled in an appreciation of the cultural importance of popular music, literature and film – that is, the study *not* of what intellectuals thought people should be reading or listening to, but what they actually *were*.[4] In the spirit of this *critique of every day life*, architectural and urban history began to discover the value of the commonplace, the ugly and the ordinary. It began to take seriously and non-judgementally the iconography of the street and how people appropriated and used the city in unforeseen and unregulated ways.[5]

France was at the epi-centre of this politico–linguistic revolution that infused social history with a new geographical and spatial narrative. The Situationists' 'revolutionary urbanism', Lefebvre's 'differential space' and Foucault's 'heterotopia', redirected our gaze to the sites of difference – of rebellion, of the covert and underground, to the places and spaces that fall outside of the normal pathologies of power and governance.[6]

It was the start of a deluge. Certeau and Auge added the transitory 'non-places' of supermodernity, such as the motorway, the airport lounge and the waiting lobby, whilst George Perec contributed *Species of Space* and 'All the bedrooms I have slept in'. Meanwhile Virillio offered an idiosyncratic index of ideas on the architecture of war, cinema and optics, and Vidler the architectural 'uncanny' and 'warped'.[7] There were many more besides, but what is significant is that urban theory and history became a lot more interesting as it began to investigate and narrate the multiplicity of spaces and places that the writers of fiction had been playing with since the nineteenth century. For novelists, the architect's and urbanist's belated discovery of the 'marginal' and 'fleeting', of the leftover spaces of everyday life must have seemed somewhat bizarre. On the other hand it was a timely reminder of the literary and political potential of exploring some of the new typologies of space thrown up by contemporary capitalism that the genres of crime, drugs and sci-fi are particularly adept at dealing with. Through such literature we can be marooned underneath a traffic intersection in Ballard's *Concrete Island* (1974), wired up on a micro-chipped inhabited bridge in William Gibson's *Neuromancer* (1984), or hanging around in the prison car-park waiting for news of Gary Gilmore's death in Mailer's *Executioner's Song* (1979).

However despite the chronotopic novelty of such modern tales, their underlying themes – murder, theft, sexual desire, narcotic pleasure and the imagination of other worlds – are strikingly familiar. In fact they are as old as literature and as ancient as the first declarations of private property. Parricide, robbery, corruption and detection have haunted the literary imagination forever, from the 'golden age' fiction of Christie and Chandler, to the Brothers Karamazov all the way back to Cain and Abel. Narratives of carnal delight, corporeal deviancy and excess have a similarly long-standing literary history. One only has to think of Chaucer's *Canterbury Tales*, Boccaccio's *Decameron* (1351), and in particular Rabelais' *Gargantua and Pantagruel* (1532) that set the template for writers from Lautreamont to Bukowski on how to explore the taboos and conventions of the world around them.[8] As for making a critique of the present through the imagination of some other state in which civilisation has either collapsed or been rebuilt in an ideal form, this too possesses a lineage that stretches back centuries. It is quite literally a bibliographic space–time adventure that begins with the classic dystopian texts of the twentieth century, passes through the dream worlds of Francis Bacon and Thomas More, and eventually arrives in the pages of Plato's *Republic*.[9]

What transforms these ancient literary examples of social criticism into recognisably *modern* genres, exemplified by the novels featured in this part of the book by Peace, Waites, Trocchi and Dick, is the *urbanisation* of their narratives. Again, this is to be entirely expected. The modern crime novel can only come of age when the professional detective first stalks the city in Dickens and Dostoevsky. The modern dystopian and sci-fi novel is only possible when the modern city has been built and found wanting. And the modern sex and drug novel emerges only when the city is complex, layered and multi-dimensional enough to hide its secrets.

True to the unsentimental realism that is typical of such genres, there are no fairy-tale endings in the *Red Riding Quartet*, the *Life of Cain*, or *A Scanner Darkly*. There may be a glimmer of hope in which the recovering addict regains keys to a home, the nasty case is resolved, and the utopian dream of the good society survives the secret police, but there is little in the way of the sort of warmth that comes from reconciliation or redemption.[10] No, these are stories that are buried to their necks in alienation, paranoia and moral corruption, in which the 'wasteland', the subterranaean 'gothic' and urban disintegration are recurring themes.[11] In Dick we stumble through entropic ruins, in Peace and Waites, urban dereliction and in Trocchi watery industrial hinterlands. These are portraits of cities that have unravelled, and that are scarred by destabilising forms of social and spatial inequality. They are cities in which the architecture of prosperity is juxtaposed with poverty and disease. They are collage cities fractured by a split reality in which subjective and social alienation from the world of work and the normal conventions of civil society are realised in real time and space; cities in which streets, urban blocks and suburban estates echo with warnings: 'No Entry – Private Property', 'Caution – Armed Guard', 'Danger – Radioactive Zone', 'Warning – This area is controlled by CCTV', 'Trespassers Will Be Prosecuted', 'Humans Only', 'No baseball caps, children, Irish and Dogs'.

The prospects for tranquillity and peace are remote in such novels. The contradictions of the capitalist city seem almost irreconcilable, such that even departure to a new planet is no guarantee of liberty or happiness. It is a form of intellectual pessimism that verges on political hopelessness. A crime might be solved but somehow the system that incubated such activities stays intact. A revolution happens but rapidly descends into surveillance hell and scarcity. The drugs provide momentary respite but the addict dies. Despite this we remain drawn to such bleak stories of unrelenting gloom. One reason for this is that tales about the restoration of reason, the realisation of social freedom, love fulfilled, and of an ideal family and home seem somehow implausible. The fear is that utopia is boring, and that a society without conflict can no longer produce exciting stories (Jameson 2005: 82).

Deeper into the urban familiar

If as detectives we were to trace the urban and architectural history of the modern crime novel our notebooks would fill with an offbeat but recognisable spatial history of twentieth-century capitalism. Symbolically the scene of the crime shifts from the 'boulevard' to the 'highway', from the affluent country house to the poverty-stricken estate, and from intoxicated gambling dens to the HQ of the corporation. A more thorough investigation would reveal a detailed inventory of familiar 'non-places', 'differential spaces' and 'heterotopias'. 'There is nothing out of the ordinary, officer.' The evidence points to crimes in bedrooms, cafes, lobbies and telephone boxes, at street corners, airports and doctors' surgeries. Two men

FIGURE 6.2 'At home with the unfamiliar', tourist bus, Cardiff

are shot outside the pub. There are deals going down in car parks, bodies buried on building sites, and fugitives pushed under trains. There are junkies in an alley with a baseball bat. Covert operatives are whispering in graveyards, unaware the dead have ears and gravestones microphones. Phone calls report that Daddy is being brutal in the kitchen or depressed with a gassy hose in the garage.

Peter Clandfield's essay underlines these quotidian themes in his survey of recent crime fiction. In *Dark Blood*, the paedophile is burnt out of his suburban home. In the *Marx Sisters* the old street is murdered to make way for finance capital and in *Red Riding* violent racists and misogynists commit the unspeakable whilst ordinary people go shopping, pay electricity bills and take the rubbish out. In such novels the mean streets and heroic detectives of the golden age are a distant memory and have long been replaced by white-collar crime and the institutionalised corruption of the body politic. The smoky backrooms of underground bars and mysterious deep throats still figure, but modern subterfuge and embezzlement can just as easily occur in the closed chamber of a covert council meeting or at a computer terminal in a thoroughly ordinary office block.

True to form these twists on the crime genre still boast high body counts, grisly murders, unexplained deaths and the strains of police procedurals. But a new twist is added. Architecture and urban development not only provide the backdrop and setting through which the crime narrative unfolds, but as arenas notorious for financial speculation, kick backs, money laundering and the suspension of democratic procedures they become the 'objects of crime', 'whose control and definition are at stake, and whose pursuit grounds individual crimes from bribery and fraud to assault and murder.'[12] It is a plotline that recalls Chester Himes' epic re-depiction of New York in the *Harlem Cycle* (1959) in which urban restructuring and urban demolition translates into a violent confrontation – 'murder the neighbourhood and you murder the Afro American' (Gifford 2010: 43–6). And it echoes Marx's description of the reconstruction of Paris as a series of 'colossal robberies committed upon the city … by the great financial companies and contractors … ' (Marx 1969: 414).

Meanwhile in the cities of late twentieth-century Britain, history is repeating itself as contemporary experiments in the privatisation and gentrification of urban space provoke their own tales of illegitimacy. Barry Maitland's description of the redevelopment of Jerusalem Lane is clearly analogous to Canary Wharf, controversially built on top of the old working-class area of east London's Isle of Dogs. Peace tells us of dodgy builders, of gypsy camps burnt down for malls, and of northern cities of the dead. Waites reserves a walk-on part for the real-life figure of T. Dan Smith, the notorious tower block speculator, and the ghost of Donald Trump hovers over McBride's Aberdeen. In such scenarios architecture and land development are the battlegrounds in which profits are sought, images sold, and crimes occur. But it is a vision of a 'modern' architecture that bears little relation to the socially progressive ideals of the modern movement that Clandfield argues have been co-opted and deformed by the financial priorities of the real estate market and building industry.

A parallel forensic search through the locational and spatial archaeology of dystopian and science fiction literature would produce a similar inventory of buildings and environments that whilst superficially strange and alien are somehow recognisably familiar. We might find ourselves searching for the miracle orb inside the spectral radioactive zone in the Strugatskys' *Roadside Picnic* (1972), but we could just as well be caught in the nightmare waiting to happen at Long Island or Chernobyl. The city might materialise, vanish and slowly atrophy in Le Guin's *Lathe of Heaven* (1971), but it remains a city we have visited. Karinthy's *Metropole* (1970) might be the archetype of an endless dystopian bureaucratic madness but it is also a facsimile of any twenty-first-century mega-city. Even on journeys to discover new cities on alien worlds in which we encounter implausibly coloured forests of flowers and hallucinogenic clouds of red dust, their geometry, spatial organisation and material structures are easily identifiable as extensions of earthly cities and phenomena. But this is to be expected. It is why Wells' Sleeper wakes in a giant version of the Crystal Palace. He could never have woken in a place made of things that have never been thought of or imagined.

However, despite the fact that we cannot dream of a science that is not already rooted in the accumulation of existing knowledge, Fortin's essay reminds us of how architects have understandably been drawn to sci-fi precisely because of the allure of new technology, and the delight in the promise of ever more astonishing and miracle-producing gizmos and tricks.[13] But this he suggests is a superficial reading of the genre. At its best such as in the work of Dick, technology and what Suvin describes more generally as the *novum* are not in fact the principal themes.

Dick's descriptions of the city and technology are far more subtle and complex than one might think or imagine. The sci-fi of Dick is not about crass new forms of gadgetry, it is about a discourse concerning the implications and limits of scientific knowledge (Suvin 1979: 65). He mentions in passing smart new technology, but it is meshed into images of ruin and urban decay and layered over the crises of identity that his characters suffer. The combination of machines for manipulating time, empathy boxes, vid phones and hover cars are more like props that embellish far more prescient antonymic themes and issues – the real and imaginary, the human and robotic, safety and fear, war and peace and crucially for an urban narrative, individual liberty and invasive surveillance.[14] In other words whilst Dick, like other science fiction writers is often imagined as an architect of futurology – his city is very much of the 'ravaged' here and now – a city on the edge of reason plagued by 'psycho-spatial' uncertainty and madness, a very special case of what Fortin describes as 'disturbanism'. This is the other side of the rational society, where technology rather than a means of social liberation becomes an instrument of domination, a mirror world where the competing interests of those who wield political and economic power tear the socially equitable planned city of reason to pieces. In this, Dick's urban environments are eerily reminiscent of the real-time urban crises of the contemporary capitalist city.

In *Do Androids Dream…* we meet Isidore in a 'deteriorating, blind building of a thousand uninhabited apartments, which like all its counterparts, fell, day by day, into greater entropic ruin' (Dick 2001: 18). In *Minority Report* we hear of tumbled miles of cheap hotels and broken down tenements, bacterial crystals and radiation tabs. In *A Scanner Darkly* we trip over McDonalds, bugs, malls, bungalows and the general detritus of suburban America. And, as Fortin highlights, scattered throughout his works is the recurring image of the large mixed-use block, the 'conapt', for many the realisation of dreams of prosperity and freedom, but for Dick and others like Ballard and Saramago, an architecture that is far more like an unsettling form of voluntary incarceration. All of this is a long way from the stereotyped wicker fence image of the American Dream Town. It is in short a literary landscape in which the realisation of utopia and the 'strivings for the de-alienation of human kind and their social life' seem very far away (Suvin 1979: 82).

Utopia seems equally distant in the literature of 'outsider angst' introduced by Boyd in the next essay. Focussing on a reading of the works of Alexander Trocchi, renowned for their explicit descriptions of sex and drug use, it is a literature that has a respectable and aristocratic history. Images of the drifter, the drop out and the rebel that hang like a ghost over *Young Adam* boast an illustrious past that would include Camus' *Étranger* (1942), Gide's *Immoralist* (1902), Hesse's

Steppenwolf (1927) and Dostoevsky's *Notes from Underground* (1864). As for narcotic adventure that riddles its way through *Life of Cain*, there is a double history. On the one hand there are stories of observation like Aldous Huxley's mescaline experiment in *The Doors of Perception* (1954), Benjamin's tales *On Hashish* (1927) and de Quincey's *Confessions of an Opium Eater* (1821), the progenitor, Boyd suggests, of Situationist-style 'urban drifting'. But on the other, there are novels that describe a far more brittle world of addiction and psychosis such as the internalised torment of Ageyev's *Novel with Cocaine* (1934), the disconnected amphetamine strip lights of Thompson's *Fear and Loathing in Las Vegas* (1974), the rabid urban dissection of Welsh's *Trainspotting* (1993) and any one of the mangled body spaces we encounter in Burroughs's *Junkie* (1953) and *The Naked Lunch* (1959).

It is tempting to think that tales of weird sex and drugs and of social and spatial alienation only happen on the periphery of the human imagination and the physical city. 'After all, it never happens here, it happens over there.' Maybe in Hellfire Clubs, in a celebrity detective's lounge, in Rhymes of Ancient Mariners, in ghettoes, crumbling squats and derelict warehouse raves, and sometimes as in the case of Trocchi, on the distant slow time of a floating barge and scow. However the truth about narcotic and sexual transgression is somewhat different. In reality whilst physical and psychological end games can take place in some subterranean urban recess under the flickering pink neon of a shady shop, they can just as easily happen on sunlit park benches, amidst the trimmed lawns of everyday suburbia, or behind the varnished doors of a thoroughly middle-class cul-de-sac.

In other words sexual and narcotic activity is geographically unrestricted which is why the archetypal 'junkie' novel is often architecturally ambivalent. As Boyd suggests, the city for Trocchi borders on the irrelevant; it has little in the way of redeeming features or any intrinsic majesty and despite his acquaintance with the celebratory urbanism of Cedric Price and the Situationists, the city for Trocchi is something to be negated or escaped from. In *Young Adam* it is a looming but opaque hinterland, an industrial behemoth that offers little sanctuary. In *Cain's Book* it is a hazy mirage, little more than a network of places for scoring drugs and pursuing other bodily satisfaction. In both novels the sense of spatial dislocation and exile illustrate Trocchi's own alienation from the world of capitalist work, and the reality of his itinerant life that took him from one urban margin to another.

> It had been the same for years. The same situations. Sometimes I thought I was learning something of my own constructions. A scow on the Hudson, a basement room in London, a tiny studio in Paris, a cheap hotel in Athens. A dark room in Barcelona, and now I was living on a moving object …
>
> *Trocchi 1992: 117*

Whether in the squat, the suburb or the salon, the architectural narrative in narcotic tales like those of *Cain's Book* and the *Naked Lunch* is not to be found in bricks and concrete, nor in romanticised Beat generation tales of travel, but in the claustrophobic frozen-time reality of the human mind and body. In this way the sensual animal architecture of flesh and the obsessive focus of a drugged mind operate as a metaphor for the modern city. It is punctured, severed, deformed, poisoned and prostituted. It is in desperate need of radical surgery and psychotherapy to prevent the complete atomisation of any belief in a practical alternative future, after which the only thing left is political nihilism or Trocchi's call for an 'Invisible Insurrection of a Million Minds', a rather conservative utopia that Boyd argues 'eschews any direct or meaningful spatial *praxis*'.

Bodies, backyards and planet B movies in the front room, this is the architectural and spatial significance of these literary genres – we are at *home* with them. The telepathic strange boy next door who knows what you are thinking is not of this world and in the future will grow up to commit unimaginable crimes whilst imbibing a vial of hallucinogens. In other words crime, drugs and dreams of other worlds are socially universal and spatially ubiquitous. Indeed the plausibility of such narratives requires that its chronotopic character, its architecture, along with the critique of our social life, is one we can recognise and identify with. In this the great popularity of such genres, especially crime and sci-fi, is suggestive of something deeply troubling and irreconcilable about our contemporary life. And it is this, the dialectic of capitalist modernity and of human civilisation in general. We gaze longingly at sunlit horizons in which social and technological progress unfolds in a narrative of increasing liberty and freedom. But hastily scribbled on the other side of the balance sheet are the badly hidden statistics of capitalism as a narrative of exploitation and alienation.

All three essays underline the relationship between crime, sci-fi, drug literature and this other history of capitalism, a truly 'noir' history extraordinaire in which 'conquest, enslavement, robbery, murder, briefly force', play the principal roles, a history that is jammed with crime scenes and provokes both dreams of other worlds and narcotic refuge in equal measure.[15] Enveloped by an overwhelming sense of helplessness, we naturally avoid dwelling on the grizzly truths of this history, which is where crime, drug and sci-fi literature have a crucial double role to play.

Such literature openly celebrates the dark side and the dark city. As a reading public we revel in it. We are voyeurs at the car crash, the murder scenes, the drug score, and it is through this simultaneous distancing and proximity that we deal with the world. Nobody likes those who wield power indiscriminately. Nobody at the time of writing likes investment bankers, pimps or drug traffickers. Which is why perhaps even if it is 'business as usual' the day after the boss is prosecuted we still look forward to the fall of the mighty. We might not be able to bring dictators to trial, but we can still read of their 'fictional' demise as we eat a TV dinner whilst watching a documentary about fraudsters, gangsters, prostitutes and aliens.

Notes

1 Reputedly uttered by W. H. Auden. See Priestman (2003:1).
2 See for example the journals *Clues – A Journal of Detection*, published by McFarland, USA and *Science Fiction Studies*, McPauw University, USA.
3 By this I mean the combination of the work of the British Marxist historians like E. P. Thompson, Hobsbawm, Hilton, Hill *et al.*, the French Annales School, the Critical Theory of the Frankfurt School, and the rise of Cultural studies, Feminist and postcolonial theory, that together helped shift both the subject and methodology of historical criticism.
4 See for instance books like Rose (2001) and Bourdieu (1989).
5 *Learning from Las Vegas* by Venturi, Brown and Izenour (1977), although clearly not driven by any revolutionary political impulse, nevertheless represented a landmark in this field.
6 Ideas explored in the classic works by Henri Lefebvre, *Critique of Everyday Life* (1947) and the *Production of Space* (1971), Foucault's *Discipline and Punish* and his essay 'Of Other Spaces – Heterotopias' (1967).
7 See for instance Auge (1995), De Certeau (1984), Perec (1999), Virillio (2009) and Vidler (1992).
8 See for instance Bakhtin's comment on Rabelais, in Bakhtin (1981: 192) 'The sexual series functions, as do all the abovementioned series to destroy the established hierarchy of values via the creation of new matrices of words, objects and phenomena. He restructures the picture of the world, materialises it and fleshes it out.'
9 There are a number of superb anthologies that subject the literary genre and its contested meaning to a critique. Two of the best are by Jameson (2005) and the groundbreaking work by Suvin (1979). There are other fine surveys by Kumar (1987), Wegner (2002) and Booker (1994).
10 See Willett (1996: 139) 'Crime fiction cannot avoid the reproduction of negative images but they may co-exist textually with utopian longings. Furthermore, the preceding examination demonstrates that redemption, the empowerment of the marginalised, the success of the underdog, even redistribution of wealth are all constitutive of the genre.'
11 See for instance Ford (2007) on the gothic allusions of Paretsky's work.
12 Clandfield – in this volume. It should be added that environmental crimes such as toxic dumping have also provided narratives for crime fiction, such as James Crumley's *Dancing Bear* (1983), New York: Vintage.
13 This connects more generally with one of the recurring themes of the twentieth century – technological fetishism and determinism – the idea that perpetual technological innovation can guarantee harmonious social progress and that therefore social revolution can be averted.
14 For a discussion on these themes see Jameson (2005: 142ff).
15 See Marx (1990) on 'The Secret of Primitive Accumulation'.

References

Auge, M. (1995) *Non-Places: introduction to an anthropology of supermodernity*, London: Verso.
Bakhtin, M. M. (1981) *The Dialogic Imagination*, Austin: University of Texas Press.
Booker, M. (1994) *The dystopian impulse in modern literature: fiction as social criticism*, Westport CT: Greenwood Press.
Bourdieu, P. (1989) *Distinction – A social critique of the Judgement of Taste*, London: Routledge.
De Certeau, M. (1984) *The Practice of Everyday Life*, Los Angeles: University of California.
Dick, P. K. (2001) *Do Androids Dream of Electric Sheep*, SF Masterworks, London: Gollancz.

Ford, S. A. (2007) 'Ruined Landscapes, Flooding Tunnels, Dark Paths: Sara Paretsky's Gothic Vision', in *Clues – A Journal of Detection*, Vol 25, No 2.

Foucault, M. (1967) *Of Other Spaces – Heterotopias Discipline and Punish.* Available on line at http://www.foucault.info/documents/heteroTopia (accessed 2 March 2008).

Gifford, J. (2010) 'There was nothing to stop the coloured people from walking across the street": Urban Renewal and the reinvention of American Detective Literature in Chester Himes's Run man Run', in *Clues – A journal of detection*, Vol. 28, No. 1.

Jameson, F. (2005) *Archaeologies of the Future – The desire called utopia and other science fictions*, London: Verso.

Kumar, K. (1987) *Utopia and Anti-Utopia in Modern Times*, London: Blackwell.

Lefebvre, H. (1971) *Production of Space*, Oxford: Blackwell.

Lefebvre, H. (1991) *Critique of Everyday Life*, London: Verso.

Marx, K. (1969) *The Civil War in France*, in *Marx and Engels, Basic Writings on Politics and Philosophy*, Feuer, L. (ed.), New York: Fontana.

Marx, K. (1990) *Capital Volume I*, London: Penguin Classics.

Perec, G. (1999) *Species of Space*, London: Penguin.

Priestman, M. (ed.) (2003) *Cambridge Companion to Crime Fiction*, Cambridge: Cambridge University Press.

Rose, J. (2001) *The Intellectual History of the British Working Class*, London: Yale University Press.

Scaggs, J. (2010) *Crime Fiction – The New Critical Idiom*, London: Routledge.

Suvin, D. (1979) *Metamorphoses of Science Fiction*, London: Yale University Press.

Trocchi, A. (1992) *Cain's Book*, London: John Calder.

Venturi, R., Brown, D. and Izenour, S. (1972) *Learning from Las Vegas*, MIT.

Vidler, A. (1992) *The Architectural Uncanny*, MIT.

Virillio, P. (2009) *War and Cinema: The logistics of Perception*, London: Verso.

Wegner, P. E. (2002) *Imaginary Communities – Utopia, the Nation, and the Spatial Histories of Modernity*, University of California.

Willett, R. (1996) *The Naked City*, Manchester: Manchester University Press.

All photos by the author.

7

ARCHITECTURAL CRIMES AND ARCHITECTURAL SOLUTIONS

Peter Clandfield

In *The Urban Experience*, David Harvey, building on Henri Lefebvre's accounts of space as something produced, not simply given, observes that '[o]nly at certain moments', such as instances of 'corruption within a system of planning permissions [...] does the nonneutrality of the creation of space become evident' (Harvey 1989: 187). These words point to the capacity of crime fiction, revolving as it does around forms of corruption, to investigate not only complexities and dangers of urban environments, but also ways in which these environments are constructed and reconstructed both physically and ideologically. Drawing on the ideas of Harvey as well as other progressive urbanists, this essay focuses on recent crime novels that link localized crimes to broader questions of justice involving the built world and its uses and users. Often making effective use of architecture in the construction of their variations on the structural conventions of the crime genre, these novels connect individual urban crimes to less directly violent kinds of spatial and environmental injustice produced by the machinations of well-placed politically powerful people such as developers, architects, planners and politicians. In investigating the 'architectural crimes' of corrupt and inequitable urban development schemes, these novels suggest valuable perspectives on the recent economic crisis produced in no small part by just such schemes.

Noir, neo-*noir*, and the privatization of modernism

One form of modernity, the rapid development and redevelopment of cities under industrial capitalism, intensified the potential danger and disorder of urban environments and shaped what Raymond Chandler famously called the 'mean streets' (Chandler 1950: 18) of the urban crime fiction which, as Lee Horsley notes, emerged in the late 1920s and 1930s at a time both of economic crisis and of 'growing evidence of illicit connections between crime, business, and politics in rapidly expanding American cities' (Horsley 2005: 69–70). Meanwhile, however, the modernism of architects and theorists such as Le Corbusier sought to design 'mean streets' out of existence. Le Corbusier's *Urbanisme*, translated in 1929 as *The City of To-morrow and its Planning*, calls industrial urbanization 'a sudden, chaotic and sweeping invasion, unforeseen and overwhelming', which 'has brought it about that the Great City, which should be a phenomenon of power and energy, is to-day a menacing disaster, since it is no longer governed by the principles of geometry' (Le Corbusier 1929: 25). Hence the need, according to Le Corbusier, for 'the "House-Machine", the mass-production house, healthy (and morally so too)' (quoted by Vidler 1992: 62). In *The Architectural Uncanny* (1992), Anthony Vidler characterises Corbusian modernism as 'a therapeutic program [...] that proposed an alliance between the hygienists and the architects that would be reinforced on every level by design', and that would produce clean, bright, airy living spaces wherein 'disease, individual and social, might be eradicated once and for all' (Vidler 1992: 62). Le Corbusier's messianic zeal was reflected by admirers like Newcastle-upon-Tyne City Planning Officer Wilfred Burns, who concludes his 1967 book on the city's redevelopment with a quotation from the Book of Revelation (21.2–3): 'And I saw the holy city, new Jerusalem, coming down out of heaven from God [...]' (Burns 1967: 96).

As Harvey notes in *The Condition of Postmodernity*, the utopian urban visions of modernism had renewed appeal following the Second World War, which was 'generally depicted (and justified) as a struggle for a safer world, a better world, a better future' (Harvey 1990: 68). Harvey allows that it would be 'both erroneous and unjust to depict these "modernist" solutions to the dilemmas of postwar urban development and redevelopment as unalloyed failures', since they 'helped preserve full employment, improve material social provision, contribute to welfare goals, and [...] preserve a capitalist social order that was plainly threatened in 1945' (Harvey 1990: 70). However, as Harvey hints, main beneficiaries of such programmes were often not poorly housed urban populations who needed them most, but those already relatively safe.[1] Public modernism began to be co-opted by private agendas. In *Film Noir and the Spaces of Modernity*, Edward Dimendberg argues that *noir* derives distinctive visual and thematic features from integral links with spatial aspects of the late modernity of the 1940s and 1950s, when utopian early modernism was increasingly being eclipsed by dystopian postwar varieties bringing 'loss of public space,' along with 'the eradication of older neighborhoods by urban renewal and redevelopment projects' (Dimendberg 2004: 7). In this unstable, disorienting urban environment, 'anxieties and phantasms of the past' (Dimendberg 2004: 8) were not purged but 'relocated in the period's most representative spatial constructions: the freeway, the suburban house, the glass office tower, the public housing project, the superblock, and the shopping center' (Dimendberg 2004: 9).

Modernist urbanism metamorphosed into 'a nightmare of spatial regimentation, consumer manipulation, and corporate economic control' (Dimendberg 2004: 14). As both Dimendberg and Vidler suggest, what becomes uncanny and menacing in late-modern cityscapes is less modernist architecture in itself than its co-option by clandestine forces of corruption and coercion akin to the ills it was intended to banish (see Vidler 1992: 11–12). Dimendberg argues that attention to the key spatial dimensions of *noir* films requires 'refusing sharp distinctions between figure and ground, content and context' (Dimendberg 2004: 7). A similar approach to more recent crime novels allows for attention to their representation of urban spaces not as fixed backdrops for crime narratives, but as important objects of crime – commodities whose control and definition are at stake, and whose pursuit grounds individual crimes from bribery and fraud to assault and murder.

While this essay focuses on novels from England, Ireland and Scotland, it will show that the tag 'neo-noir' is relevant as more than a generic marketing label, since they render cityscapes with definite resemblances to those Dimendberg evokes. Further, the forces shaping these cityscapes are often international or transnational in their origins, or aspirations, and the novels – harmonizing with Harvey's work – suggest how many contemporary urban problems stem from the sometimes criminal irresponsibility of a speculative capitalism whose practitioners lack commitment to any particular community.

Tower blocks: the new 'mean streets'?

Once the icon of utopian modernist architecture, the tower-block or high-rise apartment building has increasingly and uncannily become a familiar signifier for crime and for crime fiction.[2] In Daniel Barber's film *Harry Brown* (2009), for example, Michael Caine's title character confronts a gang terrorizing his London housing estate, but the film does not examine larger causes for the estate's deterioration, relying instead on a presumptive fit between the fictional genre of crime/police narrative and the architectural genre of modernist public housing. However, this architectural 'crime story' has been challenged both by progressive urbanists and by works of crime fiction. In *A Journey Through Ruins: The Last Days of London* (1991; 2nd edn 2009), historian Patrick Wright shows how simplistic accounts of the shortcomings of public housing estates have served as cover-stories for inequitable forms of urban development. Playing on Le Corbusier's descriptions of high modernist residential units as 'machines', Wright argues that the increasingly large public housing blocks built in many British cities in the 1950s and 1960s were '[d]evised by the large construction companies as machines for harvesting the subsidy' for high-rise residential buildings that was introduced in 1956 by Harold Macmillan's Conservative government (Wright 2009: 91).[3] Drawing on the work of historian Patrick Dunleavy (1981), Wright outlines connections between influential politicians and the construction firms which profited from government-sponsored redevelopment schemes (Wright 2009: 92). Wright expresses ideological and social divisions of late twentieth-century Britain in architectural terms, as a struggle between 'Brideshead and the tower blocks': the quasi-feudal world-view represented by the titular country house of Evelyn Waugh's *Brideshead Revisited* (1945) versus 'the hope that history could be made through the progressive works of an expert and newly enlightened State [...]'. Wright argues that '*Brideshead* has won by discrediting the [reconstruction] project of 1945, not by solving the problems the architects and engineers of that project set out, however inadequately, to address', and he cites the resurgence of homelessness in post-Thatcher Britain as the flipside of 'the kind of modernization that Raymond Williams described as "mobile privatization", whereby homes become places into which 'a television screen occasionally brings [...] distancing views of a nation that has abandoned what were once assumed to be the public duties of the State' (Wright 2009: 109).[4]

Some of these 'distancing views' may come through crime fiction, and especially through screen works like *Harry Brown* which use housing estates and related cityscapes as ready-made visual signifiers of menace. Yet, certain other films and television productions do look into causes of dysfunctional urban developments, and serve to introduce key topics this essay will go on to explore in contemporary crime novels. Caine's performance in *Harry Brown* echoes his title role in Mike Hodges' *Get Carter* (1971), a film notable for its vivid depiction and implicit critique of the particularly ambitious and particularly corrupt modernization schemes underway in Newcastle where it was shot.[5] More recently, television crime series also have shown capacities for active exposition, rather than just passive utilization, of urban settings grounding their storylines. HBO's *The Sopranos* (1999–2007) depicts New Jersey mafioso Tony Soprano's exploitation of his urban environment as systematic, ruthless, and sinister in its efficiency. Particularly in the fourth season (2002), Soprano's operations resemble the subsidy-harvesting schemes Wright outlines, as he sustains his suburban lifestyle through frauds exploiting government programmes intended to support urban renewal and low-income families in Newark.[6] Another HBO series, *The Wire* (2002–2008), offers a more explicit and sustained account of the hijacking of urban renewal initiatives, focusing on Baltimore, another American site where the unevenness of modernity's benefits has been especially evident.[7] In a pivotal moment in the third of the five seasons (episode 3.04), police detectives monitoring gangster Russell 'Stringer' Bell realize that his real estate investments are more than a means of laundering drug profits: 'worse than a drug dealer ... he's a developer.' The novels discussed below substantiate this suggestion that developers (rather than gangsters) may be the really ruthless and efficient shapers of contemporary urban space.[8]

Comparable to the screen productions just mentioned, in their capacity for nuanced investigations of dysfunctional cityscapes, are large-scaled crime novels such as the *Red Riding Quartet* (1999–2002), David Peace's alternative history of West Yorkshire from the late 1960s to the early 1980s. The first volume, *Nineteen*

FIGURE 7.1 'All great buildings resemble crimes.' Construction of the highly controversial new M74 motorway through the centre of Glasgow

Seventy-four, explicitly challenges assumptions that crime involving planning and construction is intrinsically less significant than direct abuse of people. The focal character, ambitious Leeds crime reporter Eddie Dunford, keen to cover unsolved murders of children, resents having to help his colleague Barry Gannon with 'Dawsongate', a story involving '[l]ocal government money for private housing; substandard materials for council housing; back-handers all round' (Peace 1999: 37). Dunford's view of such matters as 'crap that no-one but Barry Gannon gave a fuck about' (Peace 1999: 38) is soon altered. After an anonymous telephone tip, he witnesses a violent police assault on a gypsy camp in the city's environs:

> At the top of the motorway embankment I pulled myself up on my elbows and lay on my belly staring down into hell. There below me in the basin of Hunslet Carr, just 500 yards beneath me, was my England on the morning of Sunday 15 December, in the year of Our Lord 1974, looking a thousand years younger and none the better.
>
> A gypsy camp on fire, each of the twenty or so trailers and caravans ablaze, each beyond relief; the Hunslet gypsy camp I'd seen out of the corner of my eye every single time I'd driven into work, now one big fat bowl of fire and hate.
>
> *Peace 1999: 45*

These paragraphs, among the *Quartet*'s most important, are characteristic both in style, with the shift from a demotic, profane idiom to an archaically formal, solemn one, and in theme, with the invocation of hell. The passage also marks Dunford's shift from seeing the built space around him peripherally and in passing as fixed backdrop to important events, to perceiving it as a potential object, even product, of criminal activity.

Following Gannon's death in a suspicious car accident this same night, Dunford, recalling that his colleague 'had once said something like, "All great buildings resemble crimes"' (Peace 1999: 82), looks into the activities of Gannon's target, John Dawson, known as 'Britain's most successful postwar architect' for works such as his own lavish house, 'Shangrila'. Scouting this private utopia, Dunford is rebuffed by Donald Foster, Dawson's construction magnate crony (Peace 1999: 83), but his interest in architectural crime intensifies, as one of Gannon's informants, a hustler called BJ Anderson, tells him that 'John Dawson's just the tip of the fucking iceberg' (Peace 1999: 106), and he connects the murdered children to Foster's construction sites (Peace 1999: 116, 159). Dunford also encounters Derek Box, a gangster who declares 'ambitions towards the building trade' (Peace 1999: 181) and sets him onto William Shaw, the local councillor whom Dawson and Foster have been bribing, and whom Box attempts to blackmail via compromising pictures with BJ (Peace 1999: 185, 203–6). What emerges is a conspiracy gone wrong between Foster, the corrupt developer, and Box, the traditional gangster attracted to the development industry. Box eventually murders Foster (who, Box informs Dunford, was responsible for Gannon's death [Peace 1999: 211]). Meanwhile, Dunford, defying corrupt policemen aiming to deter his investigations, traces the crimes against children to one of Foster's foremen, George Marsh, whom he finds fatally beaten in an underground lair near his suburban house (Peace 1999: 275). Aptly, it is in the elusive architect Dawson's own palatial house that Dunford goes on to piece further elements of the plot together, after discovering the 'huge rolled-up papers, architect's plans' for the shopping centre that is to replace the gypsy camp:

> The Swan Centre:
> Shaw, Dawson, Foster.
> The Box Brothers wanting in.
> Foster fucking with the Boxes.
> Shaw and Dawson putting their various pleasures before business.
> Foster as Ringmaster, trying to keep the fucking circus on the road.
>
> *Peace 1999: 288*

As this map of links between architectural and criminal schemes illustrates, the volume has elements of a traditional crime novel – but its conclusion also sets up architectural crimes as landmarks to be revisited as the *Quartet* develops. Full exploration of the corruption Dunford has uncovered is deferred: finding Dawson and his wife dead by suicide, he laments: 'John fucking Dawson, just his works remaining, looming and haunting, leaving me […] robbed of the chance to ever know and fucked of the hope it might bring' (Peace 1999: 290). The sinister architect's evasion of a reckoning intensifies the suggestion that his influence on Leeds has been particularly pervasive and pernicious because of its clandestine nature.

Dunford proceeds to a showdown with Box, whom he shoots dead before himself dying, or committing suicide, in a car wreck. The complex narrative structure of the *Quartet*, with a succession of focal characters inheriting obsessions (as Dunford has from Gannon) and replicating actions, emphasizes the systemic nature of the corruption depicted. *Nineteen Seventy-seven* follows the investigation of the Yorkshire Ripper (or Peace's fictionalized version), as seen by Dunford's colleague Jack Whitehead and by Sergeant Robert Fraser, the earnest (though flawed) policeman with whom Dunford has shared information. Both protagonists are undone by conspiring enemies and their own weaknesses, as is the focal character of *Nineteen Eighty*, Peter Hunter, a Manchester policeman sent to Leeds to assist the stalled investigation of the Ripper murders and to uncover local corruption impeding progress. While the two volumes deal only indirectly with 'Dawsongate', they keep spatial iniquities allusively in view, for instance through passing media references to the early parole of jailed Leeds architect John Poulson (Peace 2000: 250) and to dishonest members of the metropolitan London Obscene Publications Squad as '*architects of* [a] *conspiracy of corruption*' (Peace 2001: 92; original italics).

The *Quartet* refocuses on architectural crimes in *Nineteen Eighty-three*, which juxtaposes attention to the early effects of Thatcherism with revisitings and partial explanations of events of previous volumes, conveyed through three characters: the hustler BJ; John Piggott, a struggling but principled lawyer; and Detective Chief Superintendent Maurice Jobson, who has been heavily involved in what the volume reveals as an extensive criminal conspiracy among police, yet who is also tormented by guilt. Early in the volume, at the same motorway exit where the gypsy camp once stood, Jobson observes a building site in terms at first startling from a man of his status: 'the terrifying lorries, the hysterical diggers and the screeching cranes' (Peace 2002: 21). Later allusions imply that the shopping centre planned by Dawson and Foster is materializing under other hands (Peace 2002: 45), and the hellish imagery of Jobson's perception of the site in 1983 takes on uncanny parallels with Dunford's view of the assault in 1974: both episodes involve brutal productions of privatized space. The parallel is underlined when it proves to have been Jobson (in temporary revolt against his own corruption) who tipped Dunford about the 1974 raid (Peace 2002: 281). Other architectural crime scenes are revisited through Jobson's morbid memories of 1969 and the 'skeletons' both of 'half-built semis' (Peace 2002: 82) and of Dawson's Shangrila under construction (Peace 2002: 132). This anthropomorphic perception of buildings underlines the *Quartet*'s linkage of figures and ground and emphasis on corruption built into the spaces it depicts. The *Quartet* incorporates additional suggestions that progressive modernity has never had a chance in Leeds, such as Hunter's perceptions in *Nineteen Eighty* of the city as 'A collision of the worst of times, the worst of hells – the Medieval, the Victorian, and the Concrete' (Peace 2001: 26; see also 322, 364).

Yet, if there is hope, it resides in architectural elements of the *Quartet*. Prominent passages evoke poignant aspects of the corruption of modernist ideals. Dunford's investigations in *Nineteen Seventy-four* lead him to Johnny Kelly, a rugby professional whose niece is among the murdered children, and who has dangerous knowledge of the corrupt builder Foster, his club's chairman. Finding Kelly living in a '[c]lean sixties high-rise,' Dunford 'think[s] of The Beatles and their album covers, of cleanliness, of Godliness, and children' (Peace 1999: 234). The allusion specifically evokes the covers of the Red and Blue double LPs of hits, first released in 1973 and each picturing the Beatles smiling down from the geometrically neat, yet not oppressively monumental, staircase of the EMI building in London: familiar images of a humane ideal of modernity. Dunford's optimism is fleeting, however, and he dwells on the downside of actually existing modernity ('I sat there in my polyester clothes, on the vinyl settee, staring at the Formica tabletop, in the concrete flat' [Peace 1999: 236]), while Kelly's reluctant revelation of Foster's sexual exploitation of his sister, Paula Garland, mother of the murdered child, reminds Dunford of his own sexual abuse of Paula (Peace 1999: 238). However, the glimpse of the unfulfilled promise of modernity is reprised in *Nineteen Eighty-three,* in another uncanny repetition, when Piggott replicates Dunford's call on Kelly. Both building, defaced with racist graffiti (Peace 2002: 313), and man are worse for wear, but still standing. What Piggott actually learns in the scene remains unclear, as does Kelly's exact role in the crimes of the recent past, but the episode draws attention to the plight of public housing under the divisive regime of Thatcher (radio reports of whose impending re-election Piggott hears before visiting the building) and reinforces the *Quartet*'s suggestions that modernity as a public project is not cause but victim of iniquity.

Further, to the considerable extent that crimes in the *Quartet* are committed 'over a fucking shopping centre' (Peace 1999: 294) as Dunford puts it to Box just before shooting him, rather than being compelled by forces of metaphysical Evil (as embodied by the Satanic priest Martin Laws who lurks throughout the work), they are intelligible and at least possibly remediable. Arguably, indeed, the repetitive Satanic imagery of the *Quartet* is an extended metaphor for the material and human root causes of the abuses depicted. The 'hell' of the assault on the gypsy camp is produced by earthly powers and their coercive and irresponsible manipulation of earthly space, and Peace's descriptions of what happens to the camp resonate with Lefebvre scholar Andy Merrifield's Marxist account of the 'commodif[ication] and coloniz[ation]' of space under capitalism as 'a historical geography of expropriation, both of property and of peoples, [...] written in the annals of civilization in letters of blood and fire' (Merrifield 2006: 107). Jobson reveals that police abuse

FIGURE 7.2 'The skeletons of houses.' High-rise block prepared for demolition, the Gorbals, Glasgow

of the gypsies in 1974 has included not only rendering them homeless to make way for the shopping centre (Peace 2002: 227–8), but also attempting to blame them for Marsh's crimes (Peace 2002: 134–5). The fact that the violent paedophile is a building foreman, meant to be producing safe new homes, just as the police are meant to be protecting the public instead of enriching themselves through crime, underlines the uncanny yet material way in which unsafe spaces in Leeds are produced by human vices. The *Quartet*'s most concrete suggestion is, thus, that modernity has been stolen and sabotaged, not subjugated by irreversible Evil. The work's plot architecture reinforces this suggestion, with oppressively gothic repetitions and mystifications eventually counteracted by exposition of material motives underlying crime.

'White rooms' and the potential of therapeutic modernity

Comparable to Peace's *Quartet* in both its audacious reconstruction of a recent urban past and its juxtaposition of metaphysically and materially motivated crimes is Martyn Waites's *The White Room* (2004), which re-views the modernization of Newcastle by placing (versions of) the men who led the project, pre-eminently City Council leader T. Dan Smith, alongside its fictional characters. The fictional protagonist, Jack Smeaton, is a Second World War veteran hoping to exorcize mental images of destruction and Nazi crimes in Europe by contributing to reconstruction at home. He finds a mentor in Ralph Bell, a builder with socialist sympathies (Waites 2004: 26) and connections to Smith, whose visionary schemes, evoked extensively in the text, the two men become involved in realizing (Waites 2004: 74–7). However, the text shows vices of the city's past re-emerging, particularly in the person of Brian Mooney, a psychopathic small-time gangster, abused as a child (Waites 2004: 64–5), who pimps his own common-law wife, Monica. After severely injuring one of Ralph Bell's two sons in a fight, he flees the city – but returns in 1962, six years later, having reinvented himself in London as Ben Marshall (Waites 2004: 145–7), and becomes first a ruthless landlord (Waites 2004: 203–6) and then a force in the city's redevelopment. Having helped corrupt T. Dan Smith (Waites 2004: 256–8), he infiltrates Bell's and Jack's building firm by seducing Jack's wife and blackmailing the increasingly alcoholic Bell through the desperate Monica (Waites 2004: 278–83). Marshall even employs, as an enforcer, Bell's surviving son Johnny, a sexual sadist and Nazi-admirer. While these plot events dramatize the criminal co-option of redevelopment, they also risk implying that spatial crime needs to be perversely sexed-up in order to be interesting.[9] Hence the importance of the work's own distinctive architecture.

The main crime plot plays out in surprising ways. In a scene set in Johnny Bell's tower-block flat, whose decoration with Nazi paraphernalia and other horrors underlines the corruption of modernization (Waites 2004: 349), Jack confronts Marshall with knowledge of his past, but his move has been anticipated by the gangster-developer, who leaves both him and the no-longer-useful Johnny tied up and torches the flat. However, Jack and Johnny make peace before dying, while Marshall/Mooney, gloating from the ground, is unexpectedly attacked and rendered brain-dead by the old mate he left to face blame for his earlier crimes (Waites 2004: 361–2). The city's development continues to follow its corrupted path, with successors to Marshall emerging and Smith going to prison, but the book's final section moves in a new direction, as Ralph Bell's daughter Joanne, who has been Jack's lover after his estrangement from his wife and has become an art therapist, works with Mae, Monica's (and perhaps Mooney's) daughter, institutionalized after responding to her terrible childhood by killing a playmate. The book's title and its view of modernism come into new focus in this final section: the 'white room' evokes not only a now-classic 1960s song by Cream, but also a therapeutic space and specifically, in the Jungian terms Joanne cites in the final pages, a necessary psychological reckoning that may lead to hope for Mae (Waites 2004: 389). In this context, the white room also evokes the clean spaces of modernism, and the ending thus hints that the remediative potential of urban redevelopment – perhaps with help from the 'art therapy' of inventive crime fiction – also survives.[10] This emphasis on potential for the future, however, should be read alongside another of the book's distinctive elements: its use of its version

FIGURE 7.3 'Massive cultural initiatives making the arts accessible for all.' Redefining leisure as consumption, advert, Glasgow

of T. Dan Smith to comment implicitly on twenty-first-century urban trends. During the scene where the ascendant Marshall approaches him with bribes, Smith envisions a future including 'Massive cultural initiatives making the arts accessible for all. A huge, indoor shopping centre in the middle of the city. Existing stores and banks asked to change their branded images [...] to fit in with the city colour scheme' (Waites 2004: 257). Such emphasis on continuity between the redevelopment rhetoric of the sixties and that of the present, where the rebranding of city centres as consumer attractions is widespread, implies a warning that corruption remains a threat.[11]

Crime, development, boom, bust?

Crime fiction's attention to dangerous instabilities of urban space resonates in an economic crisis triggered by unsustainable real estate speculation in a world where, as Harvey puts it in his essay 'The Right to the City', 'the rights of private property and the profit rate trump all other notions of rights' (Harvey 2008: 315), and where 'a small political and economic elite [...] are in a position to shape cities more and more after their own desires' (Harvey 2008: 329). Historian and journalist Fintan O'Toole in *Ship of Fools* exposes the particularly unrestrained speculation that fuelled Ireland's property boom in the 1990s and its collapse in the late 2000s. He outlines the exemplary career of Paddy Kelly, who accumulated property around Dublin and profited as part of a 'small oligopoly' commanding grossly inflated prices for land required for housing and infrastructure (O'Toole 2009: 103–4). Alan Glynn's *Winterland* (2009) fictionalizes a similar figure, Paddy Norton, a developer who has prospered through shady land deals and is completing a 48-storey Dublin megaproject, Richmond Plaza (Glynn 2009: 44). Anxious in the increasingly uncertain late 2000s to secure prestigious tenants, Norton panics in response to news of a safety flaw in the structure, and arranges the murder of the engineer who has discovered it, Noel Rafferty. The text conveys the developer's egotism when, uneasy about inquiries by Rafferty's sister, Gina, he calms himself by imagining the view from his project: 'the city spread out below – Liberty Hall, the Central Bank, the spire of Christ Church Cathedral, and then, farther out, the parks and greenbelt areas, the housing estates that look like electronic circuit-boards, the giant shopping centres, the new ring roads and motorway extensions' (Glynn 2009: 111). Soon after this vision, which resembles Dimendberg's survey of the representative constructions of privatized modernity, Norton invites Gina to the tower, where he talks grandly of further projects – 'Or look at Dubai […] There's no reason why we can't do *that* in this country, if we hold our nerve' (Glynn 2009: 126) – in a way that resonates with Harvey's reference to the '[a]stonishing if not criminally absurd megaurbanization projects' of the Middle East (Harvey 2008: 322).[12]

Belittling Gina's concerns, Norton provokes an argument which, it emerges, almost leads him to push her off the building (Glynn 2009: 132). As the plot ramifies further, the text pays ongoing attention to the built city, countering Norton's megalomania with Gina's sceptical perceptions of (for example) her own residential area of 'riverside regeneration' as sterile and inauthentic, 'a developer's idea of "new" city living' (Glynn 2009: 268–9).[13] In a standoff atop the tower, Gina forces Norton to admit the building's safety concerns, and uses a viral video of the admission to enforce repairs (Glynn 2009: 404). Gina continues to pursue Norton over her brother's murder, and the discredited developer dies of heart failure while waiting to ambush her (Glynn 2009: 464–6). The magnate's fate stands for that of the boom, but in the book's final pages Gina foresees renewal for the building, for herself, and perhaps for the city (Glynn 2009: 467–8), in a conclusion that evokes the utopian potential of good architecture, yet suggests that one rogue player has been responsible for what are, in fact, larger and ongoing problems.

'The Knife' and 'The Donald'

A more open-ended view of the dangerous instability produced by unscrupulous developers is emerging in Stuart MacBride's current series of Aberdeen police procedurals. Each volume centres on a violent crime and its investigation by DS

Logan McRae and his colleagues, but the police also track ongoing cases. One such concerns Malcolm 'Malk the Knife' McLennan, an Edinburgh gangster whose ambitions toward Aberdeen and opportunities presented by its oil wealth are introduced in the first book, *Cold Granite* (2005). A McLennan enforcer is discovered dead in the city's harbour, and Logan reflects on the gangster's recent activities: 'He'd turned himself semi-legitimate about three years ago, if you could call property development that [...] Recently he'd been sniffing around Aberdeen, looking to get into the property game here before the arse fell out of the market' (MacBride 2005: 135–6). Logan ties the dead man to an attempt to bribe a local planner, which foundered when the official proved to be honest, provoking the thug to push him under a bus (MacBride 2005: 136). The allusion to the corruptibility of planners is repeated later (MacBride 2005: 182), and although the plot thread then recedes, it returns in the succeeding volume, *Dying Light* (MacBride 2006: 274, 300). From this point, however, McLennan becomes something more subtle than a vehicle for broad satire of corruption. While his real estate activities are periodically noted – 'McLennan Homes strikes again,' thinks Logan upon seeing 'a development of nasty yellow-clad houses' in *Flesh House* (MacBride 2008: 208) – McLennan himself has yet to appear physically. The sense that he exists just beyond the space the texts represent directly – possibly accumulating land like the Irish speculators O'Toole describes – reflects the architectural quality of the series itself: its cunning creation of flexible virtual space. Further, McLennan's unseen influence on the Aberdeen of the series – much like Dawson's elusiveness in *Red Riding* – works as a metonym for the power of developers to shape urban space in ways not immediately apparent yet potentially crucial.

MacBride's sixth volume, *Dark Blood* (2010), mobilizes the still-unseen McLennan in order to deal pointedly with the presence in Aberdeen of an all-too-real developer, Donald Trump, an iconic figure of transnational property speculation (see e.g. Zukin 1995: 113) whose recent activities around the city have provoked controversy (see e.g. Massie 2009). The text juxtaposes Trump's development with a fictional one by McLennan:

> It hadn't taken the local press long to nickname Donald Trump's development 'Trumpton'. A vast swathe of coast was due to disappear under the bulldozers: two golf courses, five hundred houses, a four-star hotel, and nearly a thousand holiday villas. Which kind of put McLennan Homes' four hundred semi-detacheds into perspective.
>
> *MacBride 2010: 67*

Once again, there is the implication that the power of developers to re-order space makes them natural role-models for gangsters, who operate by dominating space more directly and riskily – 'The Knife' is ideological apprentice to 'The Donald'. This suggestion is cannily reiterated through Wee Hamish Mowat, the old-school

FIGURE 7.4 'The kinds of things we're building now will almost certainly be obsolete and ready for redevelopment in twenty or thirty years.' Housing for 'Luxury' on the eve of the crash, the River Clyde, Glasgow

Aberdeen crime boss who styles himself as a civilized alternative to the ruthless McLennan, against whose incursions he is trying to arm himself by befriending Logan. After remarking to Logan that McLennan's new venture '"wouldn't be happening if it wasn't for Donald Trump"', Mowat muses on the implications of Trump's presence: '"Some say it's a bad thing, that Trump steamrollered local opposition, then went blubbing to the Scottish Parliament when the planning department said he couldn't have his golf course. Others say it's a good thing – it shows that Aberdeen's open for business. Welcomes investment. Is looking to the future …"' (MacBride 2010: 89). While Mowat claims ambivalence about Trump's activities, he voices the case against them more specifically than the case for – and the further deft touch here is the suggestion that a gangster will naturally be particularly interested in the activities of a developer.

The main plotline of *Dark Blood* leads back to McLennan's development, as the escaped serial rapist Logan has been pursuing is captured by renegade officers from (they claim) the Serious Organized Crimes Agency, who plan to sell the man to McLennan: '"Your Malk the Knife's the tip of a Europe-wide smuggling iceberg:

drugs, goods, people, weapons'" (MacBride 2010: 446). While the ensuing chase draws Logan, suggestively, 'deeper into the development' (MacBride 2010: 449), the emphasis shifts once again to other matters, and the most recent volume in the series, *Shatter the Bones* (2011), makes no reference to gangster-developers. However, the indication that McLennan's activities are linked to large-scale corruption still suggests that subsequent volumes will return to MacBride's long view of 'the Knife' and his influence on urban space, and that the series will continue monitoring the developing influence of figures like Trump on its city.

Conclusion: Jerusalem lanes and future cities

Donald Trump, of course, is not himself involved in smuggling, drug-dealing or Satanic rituals. If academic discourse about urbanism is, like police forces and legal systems, bound by codes and protocols and obligations to provable fact, crime fiction can function as a kind of shady operative, able to bypass rules, rough up suspects, and supplement the factual to make a point. However, crime fiction can also accommodate notably refined takes on urban development and spatial aspects of justice, as is shown in the work of Barry Maitland, who perhaps uniquely combines careers as architect and as crime novelist. *The Marx Sisters* (1994), first book in Maitland's procedural series featuring DS Kathy Kolla and DCI David Brock, centres upon a small central London street – Jerusalem Lane – diverse in both population and architecture, where a resident, one of the three elderly sisters named in the title, who are 'great-granddaughters of Karl Marx' (Maitland 1994: 232), has been murdered. Suspects include various residents of the street, but also the powerful developers who are planning an outsize office complex on its site, and who have met resistance from the sisters; one of the survivors, Eleanor, reminds Brock of the anarchist principle that 'without robbery and murder, property cannot exist' (Maitland 1994: 144). After Eleanor is also murdered (Maitland 1994: 155), the investigation stalls, making room for further attention to questions of urban space as Kolla tells Brock about her past, which serves to recapitulate the hijacking of progressive modernism as described by historians like Wright. The suicide of her civil servant father, who had 'been speculating large sums of money with some shonky developer' (Maitland 1994: 162), left Kolla to start a new life, as a teenager, in a council high-rise. Brock suggests that the experience has been 'the making of' her as a detective (Maitland 1994: 163), and Kolla indeed uses her insights into families and spaces to solve the case.

The developers prove innocent of the murders, yet they get unflattering scrutiny when their tough Glaswegian Project Manager, Danny Finn, apparently a prime suspect in the crimes, proves disarmingly candid, mentioning that during his Gorbals youth he was 'a Thatcherite ahead of [his] time', stealing materials from building sites by night and selling them back to their owners by day (Maitland 1994: 218). Having informed the police of a deal whereby the last sister, Peg, will move to a new home near Marx's Highgate grave, while Eleanor's remains will be buried on the site of Jerusalem Lane in the foundation of the new project, Finn remarks that 'the kinds of things we're building now will almost certainly be obsolete and ready for redevelopment in twenty or thirty years' (Maitland 1994: 264). This comment sets up the novel's highly suggestive conclusion. On a last visit to Jerusalem Lane, which is already being obliterated by the new building, Kolla learns the truth from Peg: the motive for the murders has been a lost Marx manuscript that the first sister, Meredith, has wanted to sell to a career-building American academic, provoking her more idealistic siblings to embark on a murder–suicide plot (Maitland 1994: 309). Before taking her own life, Peg cites Marx's theory that 'the complete cycle of capitalist development' will pave the way for socialism (Maitland 1994: 310), and implies that his manuscript is buried with Eleanor's remains in the foundations of the new building, perhaps fairly soon to re-appear. Kolla thinks that Peg's vision is 'too silly to be taken seriously' (Maitland 1994: 311), and the fact that the Marx sisters have destroyed themselves might suggest the propensity of the left for debilitating internal conflicts. However, coming as it does at the end of the book's intricate narrative, the prospect of a Marxist manuscript emerging from the base of a capitalist superstructure remains too arresting to be dismissed. Thus, in a way that resonates with Harvey's work, the book leaves open the possibility of progressive ideas re-emerging to influence the city of the near future. In a 2006 essay on Harvey's contribution to the understanding of contemporary cities, another leading progressive urbanist, Sharon Zukin, suggests that his work 'opens the door to a more metaphorical examination of urban imaginaries than he himself may accomplish' (Zukin 2006: 104). The novels considered in this essay suggest how tropes and topoi of crime fiction contribute to such a project. Collectively, they hint that if utopian modernist urbanism is not quite thriving openly in crime fiction, it survives there in disguise.

Notes

1 On government-subsidized suburbanization, see Harvey's *Spaces of Hope* (2000), Chapter 8.
2 Andrew Burke observes that tower blocks 'are routinely associated in the popular imagination as the sites of, and symbols for, the major social problems of contemporary Britain (crime, poverty, anti-social behaviour), but such identification, by politicians and the media especially, frequently serves only as a cover for anti-working class and anti-immigrant sentiment' (Burke 2007: 178). Burke cites Thatcher's denunciation of welfare state ideals in terms of what she called the 'block mentality: tower blocks, trade union block votes, block schools', and he notes that through this 'chain of affiliation[s among] history, spatiality and ideology [...] the concrete high-rise comes to have concrete political consequences', through 'a process of dematerialisation, wherein the concrete form of the tower block circulates as a sign and visual image' (Burke 2007: 182).
3 Harvey, concurring with Wright, points out that 'it is curious that the left is now [in the early 1990s] largely blamed for' dysfunctional modernist projects 'when it was the conservatives, by cutting corners on costs of low-income housing in particular, who

perpetrated many of the worst examples of instant slums and alienated living conditions' (Harvey 1990: 70).

4 On 'mobile privatization,' see Williams's *Television: Technology and Cultural Form* (Williams 1974: 19).

5 On *Get Carter*'s critique of Newcastle's redevelopment, see Chibnall (2003: 39–42) and Clandfield and Lloyd (2002: 168–71, 175–7).

6 Maurice Yacowar offers a useful assessment of Soprano's redevelopment scams, though he focuses on details of individual dishonesty rather than on implications of systemic iniquity (Yacowar 2002: 192–95).

7 As Harvey notes, Baltimore's postwar development exemplifies problems of 'white flight' and of government-led revitalization schemes benefitting mainly those already well-placed (Harvey 2000: 150–6).

8 On *The Wire*'s investigations of development, crime and related matters, see *The Wire: Urban Decay and American Television*, ed. Tiffany Potter and C. W. Marshall (2009).

9 While the details of Smith's dealings are less lurid than the events of *The White Room*, their intricacy does make them resemble crime fiction plots, as Steve Chibnall's account highlights:

> The Trotskyist politician [...] was also a public relations consultant for the Crudens building company who won lucrative contracts for blocks of flats from the council [... and for] the Leeds architect John Poulson, whose practice was closely aligned with the construction firms Bovis Holdings, the family company of the [1962–4] Conservative Minister of Housing, Keith Joseph, and Marples Ridgeway, a firm predominantly owned by the Transport Minister, Ernest Marples. Smith also had a close working relationship with the corrupt County Durham alderman, Andrew Cunningham, whose many public roles included chair of the Northumbrian River Authority and Durham Police Authority, and membership of the Labour Party National Executive Committee [...] It was a system of mutual benefit that bridged radical political divisions and ensured that any close inspection of its undertakings was effectively discouraged.
>
> *Chibnall 2003: 40*

10 Other contemporary crime novels notably make space for attention to modernist housing in everyday use. The Glasgow novels of Denise Mina address dangers of the more ill-conceived of the city's large schemes, yet also note that the successes of progressive modernist urbanism remain underappreciated: 'Good schemes, like good families, ha[ve] no history' (Mina 2000: 59). Courttia Newland's *The Scholar* (1997) and *Society Within* (1999) centre on a fictional West London estate, Greenside, whose 'sprawling rows of buildings' are likened suggestively to 'some concrete army that had just invaded the area and was awaiting further orders' (Newland 1997: 138). While *The Scholar* does imply that drug-dealing and armed robbery are promoted in part by conditions on the estate, *Society Within* takes up the suggestion that the estate itself is neglected rather than inherently dysfunctional. The book's most sustained crime plot, an ill-fated holdup at a local drug den, is the scheme of a laid-off worker from the estate's asbestos-ridden youth centre, which has been abruptly demolished by council authorities unwilling to fund renovations (Newland 1999: 67–84; 239–51). Though he is not literally the architect of Greenside, the renegade youth worker nevertheless represents a deft variation on the theme of white-collar corruption as a threat to urban security. The final pages of *Society Within* move pointedly away from crime, focusing on routines of work and everyday life, as Elisha, a recent arrival on the estate, settles into a part-time job at a small restaurant, where she comes to feel 'completely relaxed and at home' (Newland 1999: 310). Thus, and as its title suggests, the book provides the attention to the inner lives of ordinary estate residents that works such as *Harry Brown* omit, and registers the possibility that urban public housing schemes may still accommodate the form of modernism

that Marshall Berman defines broadly as the 'attempt by modern men and women to become subjects as well as objects of modernization' (Berman 1982: 5).

11 On what Jonathan Charley has called the 'capitalisation of culture or more precisely of eating, drinking, and caffeine-injected art galleries' (Charley 2005: 9), see e.g. Zukin's *The Cultures of Cities* (1995).

12 Mike Davis hints that the urban mega-developments Harvey cites may epitomize the synthesis of speculative development and gangsterism: '[t]he platform for Dubai's extraordinary ambitions has been its long history as a haven for smugglers, gold dealers, and pirates' (Davis 2006: 55).

13 On Dublin's unsustainable boom and its production of 'truly homogenous and unsettling places,' see also Charley (2005: 11).

References

Berman, Marshall (1982; 2rd edn 1988) *All that is Solid Melts into Air: The Experience of Modernity*, New York: Penguin.

Burke, Andrew (2007) 'Concrete Universality: Tower Blocks, Architectural Modernism, and Realism in Contemporary British Cinema', *New Cinemas: Journal of Contemporary Film* 5.3: 177–88. Online, Intellect.

Burns, Wilfred (1967) *Newcastle: A Study in Replanning at Newcastle-upon-Tyne*, London: Leonard Hill.

Chandler, Raymond (1950; new edn 1988) *The Simple Art of Murder*. New York: Vintage.

Charley, Jonathan (2005) 'Boom and Slump on the Clyde and Liffey', *Building Material* 14: 8–11.

Chibnall, Steve (2003) *Get Carter: The British Film Guide* 6, London: I. B. Tauris.

Clandfield, Peter and Lloyd, Christian (2002) 'Concretizing the Seventies in Hodges's *Get Carter* and Torrington's *Swing Hammer Swing!*', *Mosaic* 35, 4: 163–80.

Davis, Mike (2006) 'Fear and Money in Dubai', *New Left Review* 41: 47–68.

Dimendberg, Edward (2004) *Film Noir and the Spaces of Modernity*, Cambridge, MA: Harvard University Press.

Dunleavy, Patrick (1981) *The Politics of Mass Housing, 1945–1975: A Study of Corporate and Professional Influence in the Welfare State*, Oxford: Clarendon Press.

Get Carter (1971), motion picture, MGM, London.

Glynn, Alan (2009) *Winterland*, London: Faber.

'Hamsterdam' (2004), *The Wire*, television broadcast, HBO 10 Oct.

Harry Brown (2009), motion picture, Goldwyn, London.

Harvey, David (1989) *The Urban Experience*, Baltimore: Johns Hopkins University Press.

Harvey, David (1990) *The Condition of Postmodernity*, Malden, MA: Blackwell.

Harvey, David (2000) *Spaces of Hope*, Berkeley: University of California Press.

Harvey, David (2008) 'The Right to the City,' *Social Justice and the City*, 2nd edn, Athens: University of Georgia Press: 315–32.

Horsley, Lee (2005) *Twentieth-Century Crime Fiction*, Oxford: Oxford University Press.

Le Corbusier (1925) *Urbanisme*; trans Frederick Etchells (1929; new edn 1987) *The City of To-morrow and its Planning*, New York: Dover.

MacBride, Stuart (2005) *Cold Granite*, New York: St. Martin's.

MacBride, Stuart (2006) *Dying Light*, London: HarperCollins.

MacBride, Stuart (2008) *Flesh House*, London: HarperCollins.

MacBride, Stuart (2010) *Dark Blood*, London: HarperCollins.

MacBride, Stuart (2011) *Shatter the Bones*, London: HarperCollins.

Maitland, Barry (1994) *The Marx Sisters*, London: Orion.

Massie, Alex (2009) 'Trumpton-on-the-North-Sea Latest: The Donald Can Still Buy Your House', *Spectator*, 1 October. Online, spectator.co.uk.

Merrifield, Andy (2006) *Henri Lefebvre: A Critical Introduction*, New York: Routledge.

Mina, Denise (2000) *Exile*, London: Bantam.

Newland, Courttia (1997) *The Scholar: A West Side Story*, London: Abacus.

Newland Courttia (1999) *Society Within*, London: Abacus.

O'Toole, Fintan (2009) *Ship of Fools: How Stupidity and Corruption Sank the Celtic Tiger*, London: Faber.

Peace, David (1999) *Nineteen Seventy-four*, New York: Vintage.

Peace, David (2000) *Nineteen Seventy-seven*, New York: Vintage.

Peace, David (2001) *Nineteen Eighty*, New York: Vintage.

Peace, David (2002) *Nineteen Eighty-three*, New York: Vintage.

Potter, Tiffany and Marshall, C. W. (eds) (2009) *The Wire: Urban Decay and American Television*, New York: Continuum.

Vidler, Anthony (1992) *The Architectural Uncanny: Essays in the Modern Unhomely*, Cambridge, MA: MIT Press.

Waites, Martyn (2004) *The White Room*, London: Pocket.

'Watching Too Much Television' (2002), *The Sopranos*, television broadcast, HBO 27 Oct.

Williams, Raymond (1974; new edn 2003) *Television: Technology and Cultural Form*, London: Routledge.

Wright, Patrick (1991; 2nd edn 2009) *A Journey through Ruins: The Last Days of London*, Oxford: Oxford University Press.

Yacowar, Maurice (2002) *The Sopranos on the Couch: Analyzing Television's Greatest Series*, New York: Continuum.

Zukin, Sharon (1995) *The Cultures of Cities*, Malden, MA: Blackwell.

Zukin, Sharon (2006) 'David Harvey on Cities,' in Noel Castree and Derek Gregory (eds), *David Harvey: A Critical Reader*, Malden, MA: Blackwell: 102–20.

All photos by Jonathan Charley.

8

PHILIP K. DICK'S DISTURBANISM

Towards psychospatial readings of science fiction

David T. Fortin

Architects and urban commentators are frequently fascinated by science fiction (SF), but it is an obsession that tends to focus on the novel, 'high-tech' and more visual aspects of the genre, often linked with film, at the expense of the broader contributions by writers such as Philip K. Dick. Dick's stories colourfully explore the complex interrelationships between us and our environments, offering unique insights into the tensions between individual autonomy and the economic and technological priorities of capitalist societies. Among his many relevant themes, Dick's comments on architecture and urbanism lucidly address one of the central dilemmas of modernity – the spatial role and use of technology in our societies – and while he may often be referred to in architectural circles as 'the guy who wrote *Blade Runner*,' his satirical critique of late-capitalist society is invaluable for all forms of cultural inquiry.

Compared to some of his contemporaries, and particularly Ursula Le Guin, Dick felt his work to be considered 'trashy' and of a lower literary form throughout his career (Sutin 1989: 277). He argued that, in general, SF was 'considered to be something for adolescents, for just high school kids, and for disturbed people in general to read in America' (Matthies 2006). Since his death in 1982, however, Dick has received increased critical attention alongside a swelling cultural fascination with his work, and while one reason for this is simply increased exposure, another perspective worth considering is that his stories are, in fact, for ordinary people increasingly disturbed by the fabricated worlds engulfing them.

His stories intimate the deleterious effects of capitalism on our urban environments, where cities and interplanetary colonies are divided into socioeconomic enclaves and one's urban experience is mediated and controlled through various technological, economic and political means. This essay explores this notion of

Dick's distinctly humanist 'disturbanism' by highlighting his critique of technology, urban planning, suburbia and the psychospatial complexities linking them, and further suggests the contemporary relevance of Dick for architectural and urban investigations into the way we might design and inhabit our built futures.

Why architects still don't know Dick about SF

Essential to understanding Dick in relation to architectural and urban issues, is the context of his writing during the mid-twentieth century. SF had been radically transformed by the advent of popular cinema during the previous decades, propelling it from its literary roots into exhilarating new forms of spatial and visual possibilities. This would have a significant influence on architecture, itself adapting to the new materials and building techniques afforded by industrialization and the cultural milieu emerging around them. While the narratives of the early films were often dystopian, for example Fritz Lang's *Metropolis* (1927), others such as William Cameron Menzies' adaptation of H. G. Wells' *Things to Come* (1936) offered an 'architecture of vigorous optimism and utopian thrust' (Albrecht 1987: xi). SF film would continue to thrive into what Vivian Sobchack describes as its first 'Golden Age' during the 1950s based 'predominantly on the fearsome and wondrous *novelty* and *strangeness* of this new [nuclear] technology – and on the new forms of *alien-ation* generated by [it]' (Sobchack 1987: 252). It was such fervour surrounding the various technologies, as colourfully explored through SF novels, comics and film, that had the greatest impact on the design and visual disciplines as artists and theoreticians such as Reyner Banham, Richard Hamilton, Lawrence Alloway and other members of the Independent Group, for instance, took keen interest.

> Powerful and emotive imagery was an important aspect of the sort of science fiction consumed by Banham and friends, and they were convinced it had a purpose and role beyond merely entertaining. According to Alloway … 'Science fiction alone does not orientate its readers in a technological and fast-moving culture but it is important among the attitude-forming channels.' Science fiction could, Independent Group members believed, provide the sort of images that shaped attitudes.
>
> *Whiteley 1990: 213*

Such techno-optimism was further embraced by architectural groups such as Archigram and their 'composite belief in pop, the future, technological innovation, enterprise, indeterminacy, and hyperfunctionalism' (Sadler 2005: 141). This is most clearly evidenced in Warren Chalk's cover design for the 1964 *Archigram* 4 'Zoom' publication illustrating a SF-like hero flying via jetpack over a futuristic city with laser gun in hand.

And yet this longstanding fixation on the visually novel and 'new' aspects of the genre is one of the inherent problems with conventional readings of SF in architecture. During Dick's most productive years, concurrent with SF film's first 'Golden Age',[1] architectural commentary increasingly split into two camps – those considering it worthy of architectural attention and those who felt 'futuristic' thinking was detrimental to the social responsibility of the profession. It was stimulating, progressive and inspiring, or fantastical, frivolous and egotistical. For example, at a cocktail party hosted by a mutual friend in the 1950s, Dick was himself ridiculed in a 'drunken song-and-dance parody of the kinds of people who wrote SF' by prominent architectural critic Allan Temko (Sutin 1989: 83). While this encounter reveals a patronizing architectural opinion of SF as a cultural form, others would assail the 'visionary' architects of the era by linking them directly to it. Robert Venturi, Denise Scott Brown and Steven Izenour, for example, famously attacked the heroic modern architect through direct association with SF, pitting it against their preferred 'social realist' position (Venturi *et al.* 1972: 149). In either case, supportive (Banham, Independent Group, Archigram) or in disdain (Temko, Venturi *et al.*), the focal point has often remained on visual and technological projection as the sole contribution of SF to architectural thinking.[2]

Yet the *novum* of SF, which Darko Suvin describes as the new concept 'validated by cognitive logic' (Suvin 1979: 63), clearly transcends these aspects of the genre, and this is paramount when considering authors like Dick. As Fredric Jameson, who refers to him as 'the greatest of all Science Fiction writers',[3] explains,

> nothing seems quite so remote from the Golden Age-type galactic and historical speculation than Philip K. Dick's world of hallucination and drug-induced vision, or the claustrophobia of his post-historical landscapes, the dreary and artificial off-worlds to which the post-catastrophe earth-dwellers have been forced to emigrate, and whose sensory and experiential impoverishment makes for a recourse to pharmacological illusion only too comprehensible.
>
> *Jameson 2005: 96*

Stanislaw Lem similarly sees Dick as the exception to most SF which he criticizes for its 'flight from the real problems of civilization'[4] (Lem 1986: 38). Furthermore, when Greg Rickman asked Dick why he enjoyed writing SF, his response was not because he wanted to create utopian techno-visions of future worlds but rather because, 'I love to just play games with time–space causality. It's my old interest in epistemology' (Rickman 1988: 44–5). It becomes increasingly apparent that the reason Dick has been often overlooked in architectural discourse is due to his very indifference to those things architects find most compelling in the genre – visual expressions of progress, technology and novelty.[5] Despite a dominant shift in SF literature during the 1960s away from the techno-utopias and towards the more 'social' and 'anthropological' aspects of the genre,[6] many architects still value it primarily for the innovative creations of the artists, film production teams and set designers, rather than the literature informing their concepts.[7]

Not-so-technological technologies

If it is epistemology and not technology that ultimately motivates Dick's writing, this suggests a reconsideration of his contribution to architectural and urban studies beyond the spectacular visuals of the film adaptations.[8] The significance of Dick for design thinking is not in technological extrapolation but in how that technology and the characters relate to one another in their selected environs. Dick often provides a future world with uncanny resemblance to the humdrum experiences of our everyday lives, his techno-scientific inserts being used metaphorically, not presciently. As his biographer Lawrence Sutin writes,

> [to] Phil, a focus on scientific probability – as opposed to plot possibilities – meant that the writer wasn't doing his job. Phil's approach to technology was, simply, to make up whatever gizmo he needed to keep his characters' reality in suitably extreme states.
>
> *Sutin 1989: 88*

FIGURE 8.1 'In Southern California it didn't make any difference anyhow where you went; there was always the same McDonaldburger place over and over, like a circular strip that turned past you as you pretended to go somewhere' (Dick 1999: 22)

The various gizmos and gadgets in Dick's stories are ultimately used to critique the role of technology in capitalist society and the dialectics of its instrumental and deterministic tendencies. As Scott Bukatman notes, it is the 'mythifying uses' of the technology, and not the technology itself, that grounds his satire (Bukatman 1994: 53). These pseudo-technologies are scattered throughout his novels and stories. For example, the mood organs in *Do Androids Dream of Electric Sheep?*, the robotic president in *The Simulacrum*, the rhetorizers and leadies in *The Penultimate Truth*, the infrared surveillance scanners in *A Scanner Darkly*, the tracking devices (microtrans and minicams) and embedded 'seed bombs' in *Flow My Tears, The Policeman Said*, the cryonic suspension in *Ubik*, and so forth. However, as Merritt Abrash notes, the technologies are introduced 'not to allow a breakthrough toward new and better societies, but to enhance the operation of existing procedures and values. Their genesis is in profit and power, never idealism' (Abrash 1983: 115). In a Marcusean spirit,[9] Dick frames technology as primarily a conservative means to protect the power-at-hand. This is exemplified in the following description of the robotic teachers and automated curriculum at the colonial school in *Martian Time-Slip*.

> For the entire Public School was geared to a task which went contrary to his grain: the school was there not to inform or educate, but to mold, and along severely limited lines. It was the link to their inherited culture, and it peddled that culture, in its entirety, to the young. It bent its pupils to it; perpetuation of the culture was the goal, and any special quirks in the children which might lead them in another direction had to be ironed out.
>
> *Dick 2008a: 63*

The result of this cultural 'embalming' in Dick's stories is the establishment of skewed social values and simplified roles, the various technologies often enabling corporate and/or Orwellian control in the proverbial SF technophobic mode.

However, Dick further complicates this in that the gradual revealing of these technological tyrannies results not in any sense of enlightenment, or truth, but rather the dissolving of the character's perception of reality as their physical and psychological worlds become irreparably detached. For example, the *Martian Time-Slip* narrative revolves around protagonist Jack Bohlen, a repairman who has relocated to Mars following a schizophrenic episode earlier on Earth. Through a series of interactions with the leader of the Water Workers' Union, Arnie Kott, and an autistic child named Manfred Steiner, Bohlen's psychosis resurfaces as boundaries between real and virtual fly asunder. This 'disturbance' is illustrated as Bohlen recalls his first schizophrenic episode during a conversation with his personnel manager back on Earth. Behind the 'façade' of a benevolent banality, Bohlen begins to see technology in place of the human qualities he had previously perceived in his world.

The man was dead. He saw, through the man's skin, his skeleton. It had been wired together, the bones connected with fine copper wire. The organs, which had withered away, were replaced by artificial components, kidney, heart, lungs – everything was made of plastic and stainless steel, all working in unison but entirely without authentic life … it was more on the order of a vision, a glimpse of absolute reality, with the façade stripped away. And it was so crushing, so radical an idea, that it could not be meshed with his ordinary views. And the mental disturbance had come out of that.

Dick 2008a: 69–71

Later, Bohlen observes similar struggles in the 'isolated' and 'lonely' children on Mars who have 'a large-eyed, haunted look, as if they were starved for something as yet invisible' (Dick 2008a: 21). The 'something' that the children seek is the world reality Bohlen witnesses in his schizophrenic episode, Bukatman arguing that this event 'permits him to perceive the spectacle *as spectacle* rather than as surrogate reality' (Bukatman 1994: 52). As in much of his writing, Dick's commentary is thus a caveat regarding the dehumanizing capacity of technology to frame our world by distorting our reality for political and/or corporate purposes.

There are many examples of this in Dick's work. The novel *Time out of Joint* (2002) involves an entire world fabricated around Ragle Gumm, a former military strategist who can predict where rebelling lunar colonists will next attack Earth. With his memory wiped clean due to his plans to emigrate to the moon, his military skills are exploited by the government until he eventually escapes the confines of the simulated town and is faced with the daunting reality of his elemental role in an interplanetary war. Similarly, in *The Penultimate Truth* (1964), the corporate elite simulate a false reality to the majority of the human population living underground in 'ant-tanks' under the impression that a world war is still occurring on the surface. In both cases, it is the explicit manipulation of the characters through strategically designed and technologically mediated environments that ultimately conceals and protects the systems controlling them.

Big bad buildings and dist(sub)urbia

Essential to Dick's reflections on these deceptive societies are the buildings and cities that the characters inhabit. For example, one of the essential causes of Bohlen's distress in *Martian Time-Slip* is attributed to the utopian artificiality of his environment back on earth.

Mars, he thought. He had cut the ties, in particular his job, had sold his Plymouth, given notice to the official who was his landlord. And it had taken him a year to get the apartment; the building was owned by the nonprofit

West Coast Co-op, an enormous structure partly underground, with thousands of units, its own supermarket, laundries, child-car center, clinic, even its
own psychiatrist, down below in the arcade of shops beneath the street level.
There was an FM radio station on the top floor which broadcast classical music
chosen by the building residents, and in the center of the building could be
found a theater and meeting hall. This was the newest of the huge cooperative
apartment buildings – and he had given it all up, suddenly … His life had no
purpose. For fourteen months he had lived with one massive goal: to acquire
an apartment in the huge new co-op building, and then when he had gotten
it, there was nothing. The future had ceased to exist.

Dick 2008a: 67–9

FIGURE 8.2 'Immediately he felt something watching: the holo-scanners on him …
Within something's very eyes; within the sight of some thing. Which,
unlike little dark-eyed Donna, does not ever blink. What does a scanner
see? he asked himself. I mean, really see? Into the head? Down into the
heart?' (Dick 1999: 22)

Bohlen's perception of this ultra-designed society, its mega-structure proudly embodying social and technological ideals of progress, is instead described as an empty and fabricated source of failed promise. The cooperative housing complex is Dick's transparent critique of the lofty expectations associated with modern utopian planning, Bukatman linking the buildings, and their politically charged counter-parts in *The Simulacrum*, to the demolished Pruitt-Igoe buildings in St Louis that Charles Jencks famously marked as the definitive end of modernism (Bukatman 1994: 50–1). These colossal buildings become increasingly central to the *Martian Time-Slip* narrative as the United Nations (UN) intends to buy a remote parcel of land on the red planet to be developed for eager immigrants. Sounding eerily like recent exploding cities such as Dubai, similarly constructed in an inhabitable environment and with recent growth founded largely on real estate speculation, Bohlen responds to an image of the buildings to be erected.

> Glancing at it, Jack saw that it was a picture of a long, thin building. He stared at it a long time. 'The UN,' Leo said, 'is going to build these. Multiple-unit dwellings. Whole tracts of them, mile after mile … All built by slave equipment, those construction automatons that feed themselves their own instructions.'
>
> *Dick 2008a: 121*

The colossal building is a common typology throughout Dick's work that he also refers to as conapts (condominium-apartments). Examples include the 'life-less' apartment of the Deckards in *Do Androids Dream of Electric Sheep?*, Runcible's prison-like residential buildings in *The Penultimate Truth*, or the conapt that traps Joe Chip in his apartment in *Ubik*, his door threatening to sue him if he doesn't deposit money into it in order to exit[10] (Dick 1984: 25). Paul Verhoeven's 1991 blockbuster film *Total Recall*, adapted from Dick's spatially non-descript story 'We can remember it for you wholesale', similarly captures the Dickian conapt by mon-taging a series of Mexico City brutalist buildings into a bustling indoor city.

Dick's sociopolitical critique of these large complexes is perhaps best described in *The Penultimate Truth*. Similar to those described in *Martian Time-Slip*, he writes,

> And then, beyond the Mississippi, he saw a manmade focus of upright, hard structures, and these, too, gave him a funny feeling. Because these were the Ozymandias-who-he? great conapt dwellings erected by that busy builder, Louis Runcible. That one-man ant army that, in its marches, did not gnaw down with its mandibles but set up, with its many metal arms, one gigantic dormlike structure, including kids' play-grounds, swimming pools, ping-pong tables and dart boards.
>
> *Dick 2004: 32*

Built for those humans remaining above the surface, or those who have wandered up to it from the ant-tanks, Dick suggests the residents are similarly trapped, not through deceptive confinement as those below, but rather by the sense of comfort provided to them by the developer, Runcible, who offers all the amenities but also uses cheap materials such as plastic imitation carpet to secure his profit. The conapt, referred to earlier as a prison, becomes synonymous with the suppression of one's autonomy in a hegemonic capitalist system during a conversation between two ant-tank escapees.

> 'Then how come,' Blair said, 'you're squatting here in these ruins instead of lounging at a swimming pool in one of those conapt constellations?'
> The man grunted, gestured. 'I just – like to be free.'
> No one commented; it did not require it.
>
> *Dick 2004: 104*

The question of why certain escapees opt for struggle and freedom over comfort recalls Horkheimer and Adorno's critique of societies structured solely around capital profit while disseminating their ideals via the various cultural enterprises. As they write, with unmistakable resemblance to Dick's conapts,

> … the city housing projects designed to perpetuate the individual as a supposedly independent unit in a small hygienic dwelling make him all the more subservient to his adversary – the absolute power of capitalism. Because the inhabitants, as producers and as consumers, are drawn into the center in search of work and pleasure, all the living units crystallise into well-organised complexes. The striking unity of microcosm and macrocosm presents men with a model of their culture: the false identity of the general and the particular.
>
> *Horkheimer and Adorno 1993: 120–1*

It is this false identity, the Baudrillardian simulated world and its human counterpart, which is central to Dick's thesis and informs the manner in which his characters inhabit their worlds.

Yet while the building-as-city plays the frequent role of spatial antagonist in Dick's stories, there is often an accompanying critique of urban sprawl. The mundane structure of Californian-bred suburban cities, along with their marital woes, job concerns, commoditized behaviours and repetitive lifestyles, are among the themes satirized by Dick, along with the fabricated and fragile worlds supporting them. This is apparent in *Martian Time-Slip* as Leo visits his son's home for the first time.

> Leo looked around. He saw a flat desert with meager mountains in the far distance. He saw a deep ditch of sluggish brown water, and, beside the ditch, a mosslike vegetation, green. That was all except for Jack's house and the Steiner house a little further on …

Being obliging, Leo said, 'Very impressive, Jack. You've got a nice place here; a nice little modern place. A little more planting, landscaping, and I'd say it was perfect.'

Grinning at him crookedly, Jack said, 'This was the dream of a million years, to stand here and see this.'

Dick 2008a: 118–19

Later, Arnie Kott's business partners refer to the 'isolated houses … way out on the goddam fringes,' (Dick 2008a: 166) where lonely housewives like Sylvia Bohlen are immobilized throughout the novel … The remoteness of such environments from human interaction and shared space is further critiqued in stories such as *Do Androids Dream of Electric Sheep?* and 'The Minority Report' as suburbanites emigrate to off-world colonies where androids are purchased to keep them company.

Dick's most intimate suburban tale, however, is arguably *A Scanner Darkly* where the outlying neighbourhood of Orange County, California, is described as 'a tract area of cheap but durable plastic houses, long ago vacated by the straights' (Dick 1999: 3). Here Dick uses ubiquitous surveillance, drug addiction and repetitive consumer patterns to construct a highly introverted and dysfunctional urban society founded ultimately on sameness.[11]

FIGURE 8.3 'In former days Bob Arctor had run his affairs differently: there had been a wife much like other wives, two small daughters, a stable household that got swept and cleaned and emptied out daily … It had been too safe. All the elements that made it up were right there before his eyes, and nothing new could ever be expected.' (Dick 1999: 48–9)

In Southern California it didn't make any difference anyhow where you went; there was always the same McDonaldburger place over and over, like a circular strip that turned past you as you pretended to go somewhere … How the land became plastic, he thought, remembering the fairy tale 'How the Sea became Salt'. Someday, he thought, it'll be mandatory that we all sell the McDonald's hamburger as well as buy it; we'll sell it back and forth to each other forever from our living rooms. That way we won't even have to go outside.

Dick 1999: 22

The book's protagonist and Dick doppelganger, Bob Arctor, attempts to escape this plastic world by breaking from the predominant suburban way of life, abandoning his lawnmower, wife and two daughters, and adopting an alternative lifestyle of informal and unpredictable relationships and situations. This attempt, however, similarly engulfs Arctor in another 'dark' world of fragmentation, uncertainty and suspicion that eventually threatens his very identity. 'We'll end up dead this way,' Arctor says, 'knowing very little and getting that little fragment wrong too' (Dick 1999: 146). In *A Scanner Darkly* the plastic city thus traps both straights (Dick's

FIGURE 8.4 'Her voice was soft, sharing her secret. Imparting it to him because he, Bob Arctor, was her friend and she could trust him. "Mister Right. I know what he'll be like – he'll drive an Aston-Martin and he'll take me north in it. And that's where the little old-fashioned house will be in the snow, north from here."' (Dick 1999: 122)

term for those abiding by cultural and consumer norms) and non-straights in an undifferentiated state of immobility and collective anxiety.

Psychogeographies undone

Whether it is the big-bad-building or the series of suburban oddities in his stories, what makes Dick especially intriguing for spatial thinking is the very lack of physical detail in his urban critiques. Jameson argues that Dick's minimalist descriptions follow authors like A. E. Van Vogt in that there is enough information presented to 'contain' the novel effect and thereby 'attenuate' its force, but nothing more (Jameson 2005: 318). Similarly, Jason Vest notes that Dick does not 'lavish much attention' on the physical environments or their 'atmospheres'.

> 'Cold, light rain beat against the pavement, as the car moved through the dark streets of New York City toward the police building' is typical of the author's environmental minimalism ... Such passages provide the reader with the barest possible details to visualize 'The Minority Report'.
>
> *Vest 2009: 128*

To compensate for the lack of descriptive scenography Dick instead offers a complex series of interrelationships and essential psycho-spatial cues linked to memory, time, subjectivity and technology. In this way, the spaces are projected as 'warped', a term used by Anthony Vidler to describe our tendency to internalize space. For Vidler, one way of understanding 'warped space' is that produced by the psychological culture of modernism, from the late nineteenth century onward, emphasizing the subjectification of space.

> Space, in this ascription, is not empty, but full of disturbing objects and forms, among which the forms of architecture and the city take their place. The arts of representation, in their turn, are drawn to depict such subject/object disturbances, themselves distorting the conventional ways in which space has been described since the Renaissance.
>
> *Vidler 2000: viii*

An apt example of this in Dick's work is a critical moment in *Martian Time-Slip* when the autistic and clairvoyant child, Manfred, draws a vision of the planned UN development on Mars.

> Well, there's no mistaking it, Jack thought. The boy is drawing the buildings that will be here. He is drawing the landscape which will come, not the landscape visible to our eyes ... There was something more in the child's drawing which he had noticed. He wondered if his father had seen it. The buildings,

the enormous co-op apartments, which the boy was sketching, were developing in an ominous direction before their eyes … The buildings were old, sagging with age. Their foundations showed great cracks radiating upward. Windows were broken. And what looked like stiff tall weeds grew in the land around. It was a scene of ruin and despair, and of a ponderous, timeless, inertial heaviness. 'Jack, he's drawing a slum!' Leo exclaimed.

Dick 2008a: 125–6

Manfred's drawing evokes similar future-oriented ruins represented in the eighteenth and nineteenth centuries, most prominently Piranesi's etchings, Hubert Robert's painting of the dilapidated Louvre overgrown with weeds, and Joseph Gandy's drawing of John Soane's neoclassical Bank of England in a state of disrepair. When the novel was first published in 1964, an image of Le Corbusier's great modern city in ruins was in stark contrast to the enthusiasm of his designer counterparts such as Banham, the Independent Group and Archigram. More consistent with writers like Jane Jacobs and the Situationists, Dick's story critiques rational utopian planning through more of a psychological lens. Most of the settlements in *Martian Time-Slip*, for example, lack urban vitality which Bohlen contrasts, in a Jacobs-like appreciation, to New Israel with its 'atmosphere of commerce and activity,' like the cities he remembers on Earth (Dick 2008a: 33), and while Bohlen makes reference to buildings that do not 'fit into' their surroundings, such as the white 'duck-egg-shaped' Public School, it is only part of a much larger commentary on the technocratic urbanism dividing the settlements into deserted and deadened enclaves. Throughout *Martian Time-Slip*, similar to other Dick narratives such as *Do Androids Dream of Electric Sheep?* and *Flow My Tears, The Policeman Said*, the Martian colony is experienced almost exclusively via helicopter, offering a technologically framed perspective of urban life, removed and abstracted from direct embodied experience. The city and its buildings, described by Arnie as seeming to 'bristle with sharp corners' (Dick 2008a: 212), are merely objects, severed from any meaningful relationship with the characters inhabiting them. Similarly, in *Flow My Tears* the Police Academy building is perceived as a possessed object when the general arrives via his 'quibble' (helicopter-like transportation). 'He liked this time: the great building, in these moments, seemed to belong to him' (Dick 2008b: 736). While the objectification of the built environment is one aspect of the detachment of the characters from their urban landscape, Palmer also suggests the strategic negation of the space between destinations in Dick's stories.

There is an absence of the experience of the kinetic, either as felt or as imagined. A trip or transportation is a mere blank, unaccompanied by enjoyment of the speed and ease of movement; one simply gets in a rocket and arrives, and, arriving, faces one's dreary, emphatically ordinary problems. To put the matter another way, that which exists between destinations is not space or

landscape but nullity. The effect might be seen as an exacerbation of a common experience of city life: the city as scatter of locations ... divided by
undifferentiated city-ness.

Palmer 2003: 52

An appropriate example of this is in *A Scanner Darkly* where the ubiquitous freeway, Coca-Cola and other brand names, McDonaldburger places, and Safeway
trucks, all begin to blur into an alienating cloud of people, products and the empty
spaces connecting them. Suggesting the resultant tension between the individual
and such consumer-fed identities, for instance, two of Arctor's friends mistake their
waitress for someone else, who they believe is named Patty. 'That must have been
a different Patty from the sandwich,' the server clarifies, 'I think she spells it with
an *i*' (Dick 1999: 27). In this way, Dick's near-future California is not dissimilar to
Rem Koolhaas's description of our late-capitalist world that he describes as 'junkspace.' He argues that junkspace is like,

> ... being condemned to a perpetual Jacuzzi with millions of your best friends
> ... a Fuzzy empire of blur, it fuses high and low, public and private, straight
> and bent, bloated and starved to offer a seamless patchwork of the permanently
> disjointed.

Koolhaas 2002: 176

In *A Scanner Darkly* the characters increasingly question their meaningful place in the
world as corporations and organizations continually manipulate and confuse their
daily roles, activities and identities. As the book ends Arctor has become the dis-
turbingly fragmented Arctor-Fred-Bruce; as a mere government pawn his identity
is ultimately linked to all and none of the names with which he has been labelled.

Designing for schizospace

The above examples provide only a glimpse of Dick's immense value in better
understanding our capitalist societies and the manner in which we inhabit the
world fabricated by them. It is not likely that we will find many useful ideas for
'new' materials or construction technologies, 'new' scientific premises for heating and cooling systems or radical cyberpunk digitalscapes in his work. But if we
recognize that in place of such radical ideas are Dick's disturbing intimations about
the world around us,[12] we are better positioned to analyze his satire in constructive
ways that might hold the potential for new avenues of critical thinking about political and spatial alternatives.[13] What Bukatman refers to as Dick's 'schizoculture' is
ultimately a set of 'disturbed' urban and interpersonal relationships that increasingly detach the characters from the worlds around them – or leave them blindly
inhabiting a Baudrillard-like simulacrum of one. The autistic child Manfred's life

FIGURE 8.5 'That had summed up to them (and still did) what they distrusted in their straight foes, assuming they had foes; anyhow, a person like well-educated-with-all-the-financial-advantages Thelma Kornford became at once a foe ... The gulf between their world and hers had manifested itself ...' (Dick 1999: 73)

in *Martian Time-Slip*, for instance, is described as a secluded one, struggling to communicate with the world due to his self-determined values and a general 'apathy toward public endeavour' (Dick 2008a: 65). The result is a highly abstracted, detached and solipsistic worldview that one could effortlessly relate to the trajectory of our current capitalist systems. One of Bohlen's final comments in *Martian Time-Slip* cogently suggests this: 'It never occurred to me before how much our world is like Manfred's', Bohlen says. 'I thought they were absolutely distinct. Now I see that it's more a question of degree'[14] (Dick 2008a: 227). This depleted urban and social experience is achieved primarily through two means: 1) capitalist hegemony and its deleterious effects on the built environment, and 2) through technologically mediated experience. In both of these cases, the urban environments surrounding the characters contribute to this ongoing delinking from the worlds surrounding them. The big bad building suppresses individual autonomy through complacency as profiteers (private developers and/or the government) exploit the masses for the small price of keeping them comfortable, quiet and complacent. Likewise, Dick's suburbia is a decentralized version of the same condition, where clustered societies are held captive by their own cyclical consumerist behaviours, social anxieties and collective paranoia. These disturbing conditions remain relevant to urban life in the twenty-first century and have made their mark on our global cities and their economic and social disparities. They represent the types of challenges and opportunities designers should seek when positing our spatial futures and are precisely why we might turn to authors like Dick for clues, beyond newness and spectacle, on how we might proceed.

Notes

1 In comparison to Sobchack's timeline for SF film's first 'Golden Age', Jameson positions its literary counterpart as starting in the 1930s and lasting until the beginning of the 1950s (Jameson 2005: 314).
2 Both Mike Davis (Davis 1992: 21) and Andrew Benjamin (Benjamin 1994: 22–5), for instance, critique *Blade Runner* specifically for its lack of prescience.
3 See Jameson (2005: 315).
4 Despite their bitter dispute over the publishing of Dick's novel *Ubik* in Poland, Lem was a vocal supporter of Dick throughout his career, heralding his work for challenging the requirement for over-description. See his chapter entitled "Philip K. Dick: A Visionary Among the Charlatans," in Lem (1986: 106–35).
5 There are, however, some noteworthy exceptions. For example, Princeton's *Pamphlet Architecture* 29, 'Ambiguous Spaces', employs Dick's *Man in the High Castle* to inspire theoretical design projects (Jackowski and de Ostos 2008). Nic Clear, in a Dickian tone, argues that a blind faith in progress 'fails to ring true in the light of economic downturn, environmental catastrophe, increased levels of crime, the threats of terrorism and global pandemics.' In this spirit, he positions authors such as Huxley, Orwell, Verne, Gibson, Dick, and most emphatically J. G. Ballard, as worthy of architectural reflection (Clear 2009: 6–10). Roger Connah similarly cites Dick and Ballard as informative sources for tangential architectural thinking (Connah 2001: 9).
6 See Jameson (2005: 323).

7 For example, David Rockwell describes his retro-futurist 'pod' at the University of Pennsylvania as a 'nod' to Kubrick's *2001: A Space Odyssey* (1968) and *The Jetsons* (see www.rockwellgroup.com) while both Charles Jencks (Jencks 1984: 77) and Banham celebrate *Barbarella* (1968) for its introduction of 'soft' materiality to the previously 'hard' surfaces of SF (Banham 1981: 134). It must also be emphasized, however, that some architectural authors have acknowledged SF literature as worthy of close attention. For example, Banham labels H. G. Wells's *When a Sleeper Wakes* as a 'sacred architectural text' (Banham 1981: 136), Anthony Vidler references Gibson's *Idoru* in discussing the digital city (Vidler 2000: 203) and Donna Haraway's cyborg in his reading of Gibson's *Neuromancer* (Vidler 1996), Greg Lynn and Bruce Sterling collaborate on a web piece called 'The Growthing' featuring Lynn's renderings of his 'Ark of the World' project in Costa Rica to supplement Sterling's narrative (Sterling 2003), Sandy Isenstadt credits Frank Herbert's 1965 novel *Dune* as a harbinger of the ecology movement (Isenstadt 2005: 165), Zeynep Tuna Ultav writes that architectural discourse should 'systematize the social and spatial clues' within SF texts, using Ballard's *High Rise* as an example (Ultav 2007), Neil Spiller derives his expressive architectural drawings based on Gibson's notion of 'slamhounds' in *Count Zero* (Spiller 2005), and Clear's volume of *Architectural Design* described above (Clear 2009: 6–10).

8 For a comprehensive look at architecture and SF film and detailed analyses of *Blade Runner* (1982), *Total Recall* (1990), *Minority Report* (2002) and *A Scanner Darkly* (2006), see my book titled *Architecture and Science-Fiction Film: Philip K. Dick and the Spectacle of Home* (Fortin 2011).

9 For example, Marcuse argues that 'technological reality' has 'whittled down' the private space needed for the individual to exert their 'individual freedom' and protect their individual consciousness 'from public opinion.' See Marcuse (1984: 10).

10 Here we are reminded of Adorno's critique of the invasion of the home by technology.

> Technology is making gestures precise and brutal and with them men. It expels from movements all hesitation, deliberation, civility. It subjects them to the implacable, as it were ahistorical demands of others. Thus the ability is lost, for example, to close a door quietly and discreetly, yet firmly. Those of cars and refrigerators have to be slammed, others have the tendency to snap shut by themselves, imposing on those entering the bad manners of not looking behind them, not shielding the interior of the house which receives them (Adorno 1974: 40).

11 Christopher Palmer calls *A Scanner Darkly* 'Dick's most powerful narrative of the loss of differentiation.' See Palmer (2003: 177).

12 As Darren Jorgensen notes, 'Dick's portrayals of the fragmentations of the psyche in mid-twentieth-century capitalism are exemplary. However, although his fiction does contain revolutionary glimpses of a changed world, it is ultimately interested in characters' attempts to deal with the world as it is' (Jorgensen 2009: 211).

13 Jonathan Charley has speculated on, and argued for, the capacity of architecture to resist such capitalist domination. See Charley (2008).

14 Recalling Vidler's 'warped space', a Master's thesis by Thomas Nemeskeri at Carleton University, for example, posits whether we may be collectively moving towards an 'autistic culture' (Nemeskeri 2007).

References

Abrash, M. (1983) 'Elusive utopias: Societies as mechanisms in the early fiction of Philip K. Dick', in R. D. Erlich and T. P. Dunn (eds) *Clockwork Worlds: Mechanized Environments in SF*, Westport and London: Greenwood Press.

Adorno, T. W. (1974) *Minima Moralia: Reflections from Damaged Life*, London: Verso.

Albrecht, D. (1987) *Designing Dreams: Modern Architecture in the Movies*, London: Thames and Hudson.

Banham, R. (1981) 'Triumph of software', in P. Starke (ed.) *Design by Choice: Ideas in Architecture*, New York: Rizzoli.

Benjamin, A. (1994) 'At Home with Replicants: The Architecture of *Blade Runner*', *Architectural Design*, Profile 112, 64: 22–25. Online. Available HTTP:http://www.baslik.com/A/A_Benjamin_BRunner_110.html (30 August 2006).

Bukatman, S. (1993) *Terminal Identity: The Virtual Subject in Postmodern Science Fiction*, Durham: Duke University Press.

Charley, J. (2008) 'The glimmer of other worlds: questions on alternative architectural practice', *arq: Architectural Research Quarterly* 12, 2: 159–171.

Clear, N. (2009) 'Introduction: A near future', *Architectural Design* 79, 5: 6–10.

Connah, R. (2001) *How Architecture Got Its Hump*, Cambridge, Mass.: MIT Press.

Davis, M. (1992) *City of Quartz: Excavating the Future in Los Angeles*, New York: Vintage.

Dick, P. K. (1984) *Ubik*, London: Panther. First published in 1969.

——— (1993) *Do Androids Dream of Electric Sheep?* Filmed as *Blade Runner*, London: Grafton. First published in 1968.

——— (1999) *A Scanner Darkly*, London: Gollancz,. First published in 1977.

——— (2002) *Time Out of Joint*, New York: Vintage. First published in 1959.

——— (2004) *The Penultimate Truth*, New York: Vintage. First published in 1964.

——— (2005a) 'We can remember it for you wholesale', in *Minority Report*, London: Orion. First published in 1956.

——— (2005b) 'The Minority Report', in *Minority Report*, London: Orion. First published in 1956.

——— (2008a) *Martian Time-Slip*, in *Philip K. Dick: Five Novels of the 1960s & 70s,* New York: The Library of America. First published in 1964.

——— (2008b) *Flow My Tears, The Policeman Said*, in *Philip K. Dick: Five Novels of the 1960s & 70s*, New York: The Library of America. First published in 1964.

Enns, A. (2006) 'Media, drugs, and schizophrenia in the works of Philip K. Dick', *Science Fiction Studies* 33, 1: 68–88.

Fortin, D. (2011) *Architecture and Science-Fiction Film: Philip K. Dick and the Spectacle of Home*, Surrey, UK: Ashgate.

Horkheimer, M. and Adorno, T. (1993) *Dialectic of Enlightenment*, New York: Continuum.

Isenstadt, S. (2005) 'Contested Contexts', in C. J. Burns and A. Kahn (eds) *Site Matters: Design Concepts, Histories & Strategies*, New York: Routledge.

Jackowski, N. and de Ostos, R. (2008) 'Ambiguous Spaces', in *Pamphlet Architecture 29*, New York: Princeton Architectural Press.

Jameson, F. (2005). *Archaeologies of the Future: The Desire Called Utopia and Other Science Fictions*, London: Verso.

Jencks, C. (1984) *The Language of Post-Modern Architecture*, 4th rev. enl. edn, London: Rizzoli.

Jorgensen, D. (2009) 'Towards a Revolutionary Science Fiction', in M. Bould and C. Miéville (eds) *Red Planets: Marxism and Science Fiction*, Middletown, CT: Wesleyan University Press.

Koolhaas, R. (2002) 'Junkspace', *October*, Obsolescence, 100: 175–190.

Lem, S. (1986) *Microworlds: Writings on Science Fiction and Fantasy*, ed. F. Rottensteiner, San Diego: Harcourt Brace Jovanovich.

Marcuse, H. (1984) *One-dimensional Man: Studies in the Ideology of Advanced Industrial Society*, Boston: Beacon Press.

Nemeskeri, T. (2007) *Autistic Culture: The Architectural Therapy*, Ottawa: Library and Archives Canada. Online. Available HTTP:http://www.scribd.com/doc/19237959/Autistic-Culture-the-Architectural-Therapy (2 August 2010).

Matthies, E. (dir.) (2006) *One Summer in Austin: The Story of Filming A Scanner Darkly*, Warner Bros.

Palmer, C. (2003) *Philip K. Dick: Exhilaration and Terror in the Postmodern*, Liverpool: Liverpool University Press.

Rickman, G. (1988) *Philip K. Dick: In His Own Words*, 2nd edn, Long Beach, Calif.: Fragments West/Valentine Press.

Sadler, S. (2005) *Archigram: Architecture without Architecture*, Cambridge: MIT Press.

Sobchack, V. (1997) *Screening Space: The American Science Fiction Film*, 2nd. enl. edn, New Brunswick, N.J.: Rutgers University Press.

Spiller, N. (2005) 'Slamhounds and other space-time creatures', *OASE* 66: 64–73.

Sterling, B. (2003) 'The growthing', *Metropolismag*, Online. Available HTTP: http://www.metropolismag.com/html/content_0103/str/index.html (16 April 2008).

Sutin, L. (1989) *Divine Invasions: A Life of Philip K. Dick*, New York: Harmony.

Suvin, D. (1979) *Metamorphoses of Science Fiction: On the Poetics and History of a Literary Genre*, New Haven: Yale University Press.

Ultav, Z. T. (2007) 'Reading science-fiction novels as an architectural research', *The 'radical' designist: Journal of design culture 1*, Online. Available HTTP: http://www.iade.pt/designist/issues/001_04.html (28 June 2007).

Venturi, R., Scott Brown, D. and Izenour, S. (2000). *Learning from Las Vegas*, Cambridge, Mass.: MIT Press. First published in 1972.

Vest, J. (2009) *Future Imperfect: Philip K. Dick at the Movies*, Lincoln: University of Nebraska Press.

Vidler, A. (1996) 'Homes for cyborgs', in C. Reed (ed.) *Not at Home: The Suppression of Domesticity in Modern Art and Architecture*, London: Thames and Hudson.

——— (2000) *Warped Space: Art, Architecture, and Anxiety in Modern Culture*, Cambridge, Mass.; London: MIT Press.

Whiteley, N. (1990) 'Banham and "Otherness": Reyner Banham (1922–1988) and his quest for an architecture autre', *Architectural History* 33: 188–221.

All photos by the author.

9

ALEXANDER TROCCHI

Glasgow through the eye of a needle

Gary A. Boyd

> More than all other towns in the country, those on the West coast of Scotland are grey, and Glasgow, the rambling metropolis of shipyards, engineering works, mining and construction companies, and endless factories, whose million inhabitants are often cut off for months on end from direct contact with the sun, is more than any other the grey city.
>
> *Trocchi 2004: 5–6*

At the beginning of *Thongs*, one of Alexander Trocchi's pornographic novels, he is perhaps most explicit about his vision of Glasgow. Here, the Gorbals is used as a metonym for the entire industrial city, a cold, miserable series of Presbyterian blocks hewn from drab stone. Against this, he juxtaposes a visceral world of ultra-violence and sexual misadventure in a series of episodes concerning blades, thongs, straps, and numerous abrasions, punctures and penetrations. Ultimately, his heroine Gertrude Gault will escape the colourless working-class Glasgow. First, to practise perverse sexual pleasures in the upper-class West End of the city, then, as the figurehead of a sado-masochistic cult, she is reinvented as *Carmenicita de Las Lunas* and wanders from the constraints of the Scottish city to experience the pleasurable freedoms of sexual pain and group sodomy (by, amongst others, a one-legged dwarf) before a ritualistic and passionately embraced death at the hands of her fellow cultists in the arid heat of Spain.

Like much of Trocchi's work, *Thongs* can be read as a critique of society that presupposes alternative spatial practices at a series of scales from that of the body and mind to that of the city and beyond. For Trocchi – as his controversial and well-documented life as novelist, literary editor, pornographer, pimp, political activist and celebrity heroin-addict testifies – this meant conscious attempts to occupy the extreme edges or interstices of mainstream space. Perhaps uniquely, he was informed in this task by consorting, exchanging ideas and publishing with figures from both of what were arguably the two most important groups of post-war spatial critics and explorers: the Beat Generation and the Situationist International. And while this would ultimately manifest itself in visionary mani- festos for a new society such as the 'Invisible Insurrection of a Million Minds' or 'project sigma', it is in the space of the novel that such ideas are arguably most intimately articulated. In *Young Adam* (written in Paris in the 1950s) Trocchi begins to explore the relationship between movement and an oftentimes con- tradictory idea of freedom. Subsequently, in *Cain's Book*, the consequences and complexities of a position *in extremis* are elaborated. In both, the protagonists are taken to settings at once separate from yet intricately connected to the urban environment. And in both, preoccupations emerge that not only inflect Trocchi's own political visions but also resonate with some of the emerging architectures of the 1960s.

Canal dreams

The majority of *Young Adam* takes place along the 'scummy waters' of the Forth and Clyde Canal which stretches through what was Scotland's industrial Black Country connecting its two principle rivers and, by extension, its two main urban centres, Glasgow and Edinburgh. The novel's main character Joe is both literally and metaphorically a drifter. He is a hired boat-hand who, at the beginning of the book, states his credentials as an outsider by disavowing the work ethic and what he sees as its inevitable consequence: stasis.

> Of all the jobs I have been forced to do I think I liked being on the canal best. You are not tied up in one place then as you are if you take a job in town, and sometimes, if you can forget how ludicrously small the distances are, you get the impression that you are travelling. And there is something about travelling.
> *1996: 30*

Joe's affirmation of the ineffable qualities of travel comes close to the ideas of another modern pioneer of movement and dislocated space, Jack Kerouac, as expressed in his own vaguely fictionalised experiences in *On the Road*.

> We all realised that we were leaving confusion and nonsense behind us and performing our one and noble function of the time, *move*. And we moved.
> *Cited in Kozlovsky 2004: 200*

But the 'loosening of a fixed identity' sought by the Beats was dependent as much on speed as it was on movement (Kozlovsky 2004: 198). *On the Road* completely

FIGURE 9.1 'It occurred to me that I was mad. To stare inwards. To be a hermit, even in company. To wish for the thousandth time for the strength to be alone and play. Immediately, there was a flower on my brow, Cain's flower.' (Trocchi 1992: 72)

embraced what Stephen Kern in *The Culture of Time and Space* has described as one of the essential characteristics of modernity: the revolutions in communications and speed that, from the telephone to the aeroplane, irrevocably transformed the human perception of space (Kern 2003). This is the context against which Kerouac undertakes a series of seemingly un-ending road-trips across the USA. But despite the speed, the vast distances involved still compelled the protagonists to spend days on end confined in the narrow spaces of a motorcar gazing outwards at an unravelling American hinterland. Trocchi, in his negotiations of a more limiting Scottish landscape employed another, altogether more archaic, vehicle to pursue the same kind of disorientating experience that only comes with a prolonged period of travel. While *On the Road* was reliant on a continental highway network that focussed or even suggested a fetish for speed, Trocchi confined his actions to a tiny piece of eighteenth-century infrastructure which, by the 1950s, was in the latter stages of a terminal decline.[1] Like those flâneurs of Haussmann's Paris, who took turtles for a walk in order to experience anew a speeded-up, altered city, Trocchi hitched himself to the slowest vehicle available in order to languish for days on end over the fifty-odd, often banal miles between Glasgow and Edinburgh.

Apart from the existence of a pub, where we stopped for the night didn't matter. There was not much to pick and choose between the small towns along the canal. A few lights after 10 o'clock at night, and they all went to bed early.

1996: 19

Displacement

The poet Edwin Morgan cites the influence that Albert Camus' *L'Étranger* had on Trocchi's writing (1997: 278). It is a relationship that can be glimpsed in the detached, dispassionate manner through which Joe narrates a series of events that seem to unfold as slowly and inevitably as the crawling passage of the boat along what he describes as the 'black tape' of the canal: Joe and Leslie, the canal boat-captain, find a female body in the river; Joe contemplates the bodily geography of the canal boat-captain's wife, Ella; Joe has sex with Ella; it turns out that the body in the river is Cathie, Joe's former lover and that he was with her at the time of death; Joe has sex with Ella's sister; and finally, he watches passively as an innocent man is tried and possibly doomed to execution for the murder of Cathie. All the while, Joe's bouts of introspection are framed within the view from the canal as it penetrates what he sees as the ubiquitous towns on its path and their unflinching Presbyterian morality.

> Close up, the church tower looked just as disenchanted as most church towers in Scotland do. Later in the evening, as we skirted the churchyard to reach the pub, I noticed the usual ugly red and black posters proclaiming the evil influence of alcohol and the imminence of the Last Judgement.
>
> *1996: 40*

To emphasise this, Trocchi gives one of these towns the fictionalised name of Lairs which, while sounding reasonable – Glasgow after all has a Cowlairs – is actually a Scots word to describe a burial-plot in a cemetery. Against these dead spaces, however, Joe describes the stirrings of life found in the landscape of the canal whose obsolescence, under-use and neglect allows another morality to emerge in the ambiguous, liminal spaces where it meets the town.

> Now, it is boring ... to crawl along a canal, ... but you see some interesting things [like] courting couples ... in the quiet places where there is no footpath and where they have had to climb a fence to get to. Perhaps it is the water that attracts them as much as the seclusion, and of course the danger. In summer they are as thick as midges.
>
> *1996: 29–30*

If the relationship between freedom, movement and modernity is made indefinite by the anachronistically slow pace of Trocchi's vehicle then it is further complicated just by adding water. It is this phenomena that draws the narrative still further from the twentieth century towards other epochs where the dominant literary motifs were not so much the motorcar and road but rather the boat and its relationships with horizontal and oftentimes large surfaces of water (Kozlovsky 2004: 212). Here, a series of other meanings and literary tropes emerge. In these landscapes, we find not so much the thrill-seeking optimisms of *On the Road* but rather more dark, disquieting and ambiguous characters. Figures such as Hermann Melville's Captain Ahab whose obsession is cast within the wastes of the North Atlantic, or Marlowe in Joseph Conrad's *Heart of Darkness*, whose psychological tensions as both a colonial agent *and* critic are emphasised by the relationship between the tightly defined European spaces of his riverboat, the disorientations of the Congo river and the vast interior of an unknown and unknowable African continent. For Trocchi, the relationship of contrasting scales between vehicle, land and water generates a sense of the uncanny where everyday forms seem to take on other, undefined significances when viewed from the unrelenting horizontality of the canal.[2]

> I could see a boom raised ahead in the distance. It looked very awkward perched there in mid air like a sign that meant nothing but was black in the thin meagre afternoon light.

> We would see the church towers of Lairs … a black cone against a red-flecked sky, a witch's hat in a haze of blood. It seemed very far away and enchanted.
> *1996: 30 and 39 respectively*

If these distant objects in space are rendered strange by viewing them from the crawl of a small craft over a flat landscape, Trocchi also finds an uneasiness in the near and immediate on the boat itself. He describes a claustrophobia and feeling of confinement experienced most acutely in his bunk: 'Often when I awoke I had the feeling that I was in a coffin.' The canal and boat increase a sense of the visceral and bodily – 'it is not exactly smell, it is closer to touch; its being touches one at the pores' (1996: 70) – which is perhaps further heightened by the contrast of the flattened visual abstractions of the landscape beyond the boat.

> Touch convinces in a way in which sight did not. I was struck by the fact that sight is hypnotised by the surfaces of things; more than that, it can only know surfaces, flatnesses at a distance, meagre depths at close range. But the wetness of water felt on the hand and on the wrist is more intimate and more convincing than its colour or even than any flat expanse of sea. The eye, I thought, could never get to the centre of things; there was no intimate connection between my eye and a plant on a windowsill or between my eye and the woman to whom I was about to make love.
> *1996: 31*

FIGURE 9.2 'But for the moment she is a forlorn figure slipping quickly through dark streets, desperate for a private place, for a burrow, for a "Castle Keep".' (Trocchi 1992: 34)

The decisive instant in *L'Étranger* – when the protagonist Meursault kills the Arab – takes place on the periphery of a city, on a beach whose shifting, nebulous limits and exposure to sun, sand and sea bear witness to his apotheosis first as a murderer and ultimately as an outsider. Trocchi takes similar care in constructing not only a troubling antihero, but one whose epiphany – which, like *L'Étranger* involves death – occurs in a fluid, ephemeral landscape at a city edge. This scene, underneath a railway truck at the canal's basin terminus, also echoes the constraints of the boat juxtaposed against an expanse of water and a wider landscape.

> The splash was contained inside my head for a few moments ... [the] quick black water ... sidled swiftly past the quay-stone and a few yards away, quietly at the surface, a few bubbles broke, like suds in a laundry.
>
> *1996: 79*

Joe's ultimate indifference is perhaps evinced most clearly in the almost forensic eroticism with which he describes the body as it re-emerges from the river and which, only later, we discover was his lover.

> She was beautiful in a pale way – not her face, although that wasn't bad, but in the way her body seemed to have given itself to the water, its whole gesture abandoned, the long white legs apart and trailing, sucked downwards slightly at the feet.
>
> *1996: 4*

It is possible to find echoes in Joe of the strange, detached behaviour of the central character in *The Private Memoirs and Confessions of a Justified Sinner*, James Hogg's tale of extremist delusion within the suffocating Calvinism of nineteenth-century Edinburgh (see Morgan 1997: 278). A summation that Joe is similarly alienated to the point of insanity (Pringle 1996: viii) is supported by a reading of the spaces *Young Adam* occupies. Joe's monologues of indifference, expressed in the intimate and intense language of the first person, emerge from a sometimes claustrophobic, sometimes uncanny environment which is itself detached and withdrawn from everyday rhythm and place. In *The Practice of Everyday Life*, Michel de Certeau describes the dislocating experience of railway travel as evoking not so much a sense of freedom but rather a type of incarceration:

> a speculative experience of the world: being outside of these things that stay there, detached and absolute, that leave us without having anything to do with this departure themselves.
>
> *1988: 112*

But it is Michel Foucault, in his seminal work *Madness and Civilisation*, who perhaps does most to unite the themes of movement, madness and water in his description of the medieval *stultifera navis*. This was both a literary construct and a real, historical 'ship of fools' whose cargo was granted no final destination but compelled to endlessly sail the waterways of Europe in what Foucault describes as a spatial paradox, '[They were prisoners] in what is the freest, the openest of routes, bound fast at the infinite crossroad' (2001: 9). On the canal of *Young Adam*, the cell-like cramped accommodation of the boat, coupled with the pre-destined and prescribed linearity of its path in full visibility across a landscape make it feel even more like the constrained and austere environment of a nineteenth-century institution of confinement.

Junkspace

The construction of an ambiguous outsider like Trocchi's Joe partly using the literary device of a boat can be understood as a received convention of writing. But what is

FIGURE 9.3 'That's the junk scene, man. Everybody gets something out of it except the junkie.' (Trocchi 1992: 77)

much more intriguing here is Trocchi's subsequent decision to locate his real self in a similar space. *Cain's Book* (first published in 1960) is an autobiographical account (Seaver 1992), written under heroin, of being a junkie in New York city. Except that he is not really in the city. Instead, using the pseudonym of Joe Necchi, he assembles, writes and narrates the book from a *scow* – a type of engineless and rudderless barge – moored in various locations around Manhattan. But the importance of the boat, so essential to the unfolding of *Young Adam*, here begins to diminish and heroin – both as a method of writing and as the subject of the book – becomes the key vehicle of a further retreat from external landscapes and a more intimate engagement with the internal sites of the body and the operations of the mind. The result is a non-linear narrative that drifts in and out of detailed descriptions of: scoring drugs in the city; the effects of heroin; reminiscences of times in Glasgow, Paris and elsewhere; harangues on drug addiction and the law; the problem of work; (bi)sexual encounters; and moments of ambiguity where the fictions of the past are apparently relived in the present – like, for example, when, half a decade after writing *Young Adam* and *Thongs*, Necchi manages to fuck a fellow scow captain's one-legged wife. All the while, his speculations are underpinned by distant visions of the city across the water.

> It's an oblique way to look at Manhattan, seeing it islanded there for days on end across the buffering water like a little mirage in which one isn't involved, for at times I knew it objectively and with anxiety as a nexus of hard fact, as my very condition. Sometimes, it was like trumpets, that architecture.
>
> *1992: 13*

The carceral significance of the boat is still not lost on Trocchi who describes it in *Cain's Book*, as a 'retreat into abeyance' and whose alternatives were 'prison, madhouse, morgue' (1992: 13). In fact, the first of these represented a very real possibility for Trocchi who had managed to choose one of the most intolerant countries in the world in which to pursue his addiction.[3] Yet he writes on the effect of heroin in similar, spatial terms describing it as a 'Castle Keep', a type of abstract, 'inviolable' institution which '[empties the questions of the here and now] … of all anguish, transports them to another region, a painless theoretical region, a play region, surprising, fertile, and unmoral' (1992: 11).

One of the most conspicuous sub-themes in *Cain's Book* is its critique of work. Necchi's disparaging attitude toward the discipline of wage labour is explored partly through remembered conversations with his father in Glasgow who, despite terminal unemployment, still unthinkingly embraces the work ethic. According to Michael Gardiner, the use of heroin in *Cain's Book* provides the alternative to work, a 'proactive, pleasure-seeking, anti-work form of action' (2006: 90). The anti-work theme is not only consistent in both novels, it is also pursued by Trocchi in his political writings on his return to Britain in the early 1960s. In 'Invisible Insurrection of a Million Minds' (1962) the author called for a cultural revolt that, perhaps using himself as a model, would reconcile art and life into a new space of non-productive, interactive play. In this he was not alone. Drawing on Karl Marx's theories on the division and alienation of labour, both Herbert Marcuse and Guy Debord had begun to analyse and critique what they saw as the passive spectacle of prescribed leisure time. Elsewhere, urban theorists like Henri Lefebvre had begun to attack the sterility of modern urban space, identifying ephemeral instants of joy as both moments of rupture and the means of resistance. In turn, this had been developed by Debord and the Situationists International whose experiments in urban drift or *dérive* became the blueprint for a new type of boundless fluid city, Constant Nieuwenhuys' *New Babylon*, where inhabitants and visitors would interact with zones of varying ambiance.

FIGURE 9.4 'Why go out when you have a bed and a floor and a sink and a
window and a table and a chair and many other things here in this
very room? After all you're not a collector …' (Trocchi 1992: 195)

Trocchi's associations with the Situationists dated from the Paris of the 1950s,
before his time in New York. Here, as editor of the avant-garde literary journal
Merlin, he had first called for the dissolving of 'all the rigid categories in criticism
and life' and between science and art to create new, limitless spaces of creative
possibility (1952 reprinted in Campbell and Niel (eds) 1997: 39–42). This was reiterated in some of the projects of a close friend and ally, the (anti)architect Cedric
Price in the early 1960s. In Fun Palace (designed with Joan Littlewood between
1962 and 1964), Trocchi's idea of 'a laboratory for the creation (and evaluation) of
conscious situations [and an] environment which is in question, plastic, subject to

change' (1963) is given form in Price's 'spontaneous leisure architecture', where one can:

> ... just walk in anywhere. No doors, foyers, queues or commissionaires: it's up to you how you use it. Look around, take a lift, a ramp, an escalator to wherever looks interesting.
>
> *Price and Littlewood 1964, reprinted in Price 2003: 58*

Price and Trocchi would go on to collaborate on a similar notion of 'spontaneous universities' which Trocchi outlined in 'project sigma' (1963) and which for Price would ultimately become the Potteries Thinkbelt project (1965) that fluid, moveable infrastructure of alternative learning (Mathews, 2006: 92). But while Price conceived Fun Palace as a 'university of the streets', Trocchi's idea of radical space ultimately differs in quite fundamental ways. This perhaps emerges most clearly in the different use of an influence shared by both Trocchi and Guy Debord: Thomas de Quincey's *The Confessions of an English Opium Eater*. While there are similarities between *Cain's Book* and de Quincey's 1822 memoirs, for de Quincey, the investigation of dreams experienced through opium was not so much a retreat from everyday life but rather another active way of engaging with it: fuelled by the drug he would explore the *terrae incognitae* of London. Thus, he introduced a new type of spatial praxis: to wander aimlessly in an active–passive engagement with the city, navigating dreamily while allowing the vagaries of urban chance to infiltrate one's thoughts and shape one's movements. Extremely influential on subsequent generations of both urban thinkers and thrill-seekers, de Quincey's techniques underpinned the psycho-geographic research of the Situationists. But despite Trocchi's admiration for de Quincey,[4] long associations with Debord and an awareness of the pleasures of the *dérive* and, despite his call for play to overtake work as the centre of human activity, there is little sense of joy in the experience of urban space in *Cain's Book*.

> It is not far from Flushing to the Village ... but again I won't go in. There's nothing for me to go there for now ... Only the citadel remains for those who aren't behind bars. The citadel, centre everywhere, circumference nowhere; lethal dose variable. It happens to many that they can no longer go outside the citadel. For one reason or another.
>
> *1992: 229*[5]

It is a withdrawal that finds a parallel in other drug-inspired literature of the twentieth century. In *Naked Lunch* (often compared to *Cain's Book*, and first published just one year before in 1959), William Burroughs – heroin addict and acquaintance of Trocchi's – discusses the overriding singularity of the junkie's existence, 'the days glide by strung on a syringe with a long thread of blood ... I am forgetting sex and all sharp pleasures of the body – a grey, junk-bound ghost' (2005: 56). Meanwhile, M. Ageyev's *Novel with Cocaine* (first published in 1934) describes a displacement of the real by the abstraction of the contemplative, 'during the long nights and long days I spent under the influence of cocaine … I came to see that what counts in

FIGURE 9.5 'We talked about how the world was just a conglomeration of rooms, other people's rooms, to wander about in. For ever and ever.' (Trocchi 1992: 108)

life is not the events that surround one but the reflection of those events in one's consciousness' (1983: 173). While the Situationists' drift is *of* and *inside* the city, Trocchi's is irrevocably apart from it. Moreover, when he does experience the city in *Cain's Book* he does so through a series of routes and spaces which are predetermined and prescribed by the need to score. Paradoxically, his drug-filled voyage to the edges of society in New York city ultimately follows temporal and spatial routines which are often as inevitable as those of an institution.

> We are perhaps the weakest minority which ever existed; forced into poverty, filth, squalor, without even the protection of a legitimate ghetto. There was never a wandering Jew who wandered further than a junkie, without hope. Always moving. Eventually one must go where the junk is and one is never certain where the junk is, never sure that where the junk is is not the anteroom of the penitentiary.
>
> *1992: 73*

Jürgen Habermas has suggested that the origins of the novel itself lie in the spatial reconfigurations that took place in the large bourgeois house of the eighteenth century. Here, as new relationships between public and private emerged, he describes a concurrent shift in expression as the intimate and subjective practice of letter writing became increasing orientated towards a larger public audience (2006: 42–51). Meanwhile, in *Imagining the Penitentiary*, John Bender (1987) explores the connection between the early novels of the likes of Henry Fielding and Daniel Defoe, and the inception of modern institutional space. Adapting the ideas of Michel Foucault, he argues that in the linear process and formation of character exhibited in these novels, one can discern the same suppositions which, decades later, will underpin a new penal order of prisons, hospitals and asylums as well as broad hints about what form these institutions will ultimately take and how they will operate. It can be argued that Trocchi – certainly through his dependency on drugs – was similarly constrained by fictive spaces. His disengagement from the city first emerges as a novelistic device, a means of occupying an oppositional space of altered morality and apparent freedom. Yet it becomes evident that, as it moves from fiction into reality, this outsider space becomes more and more a place of isolated introspection, confinement and ultimately – and ironically – a space of social conservatism.

By the 1960s, now living in London, Trocchi was obtaining heroin by prescription from the British State's National Health Service. His apparent acceptance of heroin use is problematised by William Burrough's assertion that 'addiction [is] part of the global conspiracy by the presiding powers of our world' (cited by Ballard 1993), an idea which is also articulated in Philip K. Dick's novel *A Scanner Darkly* with its description of a closed system where addiction to and rehabilitation from 'Substance D.' are both administered by the New Path Corporation. The problem for Trocchi is not the use of heroin per se but rather the State or other agency's control of that use. In his essay, 'The Junkie: Menace or Scapegoat?' (1970), he excerpts passages from *Cain's Book* to illustrate a relationship between prohibition and surveillance, 'it is impertinent … of any person … to impose their unexamined moral prohibitions on me … in every instance in which such a prohibition becomes crystallised in law an alarming precedent is created … Vigilance.' The essay also discusses withdrawal from the everyday as a means – if desired – to come off heroin.

> In such a retreat … it may or may not be an actual geographical location … the junkie would be encouraged from the beginning to involve himself in other things … The person would be encouraged to express himself in art and in a vital and active sexuality.
>
> *1970, reprinted in Scott 1991: 215*

What is of interest here is that Trocchi's ideal space (albeit one spiced with sexual promiscuity) for ending addiction is remarkably similar to his earlier visions for a new society sketched out in the essays 'Invisible Insurrection of a Million Minds' and 'project sigma': therapeutic and revolutionary space are both based on strategies of disengagement and escape. Trocchi's visions for revolution seem, then, inevitably compromised. 'Invisible Insurrection of a Million Minds' for example, eschews any direct or meaningful spatial praxis but instead, as the title suggests, sites the revolution within the consciousness of a prescribed number of 'technicians'. The catalysts for these incursions into the contemplative world would be a series of 'spontaneous universities' amongst the precedents for which Trocchi cites Black Mountain College, kibbutzim and more bizarrely, the playing fields of Eton.

> At a chosen moment in a vacant country house (mill, abbey, church or castle) … we shall foment a kind of cultural 'jam session': out of which will evolve the prototype of our *spontaneous university*. The original building will stand deep within its own grounds, preferably on a riverbank. It should be large enough for a pilot group (astronauts of inner space) to situate itself, orgasm and genius, and their tools and dream-machines and amazing apparatuses and appurtenances; with out-houses for 'workshops' large as could accommodate light industry; the entire site to allow for spontaneous architecture and eventual town-planning.
>
> *In Campbell and Niel (eds) 1997: 171 [emphasis original]*

Withdrawal from the complexities of urban space to more rarefied and controlled surroundings both as means of critique of the city and as a model for new urban forms is nothing new. Within historical examples we find the monastery, the eighteenth-century country estate, the workhouse and the nineteenth-century utopias

FIGURE 9.6 '"By the Marquis de Sade," he said. "She'd suck the fix out of your ass."'
(Trocchi 1992: 102)

of Robert Owen and Charles Fourier. The latter's phalanstery, encompassing the theory of 'passionate attraction' – free love between its inhabitants – perhaps comes closest as a precursor of Trocchi's space of retreat and revolution. The phalanstery also provided an influence for the urban visions of Le Corbusier, an architecture of 'sacred asylum' (S. Gournyi cited in Brace Taylor 1987: 132), versions of which were being undertaken even as Trocchi wrote.

The strewn ramparts of Jericho

In *The City of God*, St Augustine wrote, 'it is recorded of Cain that he built a city, while Abel, as though he was merely a pilgrim on earth, built none' (quoted in Sennett 1992: 6). For Trocchi, however, it is Cain who represents the wanderer, the (un)holy pilgrim articulated in the characters of Joe, Necchi and Gaunt but perhaps most clearly in his own life. In his desire to annihilate the physical and become a 'cosmonaut of inner space', Trocchi's occupation of neutral, frictionless zones of movement is curiously prescient. In the mid-1990s, Marc Augé identi-fied similar qualities as characteristic of what he pejoratively termed 'non-places', exemplified by supermarkets, airports and shopping malls. According to Augé not only do such landscapes profoundly alter social awareness and inhibit 'organic social life', they are also increasingly pervasive, defining what he describes as the condition of 'supermodernity'. In fact, if we return to Glasgow in the 1960s and

'70s, we can see some of these trends in embryo in the dramatic revolutions in space and time that profoundly altered its urban form. Here, the apparently static, grey city of Trocchi's writing – described melodramatically in *Thongs*, implicitly in *Young Adam* and with some subtlety in *Cain's Book* – seems to have shifted to approach something of the author's vision of alternative spatial practices. In this fluid city of movement; in the withdrawal from the pattern of streets; in the fragmentation of its forms; normalisation of its citizens' spatial dislocation and long-term unemployment: and, perhaps especially, in their confinement in ship-like, Corbusian-inspired edifices moored across its landscapes, we can find a reality as extreme as Trocchi's fictive spaces of freedom.

> I find myself squirting a thin stream of water from the eye-dropper through the number twenty-six needle in the air, cooking up another fix, prodding the hardened cotton in the bubbling spoon … just a small fix, I feel, would recreate the strewn ramparts of Jericho.
>
> *1992: 14*

Notes

1 By this date, the Forth and Clyde Canal was the only operating canal left in central Scotland. The Union and the Monklands canals, the two others which connected the Forth and Clyde, were abandoned in the 1930s and 1940s respectively.
2 The Union Canal – which connected with the Forth and Clyde Canal at Falkirk to end in Edinburgh – is a 'contour canal'. These maintain a constant level negotiating topography through aqueducts and cuttings rather than locks. The Union Canal can be discerned as a flat, constant line within the undulating landscape of central Scotland.
3 Trocchi did spend periods in jail in the USA, on one occasion prompting Guy Debord, Jacqueline de Long and Asger Jorn to write an appeal for his release, 'Hands off Alexander Trocchi', published in *Internationale Lettriste*, October 1960 (cited in Campbell and Niel (eds), 1997: 129–30).
4 See, for example, Greil Marcus's 'Do you know de Quincey?' in Campbell and Niel (eds) 1997: 250–3.
5 Coincidentally, but perhaps emblematically, Jane Jacobs' exploration and celebration of the contradictions, tensions and visceral qualities of urban life in New York, *Death and Life of Great American Cities* was written in 1961, almost exactly the same time as *Cain's Book*.

References

Ageyev, M. (1983) (trans. Heim, M. H.) *Novel with Cocaine*, London: Penguin.
Augé, M. (2006) *Non-Places: Introduction to an Anthropology of Supermodernity*, London: Verso.
Ballard, J. G. (1993) 'Introduction' in Burroughs, 2005.
Bender, J. (1987) *Imagining the Penitentiary: Fiction and the Architecture of Mind in Eighteenth-Century England*, Chicago: University of Chicago Press.
Brace Taylor, B. (1987) *Le Corbusier: City of Refuge, Paris, 1929–33*, Chicago: Chicago University Press.
Burroughs, W. S. (2005) *Naked Lunch*, London: Harper Perennial.

Campbell, A. and Niel, T. (eds) (1997) *A Life in Pieces: Reflections on Alexander Trocchi*, Edinburgh: Canongate.

Camus, A. (2000) (trans. Laredo, J.) (1982) *The Outsider* (orig. pub. 1982 as *L'Étranger*), London: Penguin Books.

Conrad, J. (1933) *Heart of Darkness*, London: Penguin.

De Certeau, M. (1988) *The Practice of Everyday Life*, Berkeley: University of California Press.

Debord, G. (1995) *The Society of the Spectacle*, New York: Zone Books.

De Quincey, T. (1997) *Confessions of an English Opium-Eater*, London: Penguin.

Dick, P. K. (1991) *A Scanner Darkly*, London: Vintage.

Dowds, T. J. (2003) *The Forth and Clyde Canal: A History*, East Linton: Tuckwell Press.

Foucault, M. (2001) *Madness and Civilisation*, London: Routledge.

Gardiner, M. (2006) *From Trocchi to Trainspotting: Scottish Critical Theory since 1960*, Edinburgh: Edinburgh University Press.

Giedion, S. (2003) *Space, Time and Architecture: The Growth of a New Tradition*, Cambridge, Mass.: Harvard University Press.

Habermas, J. (2006) (trans. Burger, T. 1989) *The Structural Transformation of the Public Sphere*, Cambridge, Mass.: MIT Press.

Hughes, J. and Sadler, S. (2007) *Non-Plan: Essays on Freedom Participation and Change in Modern Architecture and Urbanism*, Oxford: Architectural Press.

Jacobs, J. (1961) *The Death and Life of Great American Cities*, New York: Vintage.

Lefebvre, H. (1991) (trans. Nicolson-Smith, D.) *The Production of Space*, London: Wiley Blackwell.

Kerouac, J. (2000) *On the Road*, London: Penguin.

Kern, S. (2003) *The Culture of Time and Space 1880–1918*, Cambridge, Mass.: Harvard University Press.

Kozlovsky, R. (2004) 'Beat Spaces' in Colomina, B., Brennan, A. and Kim, J. (eds) *Cold War Hothouses: Inventing Postwar Culture for Cockpit to Playboy*, New York: Princeton Architectural Press.

Marcuse, H. (1991) *One Dimensional Man: Studies in the Ideology of Advanced Industrial Society*, London: Routledge.

Mathews, S. (2006) 'Cedric Price: From the Brain Drain to the Knowledge Economy', *Architectural Design*, 76, 1, 90–5.

Matteson, G. (2007) *Tugboats of New York: An Illustrated History*, New York: New York University Press.

McDonough, T. (2002) *Guy Debord and the Situationist International: Texts and Documents*, Cambridge, Mass.: October Books, MIT Press.

Melville, H. (2003) *Moby Dick*, London: Penguin.

Morgan, E. (1997) 'Alexander Trocchi: A Survey' in Campbell and Niel (1997) pp 270–82.

Price, C. (2003) *The Square Book*, London: Wiley.

Pringle, J. (1996) 'Introduction' in Trocchi (1996), pp v–xi.

Royal Commission on the Ancient and Historical Monuments of Scotland (2002) *The Forth and Clyde Canal*, Broadsheet. Edinburgh: RCAHMS.

Sadler, S. (1999) *The Situationist City*, Cambridge, Mass.: MIT Press.

Scott, A. M. (1991) *Alexander Trocchi: The Making of the Monster*, London: Polygon.

Seaver, R. (1992) Introduction to Trocchi, pp xi–xx.

Sennett, R. (1992) *The Conscience of the Eye: The Design and Social Life of Cities*, New York: Norton.

Shanks, P. (2008) 'Cain's Burden: Trocchi and Beckett in Paris', *Journal of Irish and Scottish Studies*, Issue 1, September.

Trocchi, A. W. R. (1952) 'editorial' in *Merlin*, Vols. 1 and 2. Paris, reprinted in Campbell and Niel (1997) pp 39–42.

—— (1963) 'sigma: A Tactical Blueprint', *Internationale Situationnist 8*.

—— (as De Las Lunas, Carmenicita) (2004) *Thongs*, Paris: The Olympia Press.

—— (as Frances Lengel) (1997) *Helen and Desire*, Edinburgh: Canongate.

—— (1991) *Invisible Insurrection of a Million Minds: A Trocchi Reader* (ed. A. M. Scott), Edinburgh, Polygon.

—— (1992) *Cain's Book*. New York: Grove Press.

—— (1996) *Young Adam*, Edinburgh: Canongate.

All photos by the author.

PART III

Narrative, form, space

10

ANONYMOUS ENCOUNTERS

The structuring of space in postmodern narratives of the city

Sarah Edwards

The essays in this section focus on the formal strategies, or 'building blocks', of literary narratives and examine the ways in which they both represent and shape our bodily and psychic inhabitations of the contemporary city. In these essays, narrative innovations defamilisarise both urban living spaces and the city streets to re-define concepts of public and private, while corridors, parking lots and staircases become sites of subversive and marginal activities. New versions of *flânerie* are embodied by female and gay sightseers who reclaim the streets and whose gazes are textually inscribed on maps, grids and puzzles that unsettle both literary and cartographic conventions. These essays, then, also re-consider the usefulness of twentieth-century literary and cultural theory to our understanding of everyday life and investigate relationships between the body, gender, text and space. They investigate a range of everyday activities – from a walk in the park, to recreational sex, and the chance encounter on the staircase – and illustrate how these architectural and textual spaces produce the anonymous encounters that have often been associated with the modern city.

As Inga Bryden notes in her essay on the contemporary urban short story, literary theorists have always deployed spatial terminology to describe generic features, such as structure, form or metre. More recently, writers such as Ian Sinclair and Jon McGregor have departed from earlier nineteenth-century or modernist accounts of the city (for example, the work of Charles Dickens or James Joyce), which are dominated by the gaze of their omniscient narrators or the intensely subjective stream-of-consciousness of modernist characters, who survey and map an urban panorama for their readers' consumption.[1] David Harvey, in *The Condition of Postmodernity* notes a shift in 'author(ity)', or a fundamental change in the way that architects viewed the city (Harvey 1990). Whereas modernists are identified

FIGURE 10.1 Original postcard from 1871, source unknown

with the idea of coordinated planning, postmodernists celebrated the unplanned, the accidental and the autonomous. Similarly, many postmodern writers claim that the meanings of urban space are continually produced by writers and their readers. For Roland Barthes, 'The city is a writing. He who moves about the city, e.g. the user of the city (what we all are), is a kind of reader' (Barthes 1997: 170). Cultural geographers also argue that space is both socially produced, and a condition of social production. Increasingly, literary, cultural and art and architectural critics have theorised space as 'process', as 'something linear to be narrativised' (Bryden, in this volume).[2]

Literary writers, then, have had to experiment with new formal structures that will accommodate these changing conceptions. As Stefanie Sobelle demonstrates in her essay in this volume on George Perec's *Life: A User's Manual* (1978), the late twentieth-century architectural novel emerges with the reorganization of space and everyday life that accompanies late capitalism and cultural postmodernism and 'takes for granted that the house is an extension of society and public events inextricable from the private realm'. In the works of this sub-genre, writers draw attention to the traditional literary identification of house and inhabitant and thus challenge readers to explore how and why domestic space is constituted in particular ways. For example, in Alain Robbe-Grillet's *La Jalousie* (1957), an anonymous, invisible narrator's actions and mental states are projected on to mundane household objects such as deck chairs and dinner plates, while in Mark Danielewski's *House of Leaves* (2000), a character's flight through the house not only externalises their inner turmoil but is mirrored by the layout of the page, whereby the sparse content forces the reader to 'race' through the book. As readers, then, we are forced to inhabit and to imaginatively reproduce the three-dimensional space of the book and the home. Other novelists explore the connections between pub-lic meeting-places and individual histories: in W. G. Sebald's *Austerlitz* (2001), meetings at, and memories of, the eponymous train station are the means for a biographical and literary reconstruction of a Jewish family's fate in Nazi Germany. Italo Calvino's *Invisible Cities* (1972) uses a Platonic dialogue (between Kublai Khan and Marco Polo) and prose poems on a range of cities to demonstrate how the imaginative construction of cities through conversation and literary works is vital to their realisation in architectural form. All of these works contain maps and diagrams, which draw attention to the process of literary construction, to concepts of public and private space, and to the ways in which these have been deter-mined by literary and architectural conventions and shaped human subjectivities. For example, Sobelle observes that in Perec's *Life: A User's Manual*, the apartment building is metonymic of contemporary Western society: 'many individuals living separately, yet intimately connected' in their everyday lives.

Twentieth-century urban theory has similarly viewed the city as a system of interconnected parts and many architects began focusing on the 'everyday' life, particularly in France. The theories of Henri Lefebvre (*The Production of Space*, 1974) and Michel de Certeau (*The Practice of Everyday Life*, 1984) have been hugely influential. Lefebvre identifies different types of space, distinguishing 'absolute' space (the abstract, imagined space of architects or writers) from 'social' space (the concrete, physical space which we inhabit on a daily basis). In the essays in this section, the impossibility of reconciling this dichotomy and capturing daily, bod-ily experiences of the city in prose is captured by representations of anonymous encounters and vain attempts at communication. What relationships do we form with the familiar stranger, the voyeur from the apartment block, or the veiled Muslim woman?[3] In today's world of frequent global travel, short-term employ-ment contracts, increasing numbers of single-person households, and ethnic communities which often remain isolated from each other in multi-cultural cit-ies, writers have begun to explore how literary forms evoke and comment on the shaping of these encounters. In Hanif Kureishi's *The Buddha of Suburbia* (1990), the traditionally liminal space of suburbia is transformed into a potentially alienating site of racial and class hybridity in 1970s England; but the novel adopts a traditional formal structure (and, by implication, an optimistic view of multi-culturalism) when the hero's *Bildungsroman* ends with his happy arrival in the promised city of London.[4] By contrast, writers such as Martin Amis experiment with other genres to imagine the daily experiences of urban women. Can women ever truly be anonymous, or are they always appropriated as the object of the male gaze? This issue remains problematic in Martin Amis's *London Fields* (1989), where the diary form is employed to present an apparently intimate account of Nicola who is thus revealed as a vain and manipulative character who seeks her own murder in order to avoid the stereotypically female fear of ageing.

In the essays in this section, the authors demonstrate how contemporary writers have also engaged with twentieth-century literary and cultural theory to explore the anonymity of daily life. Inga Bryden discusses the idea of the fragment as a metaphor for everyday life. The archaeological fragment is a poignant literal symbol of the obscured histories of earlier societies; it has also become a prevalent image of the postmodern condition in accounts of urban sprawl and the formation of social enclaves, of the deconstruction of the 'grand narratives' of scientific and religious systems and of the meta-narratives of literary and historical storytelling.[5] As Bryden says, 'one aspect of the fragmented, polyvalent nature of the city, and a common metaphor in urban literature, is of the city as a "babble of allusions", both architectural and linguistic'. This postmodern mixture of styles reflects ideas of freedom, individuality and choice: in Ray Bradbury's *Fahrenheit 451* (1951), a reference to a library as a Tower of Babel in the midst of a dystopian book-burning culture underscores the importance of retaining different 'languages' and discourses.

However, as Bryden says, narratives are still essential as a means of orientation through the city or the story. Many writers, then, have engaged with the idea of the text and city as a palimpsest, containing successive layers of history and meaning such as Walter Benjamin's evocative description of 'traces' that link strangers who come to occupy the same place (Benjamin 1978). Stefanie Sobelle demonstrates that for Perec, 'human history ... is a data bank of all the traces left by its inhabitants' and that he 'presents an entire building, narrating the histories of its rooms, the traces of its inhabitants, and the collections of objects that represent them'. Anthony Vidler has demonstrated that this evidence of the past still existing in the present, of the strange amongst the familiar, is a prime source of the uncanny in urban literature (Vidler 1994). In contemporary urban gothic fiction, such as Sarah Waters's *Affinity* (1990), Victorian discourses about spiritualism and the invasion of unseen spirits, and Foucauldian theories about the unseen panoptical gaze, are used to explore the experience of inhabiting a 'haunted' house.[6]

Renée Tobe, in her essay on Catherine Millet's *The Sexual Life of Catherine M.* (2001) and Renaud Camus' *Tricks: Twenty-Five Encounters* (1981), suggests that phenomenology and the 'primacy it affords to perception' enables us to understand how the contemporary novel represents the body moving in space. Both authors foreground traditionally 'othered' (female and gay) bodies. Since the 1970s, feminist, gay and queer theorists have paid increasing attention to cultural constructions of the body, from Foucault's account of the invention of the male effeminate homosexual in the late nineteenth century, to Warner's descriptions of the pervasive influence of the Virgin Mary on definitions of female sexuality as passive and maternal, to Butler's accounts of the performance of identity through bodily acts, such as clothing (Foucault 1990; Warner 1983; Butler 1986). Many of these theorists deconstruct Cartesian dualism, in the wake of declining religious belief and suspicions of grand narratives. Tobe, then, shows how both of these authors locate consciousness in the body, as well as the mind, during the act of sex; and through sexual exchange, relative strangers briefly experience an intimacy that is commonly linked to emotional connection and the private sphere. Tobe observes that in Millet's novel confined space, such as a train compartment, is 'seen almost as automatically as a filled space … referencing both the recesses of her [Catherine's] own body and the space occupied by two bodies together creating a new intimacy'. The descriptions of sexual encounters in public spaces, such as car parks and offices, disrupts literary expectations and traditional concepts of private and public by investing public spaces with this new intimacy.

Traditionally, the city has always functioned in literary works as a fluid space of sexual experimentation, free from the constraining structures of family, school and religion: exemplified by the desire of gay men and women wanting to 'come out of the closet' (a spatial metaphor that indicates the hidden and marginal status of alternative sexualities in the conventional private home – see, for example, Christopher Isherwood, *Goodbye to Berlin*, 1939 and Quentin Crisp, *The Naked Civil Servant*, 1968). For women, however, unconstrained sexual freedom has often led either to their integration into a sexual sub-culture and the formation of a monogamous partnership, as described by Audre Lorde in her 1982 work *Zami*, about black lesbians in New York; or male exploitation leading to destitution and life in a cheap Paris hotel room, a fate explored by Jean Rhys's *Good Morning, Midnight* (1939). Such portrayals have been founded on cultural assumptions about women's need for sexual and emotional connectedness.

However, Millet's novel is often compared to Henry Miller's *Tropic of Cancer* (1934), due to both authors' emphasis on fragmented body parts, multiple partners and anonymity. Millet's narrative seems an attempt to create a bodily subjectivity, and thus it repudiates many of the conventions of autobiography. Catherine's promiscuous sexual life represents her search for identity (and similarly, the tricks are the rationale for Camus' narrative and, by implication, the basis for his autobiographical identity). Millet's nonchalant descriptions of sexual acts may also be satirising the confessional, intimate tone of many erotic female autobiographies, such as Anais Nin's *Delta of Venus* (1978) and Erica Jong's *Fear of Flying* (1973). The concept of interiority, often used in autobiographical theory to refer to the mind or soul, is extended to the experience of the body in particular spaces (Smith and Watson 1998). Stefanie Sobelle similarly observes that Perec challenges autobiographical definitions of interiority when he presents only the front set of rooms in his mapping of a Parisian apartment building: 'one finds no interiority for these characters … psychology is abandoned for dimensionality' and 'memory instead is temporal, not subjective, and if it belongs to a subject, it belongs to the building itself'.

Similarly, Tobe observes that we learn about Camus as we are introduced to the spaces in which he lives and works. In both novels, the textual pleasures of sex and its locations are conveyed by the authors' use of literary devices. The identical narrative pattern of each *récit* and Camus' use of metaphor recall Roland Barthes' meditations on both the sensuous delight of reading in *The Pleasure of the Text* (1973) and the pleasures of narrating the scene.

Tobe also observes that both Millet's and Camus' conceptions of space are gendered, which lends both psychic and architectural notions of interiority another dimension of meaning. The ways in which bodily differences are perceived and represented is constituted by the ways that space produces, and is produced by, existing gender relations. Feminist geographers and architects, such as Gillian Rose and Elizabeth Grosz, have noted that the forms of the twentieth-century city are gendered (the phallic skyscraper, the female labyrinth) and that the urban landscape is not functionally adequate for women or children (due, for example, to a lack of breast-feeding facilities or women's shelters).[7] Feminist literature and theory abound in spatial metaphors of claustrophobia and visions of liberation which can be traced to nineteenth-century fictions of gothic heroines in crumbling mansions, such as Ann Radcliffe's *The Mysteries of Udolpho* (1794) and Charlotte Brontë's *Jane Eyre* (1847). One seminal work of early second-wave feminism, Sandra M. Gilbert's and Sandra Gubar's *The Madwoman in the Attic* (1979) used Brontë's literary madwoman to investigate the links between domestic confinement, female mental health and the inability to write. These novels build upon Virginia Woolf's insight in *A Room of One's Own* (1929) that only a new type of domestic architecture, which allocated private apartments to women instead of conflating them with the entire house, would enable them to become focused and productive writers. Meanwhile, Betty Friedan's *The Feminine Mystique* (1963) invented the image of the desperate housewife, segregated in American suburban domesticity, and advocated that women should adopt meaningful professional work (and, by implication, claim and re-make the professional urban sphere).

However, the essays in this section feature men and women who relate to each other in the streets, cafes and apartments of the contemporary city. Other recent autobiographies of women such as Belle du Jour (*The Intimate Adventures of a London Call Girl*, 2005) and television shows such as HBO's *Sex and the City* (1998–2004), which was structured round a New York columnist's personal observations related in voiceover, depict educated, independent women with apartments of their own where they write about, and partly define themselves by, sexual encounters with clients and/or relative strangers. With their emphasis on individuality, choice and pleasure and their re-examination of second-wave attitudes to female sexuality, works such as these can be seen as a manifestation of third-wave feminism or post-feminism.[8] Most second-wave feminists were opposed to pornographic images and writing, regarding them as patriarchal objectification (for example, Andrea Dworkin's *Intercourse*, 1987). However, both third-wave feminism and post-feminism have been identified with a 'pro-porn' stance and the recent resurgence of sexual confessional writing by women (much of it in online blogs, a new variant of life-writing in which anonymity allows for sexual experimentation with a fictional persona) plays an important role in this debate (Serfaty 2004). However, these activities remain controversial. Are women who enjoy porn duped by false consciousness? Can porn be reclaimed for women's desires and/or to subvert female stereotypes?

Much of this debate revolves around ownership of the gaze. In the quintessential theorisation of modern urban spectatorship, the *flâneur* is the anonymous walker epitomised by Charles Baudelaire and his strolls around nineteenth-century Paris, observing and later recording his fleeting encounters with the human and architectural panorama. This is the gaze of the urban planner and of the omniscient narrator, and one 'streetwalker' who has been the object of this gaze is the *passante* ('passing woman'). Critics including Janet Wolff, Rachel Bowlby and Deborah Nord argued that the concept of a female *flâneuse* was problematic, as women in the city were always vulnerable to sexual objectification (Wolff 1985; Bowlby 1992; Nord 1996). The same problem arises when a woman writes about her sexuality. The autobiographical novel enables Catherine M. to narrate her own perceptions. She employs her skills as an art critic to judge objects and spaces with detached judgement; yet through her descriptions of her body and sexual encounters, she also reinstates the role of woman as sexual object in urban space. When she writes the city, then, is she appropriating the gaze, or subjecting herself to the gaze of her readers?

The concept of *flânerie* has recently been revived in the practice and writing of the psychogeographers, as Inga Bryden discusses in her essay. Writers such as Michael Moorcock (*Mother London*, 1988), Peter Ackroyd (*London: The Biography*, 2000) and Ian Sinclair (*Downriver*, 1991; *Lights Out for the Territory: 9 Excursions in the Secret History of London*, 1997; *London Orbital*, 2002) draw on the ideas of *dérive* (purposeful drifting) that were expounded by Guy Debord and the Situationist movement in the 1960s (Debord 2000). As Sinclair's sub-title neatly describes, these novels depict narrators wandering through hidden or neglected urban areas who discover traces of local histories in pubs, cemeteries and near the M25. In these literary versions of urban spectatorship, the gaze of the walker does not encompass or 'map' the entire city. This panoramic gaze was described as being at odds with the experience of everyday life by Michel de Certeau, who in *The Practice of Everyday Life* contrasts the street-level gaze of ordinary inhabitants whose preferred routes through the city may challenge the directions of conventional maps (de Certeau 1984). Andrew Bonnett has recently discussed the 'rooted nostalgia' that the Situationists experienced for particular cities, and similarly literary psychogeographers write about their emotional attachments to sites of 'popular memory' and the 'political memories contained in buildings and streets' (Bonnett 2010: 144–5).

Writers such as Sinclair thus challenge earlier novelistic practices. In George Eliot's 'Condition of England' novel, *Middlemarch* (1871), the omniscient narrator's image of the web to symbolise the intricate relationships of society also demonstrated her all-knowing, all-seeing gaze; by contrast, works such as Sinclair's employ imagery of 'palimpsestic' hidden depths.[9] As Bryden discusses, 'unofficial' texts of the city, such as graffiti and discarded newspapers, are also recognised in these works as accounts of everyday life. The inclusion of such texts is a riposte, then, to official representations of the city, such as maps and architects' drawings that emerged alongside urbanisation and the professionalisation of architecture in the nineteenth century. These documents illustrate the Victorian fascination with organising and cataloguing every aspect of life, from people (via the census) to newly exported plants from the colonies.[10] However, they also demonstrate the attempts of an elite class to control the formal and functional roles of city streets and buildings. By contrast, many postmodern writers and architects show how the meanings and functions of these spaces are produced by their users' 'mappings'.[11]

However, Sobelle also discusses how Perec's *Life: A User's Manual* uses the grid and the jigsaw puzzle as a means of investigating how the constraints imposed by a particular building affect our daily lives, and the degree of agency individuals possess to construct their own identities and relationships. Like the Situationists with whom he was associated, Perec seems nostalgic, in this case for older apartment buildings whose grand staircases seem to imply moments of communal existence and a sense of belonging to the whole building. Instead, the transitional space of the modern staircase facilitates the anonymity of modern apartment living, where neighbours are only familiar strangers to be briefly acknowledged; or, as Tobe observes more optimistically, where people can construct alternative identities (for example, as sexual risk-takers) which can be briefly indulged 'in between' their primary roles as writer or wife.

Inga Bryden's essay deals specifically with the short story, a form often associated with the depiction of fleeting moments. The short story is a product of modernity, developing in the nineteenth century alongside the magazine and periodical market in world cities such as London and New York, which sought to meet the reading demands of an increasingly literate population.[12] Unsurprisingly, then, the short story has from its inception reflected and shaped experiences of the modern city. The formal qualities which can be seen in early examples such as Edgar Allen Poe's *The Fall of the House of Usher* (1837) and which are outlined in *The Philosophy of Composition* (1846) – the structuring of a story around a single event, the compression of language and imagery, and elsewhere the frequent use of transitory environments and visual metaphors – all lend themselves to the theme of the city.[13] Indeed, short story theory abounds in visual and architectural metaphors. Sherwood Anderson described his readerly response to a good story thus: 'in a crowd of faces in a crowded street one face suddenly jumped out. It had a tale to tell, was crying its tale to the streets but at best one got only a fragment of it' (Shaw 1983: 15).[14] This reference to the fragment acknowledges the short story's likeness with many urban encounters: momentary, not all-encompassing and merely one of many accounts of the city (and, indeed, short stories are often published in collections).

By contrast, Elizabeth Bowen commented scathingly on Henry James's and Thomas Hardy's stories, claiming that 'they are great architects' fancies, little buildings on an august plan' (Bowen 1976: 153). Bowen's dismissive comment illustrates the traditional prestige of the novel and draws attention to the parallels between literary and architectural conceptions of authorship, canon and genre hierarchy.[15] In twentieth-century modernism, the urban short story was similarly overshadowed by the novel, although, as Dominic Head has claimed, its fragmentary nature seemed to chime with modernist thinking about symbolism, the compression of time and, furthermore, the links between modernity and urban life (Head 1992).[16] However, in the new urban gothic fiction of the 1880s and 1890s, such as Robert Louis Stevenson's *The Strange Case of Dr Jekyll and Mr Hyde* (1886), the use of brief contrasts of light and dark evoked the uncanniness of the familiar city at night while the equally terse and metaphorical descriptions of Hyde conjured up fears of the anonymous, random killer. These features were adopted by twentieth-century short story writers such as John Cheever in *The Housebreaker of Shady Hill* (1958) and by writers of detective fiction, such as Arthur Conan Doyle who often chose the short story form for his London detective Sherlock Holmes. In all detective stories, the city setting facilitates an exploration of the urban themes of moral and physical corruption, the anonymity and mobility of criminals and victims, as we have seen in the previous section; in addition, the short story form lends itself to the minute details of criminal acts and investigations and to depictions of sudden, violent and suspenseful encounters.

Finally, postmodern and magical realist writers have deployed the short story form to revise and re-write urban myths from feminist and post-colonial perspectives. These myths are often derived from fairy tales, oral narratives or essays that also depend on striking visual images: for example, 'Black Venus' Jeanne Duval, mistress and muse of Charles Baudelaire's *Les Fleurs du Mal* (1857), whose ambiguous racial heritage and subjective experience of nineteenth-century Paris are explored by Angela Carter (*Black Venus*, 1985). In the recent collection, *The New Uncanny: Tales of Unease* (2008), writers including Hanif Kureishi and Ramsey Campbell explore Freud's seminal essay in a series of marginal urban settings, including suburbia; while Shaun Tan's *Tales of Outer Suburbia* (2008) draws on science fiction conventions and images to explore sudden and strange encounters with aliens in the suburbs.

The essays in this section, then, explore some of the many rich interconnections between contemporary urban space, everyday life and the evolving forms of literary narrative (novel, autobiography, short story) that document these connections, and also show how these disciplines shape and respond to each other.

Notes

1 See, for example, Charles Dickens, *Oliver Twist* (1838) or James Joyce, *Ulysses* (1922).
2 For an overview of debates about space in the field of cultural geography, see Hubbard *et al.* (2004).

3 See Milgram (1992) on the 'familiar stranger'.
4 For an account of literary representations of suburbia, see Hapgood (2005).
5 For an overview of the ways in which the fragment has been used as an image of urbanism, see Graham and Marvin (2001); in relation to epistemology, see Foucault (1982); in relation to gay history, see Monette (1988).
6 For an account of the panopticon and its role in modern society, see Foucault (1995).
7 The recent critical debates on gender, sexuality and space are usefully outlined in Rendell *et al.* (2000); Colomina (2000); Rose and Blunt (1994); Grosz (1991).
8 For an account of the different strands within the 'third wave', see Gillis *et al.* (2007).
9 See also Foucault (1990) on the 'web of power', which discusses how power is dispersed and shifting within a society; and Foucault (2002) for his account of subterranean histories and discourses. See also Baker (2003) on psychogeography and the concept of the underground.
10 For example, Henry Mayhew, *London Labour and the London Poor* (1861).
11 See Moretti (1998) who uses maps to demonstrate how narratives are linked to specific routes and journeys.
12 See Shaw (1983) for a history of the short story.
13 See, for example, the short stories of Ernest Hemingway, which are often set in cafes, waiting rooms and station restaurants (Hemingway 1995).
14 See Sherwood Anderson, *A Story Teller's Story* (1924), Ann Arbor: University of Michigan Press; Brander Matthews, *The Philosophy of the Short-Story* (1901), Longmans, Green and Co. Matthews coined the term 'short story' in the same year.
15 By contrast, the short story was popular in France, Russia and America during the nineteenth century, where its practitioners included Emile Zola, Anton Chekhov and Nathaniel Hawthorne.
16 Both Virginia Woolf's *Mrs Dalloway* (1925) and James Joyce's *Ulysses* (1922) were originally conceived as short stories. For examples of the modernist short story, see Mansfield (2006) and Joyce (2000).

References

Anstey, T., Grillner, K. and Hughes, R. (eds) (2007) *Architecture and Authorship*, London: Black Dog Publishing.

Baker, B. (2003) 'Maps of the London underground: Ian Sinclair and Michael Moorcock's Psychogeography of the City', *Literary London*, 1.1 Online. Available www.literarylondon. org/london-journal/march2003/index.html (accessed 27 May 2011).

Barthes, R. (1980) *The Pleasure of the Text,* New York: Hill and Wang.

—— (1997) 'Semiology and the Urban', in N. Leach (ed.) *Rethinking Architecture: A Reader in Cultural Theory*, London: Routledge.

Benjamin, W. (1978) 'Paris, Capital of the Nineteenth Century', in P. Demetz (ed.) *Reflections,* New York: Schocken Books.

Bonnett, A. (2010) *Left in the Past: Radicalism and the Politics of Nostalgia*, London: Continuum.

Bowen, E. (1976) 'The Faber Book of Modern Short Stories' in C. E. May (ed.) *Short Story Theories*, Cincinnati: Ohio University Press.

Bowlby, R. (1992) 'Walking, women and writing: Virginia Woolf as *flâneuse*', in I. Armstrong (ed.) *New Feminist Discourses: Critical Essays on Theories and Texts*, London: Routledge.

Butler, J. (1986) *Gender Trouble: Feminism and the Subversion of Identity*, London: Routledge.

Colomina, B. (ed.) (2000) *Sexuality and Space*, New York: Princeton Architectural Press.

Debord, G. (2000) *The Society of the Spectacle*, St Petersburg: Black and Red.

de Certeau, M. (2002) *The Practice of Everyday Life*, San Diego: University of California Press.

Foucault, M. (1982) *The Archaeology of Knowledge and the Discourse on Language*, London: Vintage.

—— (1990) *The History of Sexuality* (trans R. Hurley), London: Vintage.

—— (1995) *Discipline and Punish: The Birth of the Prison*, London: Vintage.

—— (2002) *The Archaeology of Knowledge*, London: Routledge.

Gillis, S., Howie, G. and Munford, R. (eds) (2007) *Third Wave Feminism: A Critical Exploration*, Basingstoke: Palgrave Macmillan.

Graham, S. and Marvin, S. (2001) *Splintering Urbanism*, London: Routledge.

Grosz, E. (1991) *Space, Time and Perversion: The Politics of the Body*, London: Routledge.

Hapgood, L. (2005) *Margins of Desire: The Suburbs in Fiction and Culture 1880–1925*, Manchester: Manchester University Press.

Harvey, D. (1991) *The Condition of Postmodernity: An Enquiry into the Origins of Social Change*, Hoboken, NJ: Wiley-Blackwell.

Head, D. (1992) *The Modernist Short Story: A Study in Theory and Practice*, Cambridge: Cambridge University Press.

Hemingway, E. (1995) *The Collected Stories*, London: Everyman.

Hubbard, P., Kitchin, R. and Valentine, G. (eds) (2004) *Key Thinkers on Space and Place*, London: Sage.

Joyce, J. (2000) *Dubliners*, London: Penguin Modern Classics.

Lefebvre, H. (1991) *The Production of Space*, Hoboken: Wiley-Blackwell.

Mansfield, K. (2006) *The Collected Stories of Katherine Mansfield*, London: Wordsworth Editions.

Milgram, S. (1992) 'The Familiar Stranger: An Aspect of Urban Anonymity' in S. Milgram, J. Sabini and M. Silver (eds) *The Individual in a Social World: Essays and Experiments*, McGraw-Hill Humanities.

Monette, P. (1988) *Borrowed Time: An AIDS Memoir*, Boston: Mariner Books.

Moretti, F. (1998) *Atlas of the European Novel 1800–1900*, London: Verso.

Nord, D. (1996) *Walking the Victorian Streets: Women, Representation and the City*, Ithaca: Cornell University Press.

Rendell, J., Penner, B. and Borden, I. (eds) (2000) *Gender Space Architecture*, London: Routledge.

Rose, G. and Blunt, A. (eds) (1994) *Writing Women and Space: Colonial and Postcolonial Geographies*, New York: The Guilford Press.

Serfaty, V. (2004) *The Mirror and the Veil: An Overview of American Online Diaries and Blogs*, Amsterdam: Rodopi.

Shaw, V. (1983) *The Short Story: A Critical Introduction*, London: Longman.

Smith, S. and Watson, J. (1998) *Women, Autobiography, Theory: A Reader*, Milwaukee: University of Wisconsin Press.

Vidler, A. (1994) *The Architectural Uncanny: Essays in the Modern Unhomely*, Cambridge, MA: MIT Press.

Warner, M. (1983) *Alone of all her Sex: The Myth and Cult of the Virgin Mary*, London: Vintage.

Wolff, J. (1985) 'The invisible *flâneuse*: women and the literature of modernity, *Theory, Culture and Society*, 2.3: 37–46.

11

THE NOVEL ARCHITECTURE OF GEORGES PEREC

Stefanie Elisabeth Sobelle

> To live is to pass from one space to another, while doing your best not to bump yourself.
>
> *Georges Perec*

An evocative sub-category within late twentieth-century fiction privileges domestic architecture as an organizing principle for narrative construction.[1] The 'architectural novel', which emerges with the reorganization of space and its impact on everyday life, takes for granted that the house is an extension of society and public events inextricable from the private realm. The most exemplary versions of the architectural novel enact socio-political transitions through the architecture both in and of the novel, exploring the political implications behind the arrangements of inhabited space. This essay examines one such novel, Georges Perec's seminal *La Vie mode d'emploi* (1978; *Life A User's Manual*, 1987), a complex and mammoth work that constitutes a web of interwoven stories tracing the past and present lives of the inhabitants of a fictional Parisian apartment house at 11 rue Simon-Crubellier. Perec exploits the tension between the rigid structure of a building and the imaginative processes that take place within it and engages with the possibilities offered by imaginative depths not available in the two dimensions of the page. This particular architectural novel functions as a national allegory of France in the second half of the twentieth century.

Perec's allegory responds specifically to the transformation of French national identity and social relations in the aftermath of 1968, particularly as it presents the problem of finding one's place in history. With *Life*, written between 1969 and 1978, Perec turns to domestic space in response to the 'Unitary Urbanism' of the late 1950s (and its subsequent impact on May '68), the Situationists' reaction against a perceived stagnation of everyday life. Unitary Urbanism advocated the '*dérive*' (an aimless wandering) and 'psychogeography' (the effect of an environment on a subject's behaviour and psychology). Perec explores ever-shifting social relations within the confined space of a single building. This building, a nineteenth-century structure, no longer displays the class relations it was once designed to shelter, and as such questionably accommodates postmodern dwelling. In his short essay 'The Apartment Building', Perec plainly describes his plans for *Life A User's Manual*:

> I imagine a Parisian apartment building whose façade has been removed … so that all the rooms in the front, from the ground floor up to the attics, are instantly and simultaneously visible. The novel – whose title is *Life A User's Manual* – restricts itself … to describing the rooms thus unveiled and the activities unfolding in them, the whole in accordance with formal procedures … try to imagine on what a collective existence might be based, within the confines of this same [the reader's] building.
>
> *Perec 1998: 40; 44*

Perec claims here to imagine collectivity as a fundamentally interior, domestic project, but on what might a collective existence be based within a building for which only the front line of rooms is described? Surely a collective existence in a large building would be determined by all rooms and all inhabitants – all modes of dwelling. Perec, who lost both parents to the Nazis, understands, however, that all modes of dwelling are inaccessible. He writes mournfully of loss in *Espèces d'espaces* (1974; *Species of Spaces*, 1998):

> I would like there to exist places that are stable, unmoving, intangible, untouched and almost untouchable, unchanging, deep-rooted … such places don't exist, and it's because they don't exist that space becomes a question, ceases to be self-evident … I have constantly to mark it, to designate it. It's never mine, never given to me, I have to conquer it.
>
> *Perec 1998: 91*

However romantic, for Perec, 'spaces are fragile: time is going to wear them away, to destroy them. Nothing will resemble what was … Space melts like sand running through one's fingers. … To write: to try meticulously to retain something, to cause something to survive' (Perec 1998: 91–2). In *Life*, he negotiates his incessant yearning to identify and hold onto human existence through an obsessive exploration of domestic spaces. His home exists in the realm of the imagination; Perec dwells in narrative itself, slipping between the theme of domesticity and the materiality of textual space. Yet this project is not only personal and mnemonic; according to Perec, the apartment building is synecdochic of society – many individuals living

separately, yet intimately connected. He suggests that it is in the apartment building, the '*immeuble d'habitation*', and not in the street that we can best understand not
only a new society, but even that society which has been lost to space and time.

Perec examines these issues through an architecture that performs the reading
experience, one of imagination, surveillance and limited accessibility. He offers no
detailed scenes of domesticity but rather an array of anecdotes about fantastic and
absurd individuals. One finds no interiority for these characters or for the apartment
building; Perec abandons psychology altogether. His primary concern is instead
with dimensionality. Perec's brief statement about his ideas for the novel reveals
several significant qualities of his depiction: the apartment building's rooms, which
comprise the organizing device for the novel's stories, are 'instantly and simultaneously visible'; the novel describes only that which occurs in those visible front
rooms, neglecting anything that might occur in the building's interior. The building
Perec describes is, like a painting or a page, exposed, yet its depth is not revealed.
For Perec, dimensionality is both a theme in the novel and a formal device. He layers stories upon stories – within the building's storeys upon storeys – connected by
staircases and a reader's horizontal and vertical movement across the page.[2] Perec
sees in the staircases – in the spaces between spaces – potential for human existence
– a challenge to a staid society – just as, ultimately, he admits its futility.

Perec, a dedicated puzzle-master, crossword editor, and Oulipo member,[3] navi-
gates the shifting patterns of France by designing his own puzzles for constructing
Life. To construct the novel's form, Perec devised three primary constraints, constraints that motivate a kind of conceptual thinking in parallel with that of any
architect. First, he used a 10×10 Greco-Latin bi-square or Euler square, which is
a grid wherein each cell contains a pair of elements that derive from two distinct
lists.[4] Each element from list A, in other words, is paired with each other element
from list B, without any combinations repeating. Here, the Greco-Latin bi-
square is envisioned as a Saul Steinberg-inspired section of an apartment building.
The novel's ninety-nine chapters (the 100th of the 10 x 10 board is missing) are
named for apartments and spaces within the building, sometimes appearing once,
other times repeated, each offering its own often fantastic, sometimes devastating,
vignette. Second, Perec incorporates into these laws an organizing, 'permutating
"schedule of obligations"' (Mathews 1998: 170): forty-two themes which include
furniture, objects, characters, allusions, quotations, and so on that must be used
repeatedly throughout the novel and that make up the elements belonging to each
block of the bi-square.[5] Third, he treats the grid/building as a kind of game board
and narrates through it via a Knight's tour (a play in chess that involves moving the
knight through every square of the board without it ever landing in the same place
twice), which determines the order of the chapters.

Perec considers the grid, and how one negotiates through it, as a mirror for how
one lives daily life. Habitation constitutes a complex system of interacting relations
within a fixed place: we brush our teeth, we cook our meals, we read our books,

	1	2	3	4	5	6	7	8	9	10	
1	1 1	7 8	6 9	5 10	10 2	9 4	8 6	2 3	3 5	4 7	
2	8 7	2 2	1 8	7 9	6 10	10 3	9 5	3 4	4 6	5 1	
3	9 6	8 1	3 7	2 8	1 9	7 10	10 4	4 5	5 7	6 2	6
4	10 5	9 7	8 2	4 4	3 8	2 9	1 10	5 6	6 1	7 2	5
5	2 10	10 6	9 1	8 3	5 5	4 8	3 9	6 7	7 2	1 4	4
6	4 9	3 10	10 7	9 2	8 4	6 6	5 8	7 1	1 3	2 5	3
7	6 8	5 5	4 10	10 1	9 3	8 5	7 7	1 2	2 4	3 6	2
8	3 2	4 5	5 4	6 5	7 6	1 7	2 1	8 8	9 9	10 10	1
9	5 3	6 4	7 5	1 6	2 7	3 1	4 2	9 10	10 8	8 9	R de C
0	7 4	1 5	2 6	3 7	4 1	5 2	6 3	10 9	8 10	9 8	5/5

FIGURE 11.1 10×10 Greco-Latin bi-square from Mathews (1998), redrawn from original

and these movements vary infinitely, even if the rooms in which we perform them remain stable. Perec offers the crossword puzzle as a further example of the function of a grid. His character Lord Ashtray obsesses over puzzles, subscribing to every newspaper in the world so that he can play the crosswords, even having his bedroom re-wallpapered weekly in grids designed by his 'favorite cruciverbalist' for inspiration (Perec 1987: 452–4). One might consider Ashtray's wallpaper a metaphor for the dimensionality of Perec's building itself: a crossword puzzle seems to be two-dimensional – a flat grid into which one enters letters, themselves nothing more than intersecting lines. But what of the mental space involved in solving a crossword? If, to give an easy example, the clue is 'Dante's city', one's mind goes to Florence and to any images one has of that city. Depth, in this case, exists in memory or imagination – just as it does in the act of reading the flat page of a book. Perec asks, 'what is there under your wallpaper?' (Perec 1998: 211). He requires the reader to take initiative, to look beyond the flatness and to depth, complexity – beyond big events and into the infinite details that inform them. He depends, in this sense, on the reader's imaginative capability.

Perec's removing the façade from the apartment building not only allows him to see all its inhabitants living simultaneously but also destabilizes the building's structure. Perec responds to places that are forever changed yet rigidly the same – places evident and available yet unattainable and impossible. Perec mourns his personal lost France: 'Spaces have multiplied,' he muses, 'have been broken up and diversified': 'it has been decided that everything found *inside* this dotted line should be coloured violet and called France, while everything found *outside* this dotted line should be in a different colour' (Perec 1998: 6). As the places of modern society become increasingly unfixed, increasingly globalized, the relations that move through them are also constantly changing.

Perec then exercises the two-dimensional to access the multi-dimensional – the flat surface to tell the complex tale. The full implications of the geometric structure of *Life* are revealed when the apartment house, superimposed on a flat bi-square, is understood as fundamentally a two-dimensional grid. A year after *Life* was first published in France, Rosalind Krauss, in her essay 'Grids' for *October*, famously argues, 'although the grid is certainly not a story, it *is* a structure, and one, moreover, that allows a contradiction between the values of science and those of spiritualism to maintain themselves within the consciousness of modernism' (Krauss 1979: 55), citing artists such as Chuck Close and Piet Mondrian as examples of the prevailing structure of the grid in Modernist art. Perec complicates the clean rigidity of modernist axes; he does not use the grid as Chuck Close does, to plan hyper-realist representation, nor as Mondrian does, to remove representation altogether. Much like the maps he describes above, Perec's grid is the space within which the mathematical and the imaginary coexist in tension with one another, creating an impossible architectural space. The grid *is* the story.[6]

While in architecture, the grid would most likely be a plan, for Perec, the fixed square rises into storeys. A building's inhabitants cannot move only through the front visible rooms, and yet they are forced to by Perec's design. Because the constraint prevents him from exploring the rooms unseen in the section, which would violate the flatness of the bi-square, the author must instead explore the histories of the rooms and characters that *can* be seen. Perec himself gives the following example: among his long list of elements for the bi-square are quotations from Jules Verne – Captain Nemo's library and the contents of the trunk in the Miraculous Island; and James Joyce – the house Leopold Bloom dreams of at the end of *Ulysses*.[7] These appear together in the flat of a certain Madame Moreau, who has decorated an area in her residence for foreign business travellers. Nemo's library, a rectangular room, becomes an oval one, and Bloom's house becomes a dollhouse representing an English cottage (Perec 1987: 99). In narrative, when the gridded story is transferred from the bi-square to the apartment building, the content itself morphs from ordinary objects and familiar occurrences (in the same chapter, these include the Middle East, posters, a triangle, the color red, and wool [Perec 1987: 172–3]) into extraordinary objects or fantastic occurrences ('dark red woollen carpet with triangular motifs in an even darker red', a facsimile of a Hayden Symphony score [Perec 1987: 100], and old tools bearing the monogram

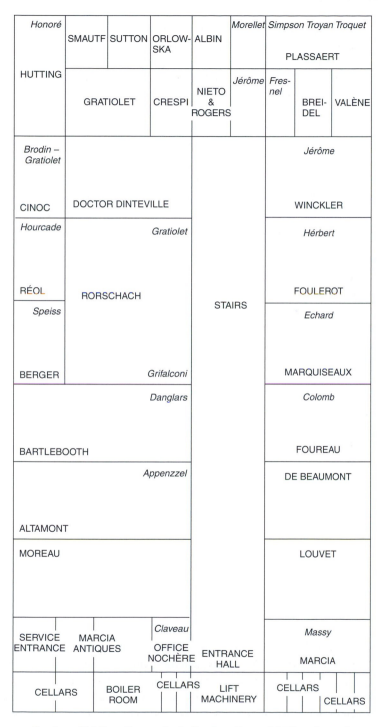

FIGURE 11.2 Section of 11 Rue Simon-Crubelier from Perec (1987), redrawn from original

of the Suez Canal [Perec 1987: 99]). Perec's brand of spatial distortion is what happens to space when generative constraints are in play. Imaginative space becomes an alternative to the rigidity and confusion of mapped, constructed space.

What is particularly unusual about Perec's use of the grid, then, is his move from the two-dimensional grid to the three dimensions of a building. He complicates his own constraint of the two-dimensional bi-square with the notion that movement through the grid will be defined by the knight's moves; he seemingly plays chess in three-dimensions. Perec gives the grid dimensionality, but not one that abides by geometry's rules.[8] Just as Perec's characters have no psychological interiority, the apartment building's 'z' or depth axis is not represented either – only the rooms on the plan itself – an architecture that is impossible. Characters are rarely seen moving between rooms at all, nor does Perec represent or allude to what is behind the rooms on the diagram. In the grid, Perec's knight can move into any represented square, but his movement is restricted by the rules of his tour of diagonals; while in the building, Perec's characters can only move through the spaces to which they have access as determined by their own social relationships, even if their movement itself is presumably organic. In addition, the building's apartments themselves have been configured and reconfigured over time – walls moved and taken down – to accommodate the needs of new inhabitants. Therefore, the stories that begin within the fixed walls of a particular place soon breach their own boundaries when they digress into past lives or past configurations within the building.

When reading, one scans the horizontal and vertical axes of a page and moves into the three-dimensional book object, but one is not physically transported into the depths of the stories themselves. For the reader to follow the knight's moves through the novel, he or she must move mentally, and therefore spectrally, through walls and floors and ceilings – even through time itself. Perec's representation of the building's architecture too begins to mimic the very act of reading a novel. In spite of any absence of geometrical depths, the 'z' axis functions in *Life* through history, memory and imagination. The play between depths and grids is allegorized in chapter ninety, which takes place in the building's 'Entrance Hall'. In this segment, Perec devotes several pages to the aforementioned Lord Ashtray in an anecdote within a chapter given to the flat of Madame Moreau. Ashtray is the current employer of Moreau's former cook and is obsessed with glass, a satire on imaginative depths; Ashtray has 'so many windows, glazed doors, and mirrors in his property that he employs four servants solely for their maintenance, and that since he couldn't get enough replacement glass to keep up with repairs he solved the problem by simply buying the nearest glassworks' (Perec 1987: 452–3). How exhausting it must be to maintain so much glass! If realism is a window on the world, Ashtray is a joke on its effectuality. The flat surface of glass, whether reflective or transparent, offers the illusion of depth so much so that its surface itself is often forgotten.

Throughout the novel, Perec is concerned with boundaries – between transparency and reflection, present and past, individual and collective. As idealistic as it may be, his removing the façade from this Parisian apartment building also exposes both the past and present lives within, signifying a breakdown of privacy in a post-war climate and threatening the stability of private space. 'But where is our life?' he asks in an essay, 'Where is our body? Where is our space?' (Perec 1998: 210). Perec's removing of the façade suggests a postmodern ontological crisis, if we are to abide by the distinction that Brian McHale outlines for us in his 1987 *Postmodernist Fiction*. Perec then also represents a kind of voyeurism, a Foucaultian allegory of reading; the viewer is in a position of power over the viewed, who cannot see that they are being watched. In the plot of the novel itself, the building is being 'narrated' by the artist Serge Valène, who paints its rooms and those who dwell in them. By transcending the boundaries of the lines of the grid, Perec addresses and then rejects such institutionalized power.

If the prevailing act of this novel is one of voyeuristic power play, Perec's work not only shares with visual art the use of the grid but also a sense of exposure, a common thread running through postwar culture. It is in this way that his ideas of relationality most intimately correspond with those of his contemporaries about how we interact with the spaces we inhabit. Prevailing urban theory at the time saw the city as a system of interconnected parts and as the site for potential revolution, just as architects began focusing on the 'everyday', particularly in France. Both Henri Lefebvre and the Situationists, with whom Lefebvre associated, prioritized the experiential, whether it be Lefebvre's 'moment' or the Situationist *dérive*. Even if their ideas were rampant in the cultural climate of the time, Perec was most likely introduced to the ideas of the Situationist International by Lefebvre, with whom he was close and whose *Critique of Everyday Life* (1947–81) directly influenced his earlier novel, *Les Choses: Une histoire des années soixante* (1965; *Things, A Story of the Sixties*, 1990), a cataloguing of the objects owned by a Parisian couple in the sixties.

Lefebvre, in *The Production of Space*, designates levels of space, distinguishing abstract or 'absolute' space – the represented or imagined space of architects, for example – and 'social' space – the space in which we actually live. Lefebvre privileges the city as *the* site for lived experience, and it was in a similar vein that the Situationists believed the transformation of architecture was a means to revolution. Where for both Lefebvre and for the Situationists, however, social space is best experienced in an urban environment, Perec suggests that it is in private life that we 'live' most intensely. Perec's interest in the dimension added by time, memory and imagination distances him from the relationship between space and the psychological so insisted upon by the Situationist concept of psychogeography. Depth in this novel, in fact, is not particularly psychological at all – characters get no psychology, no interiority. Memory instead is temporal, not subjective, and if it belongs to a subject, it belongs to the building itself.

David Bellos claims that '[the Situationist International's] influence on Perec's attitudes is … certain. He was familiar with the ideas of *dérive* and *détournement* in the early 1960s, and these notions informed his reinvention of the art of seeing as well as the art of writing' (Bellos 1993: 281). However, Bellos also confesses that Perec was still no 'prisoner of Situationist contestation', suggesting that he identified an inherent hypocrisy in left-wing intellectualism, having once stated that 'there is no art of living that is not bourgeois, and there's nothing I can do about it' (in Bellos 1993: 282). While Perec may be in line with figures such as Lefebvre, (even when only conceptually), he resisted what Kristin Ross has called in her study of postcolonial French identity, the 'highly destructive' modernization of postwar France (Ross 1996: 21) with an almost obsessive construction through his use of gridding and diagramming as formal constraint. Even if openly interested in *détournement*, Perec is fundamentally anti-*dérive*: *Life's* movement is determined, not drifting – it is through this determination that Perec emphasizes the need to privilege the quotidian.

In Perec's veering away from the events of the extraordinary toward the mundanity of what he calls the '*infra-ordinaire*', he finds potential in the antiquated, ignored, destroyed, defunct.[9] He asserts, 'There are few events which don't leave a written trace at least. At one time or another, almost everything passes through a sheet of paper' (Perec 1998: 12). Walter Benjamin reminds us that 'to live means to leave traces' (Benjamin 1978: 155). The human subject itself is often absent or gone missing in Perec's work, signifying the loss of life in his own autobiography: human history for him is a data bank of all the traces left by its inhabitants. Such traces of living are found in the spaces in between and are marked by the seams of the architecture he has constructed. Perec thus presents an entire building, narrating the histories of its rooms, the traces of its inhabitants, and the collections of objects that represent them. In order to present private life, he suggests that we live, even when in seclusion, in an intricate coevality with others.

For Perec, domestic living operates like the squares of the grid, occurring in what he calls in 'The Apartment', 'the functional relationships in between the rooms' (Perec 1998: 31), and in the ways interaction between subjects takes place in those transitional spaces. As such, Perec's knight's tour lands the reader in the various apartments of the building, but apartments are not the only significant spaces of the building; whereas the spatial movement of the knight links the squares together, the places of connection within the building are also present. The reader lands most often in the stairways, which are given twelve chapters in the novel. The first staircase in *Life* constitutes the first chapter, and the narrator describes it in lyric detail:

> [the staircase is a] neutral place that belongs to all and to none, where people pass by almost without seeing each other, where the life of the building regularly and distantly resounds. ... The inhabitants of a single building live a few inches from each other, they are separated by a mere partition wall, they share the same spaces repeated along each corridor, they perform the

same movements at the same time, turning on a tap, flushing the water closet, switching on a light, laying the table, a few dozen simultaneous existences repeated from storey to storey, from building to building, from street to street. They entrench themselves in their domestic dwelling space – since that is what it is called ... *For all that passes, passes by the stairs, and all that comes, comes by the stairs*: letters, announcements of births, marriages, and deaths, furniture brought in or taken out by removers, the doctor called in an emergency, the traveler returning from a long voyage. *It's because of that that the staircase remains an anonymous, cold, and almost hostile place.* In old buildings there used to be stone steps, wrought iron hand rails, sculptures, lamp-holders, sometimes a bench to allow old folk to rest between floors. In modern buildings there are lifts with walls covered in would-be obscene graffiti, and so-called 'emergency' staircases in unrendered concrete, dirty and echoing.

Perec 1987: 3 (author's emphasis)

The two italicized assertions above are contrary; the first suggests all the humanity and human connection the staircase facilitates and witnesses, referring to the grand and central staircases of the nineteenth century; yet the second unexpectedly dismisses it as cold, lamenting the modern staircase relegated to hidden wells and used only on rare occasion. Perec is nostalgic for 'old buildings', whose staircases facilitate a slowing down, a giving time to notice one another. The modern staircase is shut away and forbidding. Yet *Life*'s nineteenth-century staircase 'declines in terms of middle-class respectability as it rises from floor-to-floor: two thicknesses of carpet as far as the third floor, thereafter only one, and none at all for the two attic floors' (Perec 1987: 4). Now the rooms on those top two floors, once used as servants' quarters, are merely apartments like any other, yet a vestige of social hierarchy remains: 'Even if there are people upstairs much richer than those downstairs, that does not prevent it being the case that from the point of view of downstairs people those upstairs people are somehow inferior' (Perec 1987, 214–15). The property of staircases made evident here is that while they may no longer determine class distinction, they still codify it.

Still, for Perec, the modern staircase represents a breakdown of the aforementioned collective existence, and he repeats this notion in 'The Apartment': 'We don't think enough about staircases. Nothing was more beautiful in an old house than the staircases. Nothing is uglier, colder, more hostile, meaner, in today's apartment buildings. We should learn to live more on staircases. But how?' (Perec 1998: 38). A staircase traces the passage from one space to another, while hidden neighbours can be heard from behind locked doors, living parallel but discrete lives. A flight of steps is a neutral site of interconnection only theoretically, as staircases signify the seams between these private apartments. To view the inhabitants all at once in their rooms is to see simultaneity and repetition of a sort that skews the possibility of seeing them as individuals. They may engage in similar activities, but because ensconced in different apartments, they are alienated one from the next. However, in Perec's idealized stairways, the exchanges that constitute life take place, which both offer a genuine sense of individuation, insofar as the participants act according to the law for the distribution of social positions, and, in turn, give us a picture of the whole.

Staircases, however, are not hallways – they do not connect rooms to one another. The function of a staircase, architecturally, is usually to transition subjects from storey to storey (as in landings), and thus analogically, in Perec's version, from story to story (as in narratives). The function is one of movement. It follows that Perec is drawing an analogy between the form and content of a novel and the form and function of architecture. Staircases – the transitional spaces, the much ignored entopic spaces – preserve the moments of individuals coming together, even passing one another by, and they show us the pattern of the whole well after the meeting has taken place, no matter how fleeting. One may examine individuals one by one in order to discern the structure of the whole, but they do not display the pattern or the law of their organization, except in those rare places or times where they coexist. For many of his Situationist contemporaries, such interactions would need to have happened on the street, but for Perec, they need to happen in places like the staircase.

Perec understands that staircases are not utopian places; passing by one's neighbours can be terrifying as well as communal. In the second stairs chapter, we are reminded that 'on the stairs the furtive shadows pass of all those who were there one day' (Perec 1987: 59); a staircase, after all, transports one up and across spatially and forward temporally, and its architecture can reflect a set of relations lived therein well beyond the time when those particular class relations hold, yet this being so will still occasionally determine a set of relations between individuals despite their efforts to live the contrary. For on the stairs are not only those who travel there, but everything they carry with them – memories, experiences, feelings: 'the stairs … were, on each floor, a memory, an emotion, something ancient and impalpable, something palpitating somewhere in the guttering flame of his memory: a gesture, a noise, a flicker' (Perec 1987: 61–2). When dimensions multiply, coexistence becomes uncanny. As such, the traces of living are not always tenable. The novel maintains a particular narrative thread, which for the most part constitutes the career of a rich eccentric puzzle-solver named Percy Bartlebooth, who has travelled the world to paint a series of 500 watercolours. Bartlebooth, perhaps the novel's most global figure, then commissions a sinister craftsman, Gaspard Winckler, to transform the paintings into complex jigsaw puzzles that he will later reassemble. Bartlebooth's strict game is another subversion of Situationist drifting, yet he is, perhaps, Perec's most explicit postcolonial figure, in that for all his travels, he does not really see the places he encounters but for anything other than the paintings he can make of them and the puzzles they can become. When Bartlebooth completes each puzzle, a special solvent will return it to its original state as a blank page. Time and its passing, event and consequence, climax and resolution, do not exist here. Bartlebooth dies before finishing his project; Valène's canvas, in the novel's final paragraph, is 'practically blank: a few charcoal lines had been carefully drawn, dividing it up into regular square boxes, the sketch of a cross-section of a block of flats which no figure, now, would ever come to inhabit' (Perec 1987: 500). In the end, all Valène leaves behind him is the very layout Perec used for the novel – a blank grid.

Perec, in this sense, acknowledges his own limitations as author and as architect: who can write a manual for life, after all? If this novel is, in essence, one about life and living, its intent is in part ironic. We learn at the beginning that what happens in the common areas are 'embryos of communal life which never go further than the landing' (Perec 1987: 3) – for all their adhesiveness, staircases rarely offer the convergence or emergence that they promise. Whether referring to the novel or society itself, Perec insists on the potential rather than the processed; he yearns for and embraces that which he cannot attain. The only way he knows how to establish the connection between domestic space in the novel and the space of the novel as such is through writing fiction. For Perec, both literary and social spaces are complex game boards, performative, not fixed. He considers literature as architectural – meta-phorically, as in we might find ourselves 'at home' in a novel, or more literally, in that the book object is another three-dimensional structure to inhabit. Yet traditional narrative, home, society and nation are all structures that no longer accommodate contemporary life. By subverting traditional narrative through literary experimenta-tion, Perec challenges the authority of these often uninhabitable structures and offers the architectural novel as an alternative space of imagination and possibility, propos-ing radical perspectives on – and sometimes solutions to – the uninhabitable.

Notes

1 In *Postmodernism or, The Cultural Logic of Late Capitalism,* Fredric Jameson famously argues that 'a certain spatial turn has often seemed to offer one of the more productive ways of distinguishing post modernism from modernism proper' (Jameson 1999: 154), implying that postmodernism privileges space even more aggressively than Joseph Frank claimed for modernism in 'The Idea of Spatial Form'.

2 At one point in the novel, Perec demonstrates this in the very writing on the page, with acrostics running diagonally like staircases.

3 The Oulipo is a France-based literary workshop known for designing constraints for generating literature, the idea being that when the author releases control over content, writing takes on an imaginative power otherwise impossible.

4 According to both David Bellos (1993) and John Sturrock (ed. *Species of Spaces and Other Pieces*), Raymond Queneau first used this type of bi-square to generate poetry; Oulipians thus call this constraint a 'quenine'.

5 See entry for '*Life A User's Manual*' in the *Oulipo Compendium* (Mathews 1998). Here, Perec gives his explanation for the construction of the novel. David Bellos also offers some useful information in *Perec* (Bellos 1993: 507–17).

6 Perec used the grid as a plan for several of his works; Motte (1984) parallels the gridding of *Life* with that of the project on which Perec was working when he died: *Les Lieux*

(The Places), wherein the novelist chose twelve Parisian locations that were personally significant and described two of them per month – the first he would write at the location itself, and the second he would describe from memory. Over twelve years (one year per place), each place would therefore be described twenty-four times, twelve from memory and twelve by what he called 'simultaneous description'. For *Les Lieux*, Perec used a bi-square of 12×12, with 144 elements with the result of 288 texts (Motte 1984: 830), each text signifying a moment of stasis within a particular geographic location – whether literally or imaginatively. *Les Lieux*'s grid is then, perhaps, a most extreme example of Perec's geometry, in that unlike in *Life*, the author is also character, moving across the city he describes like a knight across a chessboard. The knight's tour is then how an individual moves through society; Perec's grids are irrelevant without movement through them.

7 See Mathews (1998).

8 My thanks go to Erik Ghenoiu at Pratt Institute for pointing out to me that even the building itself, described as a nineteenth-century Hausmannian structure, is impossible: it has seven storeys, two attics and a basement, whereas a 'proper' building of the time, before lifts became common and also to keep with the city's rooflines, would never have reached above seven (including the attics). Perec's plan abides by the Oulipian quenine, however – reality was of little concern.

9 Perec's interest in the 'ordinary' underlies all of his writings on interior space. He opens his essay '*L'Infra-ordinaire*', his manifesto of sorts on the vitality of the quotidian, with:

> What speaks to us, seemingly, is always the big event, the untoward, the extraordinary ... [but] let's not leave out the essential: the truly intolerable, the truly inadmissible. 'Social problems' aren't 'a matter of concern' when there's a strike, they are intolerable twenty-four hours out of twenty-four ... How should we take account of ... the banal, the quotidian, the common, ... the habitual? To question the habitual. ... We sleep through our lives in a dreamless sleep. But where is our life? Where is our body? Where is our space? (Perec 1998: 209–10).

References

Bellos, D. (1993) *Georges Perec: A Life in Words*, Boston: David R. Godine Publisher.

Benjamin, W. (1978) 'Paris, Capital of the Nineteenth Century', in P. Demetz (ed.) *Reflections*, New York: Schocken Books.

Jameson, F. (1999) *Postmodernism or, The Cultural Logic of Late Capitalism*, Durham: Duke University Press.

Krauss, R. (1979) 'Grids', *October*, 9: 50–64.

McHale, B. (1987) *Postmodernist Fiction*, London: Routledge.

Mathews, H. (ed) (1998) *Oulipo Compendium*, London: Atlas.

Motte, Warren F. (1984) 'Georges Perec on the Grid', *The French Review*, 57.6: 820–32.

Perec, G. (1987) *Life A User's Manual*, trans. D. Bellos, Boston: David R. Godine Publisher.

Perec, G. (1998) *Species of Spaces and Other Pieces*, ed. and trans. J. Sturrock, New York: Penguin Books.

Ross, K. (1996) *Fast Cars, Clean Bodies: Decolonization and the Reordering of French Culture*, Cambridge, MA: An October Book, MIT Press.

12

SEX HAPPENS

A phenomenological reading of the casual encounter

Renée Tobe

As we read, we gather together our knowledge and experience and we picture the situation and surroundings sketched out in writing. We picture a world not there, rendered in words as 'experience'; the act of reading sustains these conflicting conditions. Memory and sensuality are intertwined with the settings in which particular events not only transpire or in which they are remembered to have happened, but also in which they might be imagined to take place. We enter the world through the boundary between our imaginations and the given world and phenomenology provides the language or means to describe it. It also helps us to understand the role of architecture in this discussion. Reading combines mimetically the mystery of language with architecture's unique capacity to signify order (Pérez Gómez 2006). The phenomenological discussion implies spatial awareness and a 'there' brought to life in words. We get 'lost' in a novel, not because the words, grammar or structure confuse us, but rather the opposite; the world of the novel is such an ordered, formal and deeply comprehensible 'place' that we have lost, for the moment, connection with the physical world around us.

Two contemporary volumes, *The Sexual Life of Catherine M.* by Catherine Millet and *Tricks: Twenty-Five Encounters* by Renaud Camus, focus on explicit descriptions of casual sex (Millet 2001; Camus 1981). The spatial evocations of the locales in which the events take place include public parks, bedrooms, night clubs, circulation spaces and thresholds such as staircases and doorways. Conjuring up images of what locations are like, whether inviting or claustrophobic, bright or ill-lit, relies on the reader's imagination and our lived experience grounds us in the writer's world. Expressions of architectural form in literature disclose peculiarities of spatial experience, such as how small is small, how dark is dark, or how open is open. One person's experience of an intimate corner is another's claustrophobic enclosure, so

FIGURE 12.1 'Our movements took up no more space than our tightly joined bodies. The light went back on again two or three times. In the intervals between it was as if the darkness were hiding us (…)' (Millet 2001: 118)

that Millet's description of an area that needs to be only large enough to enclose two bodies together, offers a vast range of imaginative possibilities depending on each reader's experience and preference. Camus describes a room where he often takes his tricks, but prefers not to spend the night, as unwelcoming: the bed is cold, there is no hot water, and no shade for the lamp. Architects' intentions are to design appropriate settings for designated events utilising both quantitative and qualitative predetermined criteria. By contrast, literature creates these events in the imagination in as many different ways as there are readers.

Form, purpose and structure are inherent in how architects 'plan' buildings. Casual sex implies connections that are unplanned, formless, capricious or unsorted and correspond to the circulation spaces that often provide a location for these expeditious activities. Similarities between primary areas (such as bedrooms, kitchens, boardrooms or galleries) and our relation to them and the sensual experience of the world, find themselves mirrored in the correspondence between the supporting ones (such as circulation spaces, hallways, stairwells, doorways, closets or storage areas) and Millet's and Camus' promiscuous, and sometimes random, couplings that take place there. These auxiliary places include a maid's room, a *chambre de bonne*, rooms that occupy the top floor of Parisian apartment houses. Museums preserve and display artworks and artefacts for public consumption, but Millet excludes descriptions of formal exhibition halls in favour of the supporting regions. It is as if these actions, that are in between the authors' primary identities as writer, in Camus' case, or art critic, in Millet's, can only take place in 'in-between' spaces.

Similarities and differences

In their writing, Millet and Camus both question the distinction between public and private environments and through the act of reading, summon the hidden inner world of the reader's imagination. Other similarities include the manner in which the writers examine the spaces in which their brief encounters take place. Both writers reference cinema, mentioning films that all reference sexual power games and include *Le Mépris* (Jean-Luc Godard, 1963), *Belle du Jour* (Luis Buñuel, 1967) and *La Collectionneuse* (Eric Rohmer, 1967). Both writers write in the first person, although, as Millet suggests, to write in the first person turns the narrator into the third person (Millet 2001: 156). Just as we look at text on a page, a collection of familiar letters arranged and rearranged in sometimes familiar and sometimes foreign combinations, which we form into a narrative, both authors assemble a multitude of lovers, body parts, places and observations to construct a complete image of a whole world.

Although each author explains what, for them, constitutes a casual encounter, these explanations are as distinct as their styles of writing. For Millet names, physical appearance and even cleanliness are entirely unimportant. Her focus is on body parts: hers, and others, how they connect, and where. She never has sex with men whom she meets accidentally in toilets or on public transportation and discourages the men who approach her in these places. She prefers arranged meetings by telephone, even if she has not previously met the person, as her predilections are well known, and she often meets interested men at parties. Her preference is to get together with a man to whom she has been suggested by another.

By contrast, Camus's lovers almost always have a name, or at least a signifying nomenclature, such as 'plaid shirt' or 'the cowboy'. Each chapter describes an individual, their personality, where they are from, as well as their physical characteristics. Camus is clear as to what constitutes a trick: the person must be previously unknown to the author, although they may later form an acquaintance or friendship. He suggests that the introduction to someone new is what constitutes the narrative.

Camus and Millet both have long-term relationships. Camus introduces his partner with a jealous and possessive 'Tony? *My* Tony?' (Camus 1981: 9). Other similarities include the explicit language used to describe each physical detail in such a way that the external world, beyond that which is touched by the body, evaporates from our consciousness. The book explicates the sexual acts while the use of language implies spatial consent as if the places described are present expressly to gratify the pursuit of pleasure. Millet calls to mind Michel Foucault who argues for the emancipatory power of the pleasure principle to be found in heterotopias, the privileged, sacred or forbidden places that are gifted with meaning by the activities that take place there (Foucault 1984). As Foucault suggests, sexual activity and sexual pleasures initiate the aesthetics of existence and to keep pleasure undimmed desire must be satisfied (Foucault 1985: 55–6). Physical intimacy implies spatial proximity and a sense of enclosure. As we, the readers, imagine the activity described in the text, our spatial imagination converges with our knowledge, memory, feeling and understanding of being in the world. The intimate acts at public locales provide spatial analogies that demonstrate how our spatial imagination converges with our presence in the world. Millet concludes with a discussion of the body and the image, while Camus' clever use of literary interruption and *mise en abyme* illustrates the actuality of the encounters in metaphor. A description of sexual congress in public spaces presents a means to 'measure' or compare by contrasting that which is designed for public use, but explored here through sex, and includes bare skin exposed out of doors, two bodies pressed together on a stair landing or threshold, or a gap in a hedge.

The written works of Georges Bataille and Roland Barthes inform these two texts. Without explicitly referencing a specific novel Millet suggests that in their youthful zeal she and her friends 'found a ready made philosophy reading Bataille' (Millet 2001: 38). In Trick Sixteen, 'Albert le Quebecois', Camus uses a note taken at a seminar by Barthes he attended the previous winter to describe the 'delicate insignificance' of the encounter (Camus 1987: 94). In Trick Twenty Three, 'Jeremy', Camus explains to his trick that Barthes reminds us that 'there was something else in writing which was precious, which had to be preserved at all costs,

FIGURE 12.2 'In that dark storeroom with my body bent double between two other bodies and my eyes staring vertically down, I was well hemmed in.' (Millet 2001: 68)

and which was pleasure' (Camus 1979: 224). Both texts proffer Marquis de Sade as silent companion because, as Barthes (who wrote the introduction to Camus' novel) suggests, 'Sade laid the foundation for all erotic narrative' (Barthes 1979: 124). Millet's suggestion that there is a pleasure in telling suggests the foreplay of the prefix in the words discourse and intercourse. Her intercourse is also her discourse with the world.

We relish 'reality' while our imaginations fill in the details of the scenes presented, in which we, the readers, may take our place. According to Barthes, the reader takes pleasure in representations of daily life and the satisfied curiosity of the kind of small details that both Millet and Camus describe. Their text is sparse, detailing their physical activities, and each takes the time to describe the places where the clothing as well as the activities come off. Millet, an art critic, examines how the space around us relates to our bodies and ourselves. Camus details how the rooms are furnished, and where they are, what they are like spatially, before describing the activities that occur within. While Camus' encounters all take place in a single year, and are carefully dated and told chronologically, Millet's narrative moves back and forth in time. Sometimes the same 'episode' appears in different places to illustrate different concepts, such as freedom, or out of doors, or interior décor. Camus' daily life seems relaxed, and unstructured; he sleeps late and rarely has to be anywhere at any particular time, but his book is an ordered, organised, methodical 'list'. Millet's writing is more discursive, occasionally seeming somewhat random, although she writes that she likes lists, and creates them.

Millet's *La vie sexuelle de Catherine M*

Millet is an art writer, and founder and editor of *art press*, an art critical journal. In her personal novel she takes us, the readers, from abstraction to the fully dimensional world we create for ourselves. After climbing as she describes, through the picture frame into the world depicted on the other side, we crawl into niches, gather our intimacy around ourselves and linger in forgotten corners.

Millet's literary text takes us from the immeasurably large to the fragment. Written more than ten years after her book, *the art critic exposed*, Millet describes her sexual activities with not only a directness of language, but with the language of the art critic. Her book is structured as an architect devises a plan and section, from the universal to the particular. The sections begin with 'Numbers', where individuals and activities are subsumed in categories, followed by 'Space', then 'Confined space' and then 'Details', as if moving from an art listing of what happened and where, to the Renaissance perspective discovery of 'space' through representations of architecture and enclosure, and resolving with the feminist art historical theory that depictions of women represent them 'cut up' into body parts.

Each chapter draws to its conclusion with a discussion that introduces the subject of the next chapter. Thus, 'Numbers' ends with a discussion of wide open

FIGURE 12.3 'As soon as it had been decided that we would go home together, I regretted this choice.' (Camus 1981: 97)

spaces and distances. The chapter on 'Space' concludes with a discussion of hidden spaces, of being in bed with the sheet pulled up over Millet's head and of flimsy partitions; the subject of the next chapter, 'Confined space' which itself finishes with an image of hips, thighs and tongue, the body parts that insert themselves into and in-between others.

Numbers

In the opening chapter, Millet references the very book she writes. 'Would I ever,' she asks, 'have thought of writing this book which opens with a chapter called "Numbers" if I had not once experienced being a minute satellite which suddenly left the orbit where it had been held by a whole network of connections (…)?' (Millet 2001: 69) Later, she suggests that were she ever to write a novel about her life it would have to be called *The Sexual Life of Catherine M.* (Millet 2001: 71). Millet's novel opens not unlike other personal narratives, with a memory of her childhood. 'As a child I thought about numbers a great deal,' she begins, and then continues to discuss unknown quantities, and enlarges on other, even larger questions, about God as an overwhelming if invisible presence, before promptly relating in detail a story about getting a venereal disease. The sudden introduction of the 'clap' is like a thunderclap that brings us abruptly to reality from these abstractions and affirms the sexual persona that underpins both this network of numbers and this narrative.

'Numbers' includes first times (implying there are many), and the pleasure of telling by which each experience is repeated. Although she takes pleasure in communities, both artists' networks and the sex community, Millet looks forward to an evening alone curled up on a comfortable armchair: 'There is something delicious about those moments when the emptiness around you opens up not only the space around you but also, somehow, the enormity of the time ahead' (Millet 2001: 46). For Millet, the expanse of space is required only for her gaze; to draw her in, or out of herself.

Millet describes her desire to always be somewhere else once she arrives in a particular location. She openly employs metonymic metaphors for space, place and sex. For example, she proffers the phrase 'having it away' as metaphor for the act of sex, and moving in space or travelling. The final paragraph of 'Numbers' also suggests her wish for new, or rapidly multiplying, experiences:

> On a walk I hate coming back the same way that I set out. I study maps in minute detail to find a new way of getting to some piece of countryside, an edifice or a curiosity I haven't yet seen. When I went to Australia the furthest I could get from home on this earth, I realised that my perception of this distance could be compared to the concept of having no sexual barriers.
>
> *Millet 2001: 72*

Space open and closed

The chapter 'Space' begins with an account of why art historians analyse space represented in painting and suggests the notion of *abyme*, the gulf of paradox and the description of the spaces of the imagination, where space unfolds endlessly. In Millet's description:

> Surely someone ought to write a study of the reasons why, during the course of their careers, eminent art historians (...) have focused increasingly on architecture? How did their analysis of the space represented in a painting mutate into an analysis of the way real space is organised? In my role as an art critic I might have felt more inclined to follow their example if I had not come across modern and contemporary pictorial works which could be said to inhabit the cusp between an imaginary space and the space in which we live, be they Barnett Newman's vast coloured expanses (Newman himself said: 'I declare space'), the radiant blues in the work of Yves Klein (who called himself the 'painter of space'), or even Alain Jacquet's topological surfaces and objects which juxtapose paradoxical abysses. What characterises these works is not the fact they open space up, but that they both open and seal it – Newman with his closing zips, Klein by crushing his anthropometric forms, Jacquet by binding the ends of Mobius's ring. If you allow yourself to be led, it's like the boundless inner surface of a lung.
>
> *Millet 2001: 75*

Immediately after this introduction that purports to instruct us on the different means by which we expose and express the unfolding spatial imagination of artist, writer and architect, Millet plunges into the Bois de Boulogne, where men and women meet to engage in intended and easygoing, sexual congress.

Millet contrasts the countryside and the city. The former she describes as enticing, where the open air penetrates and embraces her body. She experiences the vastness of the world as adhering to the surface of her skin like a 'myriad tiny suction pads' (Millet 2001: 92). Natural spaces do not fuel in Millet the same fantasies as urban spaces, which are, by definition, social spaces and presuppose the presence of others (Millet 2001: 115). The city is a 'territory in which we express a desire to transgress codes with our exhibitionistic/voyeuristic impulses; it presupposes the presence of others (...)' (Millet 2001: 80). Millet also introduces Marc Augé's idea of non-places where she describes:

> (...) terraces, roadsides, stretches of open country, and in any space designed merely to be crossed, such as concourses and car parks, all of these are places (or non-places as Marc Augé calls them) where it feels good to me to follow their example and be open.
>
> *Millet 2001: 81*

FIGURE 12.4 'When he came back, I was lying on the bed, my shoes and socks off. He sat down beside me.' (Camus 1981: 72)

Non-places include parking lots, where people come and go, but also the *portes* of Paris, gates through which one would enter the medieval boundaries of the city, but which for Millet lead outwards beyond the periphery.

Millet suggests that phenomenology and the primacy it affords to perception enables us to look at the 'empty' or 'bare' space of modernity, where ornament is considered a crime, or what she refers to as *'l'espace nue'*. She describes a 'sparse interior that would make a Quaker feel at home' (Millet 2001: 67). She visits a flat with 'furniture arranged like a painting by Mondrian', where carpet, wardrobe and bed are one continuous unit with homogenous proportions. She prefers the large rooms of Italian apartments where the furniture looks out of scale so that the space enlarges around it and around her. She experiences these high-ceilinged rooms voluptuously.

Being out-of-doors plays an important role in the text's conception of space. In descriptions of open-air intimacy, Millet evokes what she describes as the 'rules in paradise, harmony between humans and nature' (Millet 2001:120). Millet's out-door encounters generally take place in the daytime when she can meditate on the unfolding hills fading away in the distance, the smells, the feeling of the movement of air, and distant lights from a village. The fresh air caresses her like a lover, sur-rounding her in the sense of the French term: *plein air* or the full of the air. *Plein air* may be translated as open space or an area that is 'full' of space. Millet appropriates this space for herself (Millet 2001: 150). For Millet, rubbing up against the anony-mous space is like rubbing up against anonymous men.

Enclosed space

'Confined space' (in French it is literally enfolded space) begins with a section entitled 'A variety of havens' in English, but *'divers niches'* in French, which evokes more intimately the hidden recesses of her own body. The next section, entitled 'Illness, dirt', suggests that in a confined area the body knows a fulfilment inversely proportional to the available space, while the following section, 'In the office', expounds on the pleasure of mixing personal acts in the space of generalised oth-ers. Generalised others, a phrase from sociology, represent the implied or learned norms that prevent us from acting in a manner a particular society would deem inappropriate, or as Millet might describe, confined. This chapter on the con-strained includes a discussion of 'Taboos', and then, once these are broken, on 'Trusting'.

If 'space' is the open sky or desert, a confined space is 'seen almost as automati-cally as a filled space', as Millet suggests, referencing both of her own penetralia and the space occupied by two bodies together (Millet 2001: 124). As Bataille reminds us, the transgression of the cultural taboo is no less subject to rules as the taboo itself (Bataille 1987: 65). Millet describes one such transgression, sex in the conjugal bed (Millet 2001:158). Before describing what she was doing or where, she describes her partner entering not only the large bourgeois apartment into which she has just moved with him, but specifically the 'spare room' or, in French, the 'friend's room' next to the entrance where she is *in flagrante*. This sentence offers a great deal for our investigation: the use of the word *penetra* to enter the 'friend's' room, next to the entrance, where a friend is penetrating her, and into which her partner immediately 'penetrates'. Furthermore it is an apartment into which she has just moved and so she is not yet 'at home' there. The erotic encounter transmutes the 'there' of the unknown space to the 'here' of where we are at home. She never states how long they stayed or if she ever did feel at home there.

The chapter *L'espace replié* is translated into English as 'confined space', and in English this word, 'confined', has a suggestion of restraint while in the original French text many other, more evocative words are used.[1] The title, *replié*, implies folded up, or tucked in, suggesting Freudian overtones, as well as the Deleuzian fold that brings disparate things together. In this chapter she describes a tiny, demanding space in which four to five people are brought together in a niche, or tiny apartment alcove. Other enclosed spaces include train compartments, peep shows, secrecy, hiddenness and privacy.

One of the enclosed spaces is a staircase in an apartment block on boulevard Exelmans. This occurs during *l'heure de voleurs* or, in the English translation, the 'witching hour when thieves are out' (Millet 2001: 158). This is an elaborate tale that is related over three pages although we are told that the action itself only took as much space as two bodies together. This *mise en scène* is not one continuous motion, but, like the pumping of the fellatio she describes, stops and starts with the light of the stairwell going on and off.

The section 'In the office' contrasts opposites of private and public space, between cultural and useful space, and the space of leisure and that of formal employment (Foucault 1984). Having sex the maximum number of times in the most familiar of spaces, her workplace, stitches together the interior and the exterior of her body (Millet 2001: 127). She likes the atmosphere of the deserted office after work has ceased, where intimate space and public space converge and she can eroticise the topography of the workplace, or as Millet describes 'laying out the markers of a sexual territory within a professional location' (Millet 2001: 128). As Bernard Tschumi also suggests, even the most rational buildings can be overcome with sensuality (Tschumi 1979).

This section also contains many of the taboo activities that restrict our actions and certainty (the discussion of the sex in the spare room and the partner walking in). In the section 'Trust', Millet suggests that she must trust her lover's gaze. In this longest episode of the novel, Millet walks naked in the cemetery where Walter Benjamin is buried at Port Bou, on the border between Spain and France. She poses naked for her photographer partner Jacques. She describes entering this picturesque town, where the train station opens onto a little terrace 'graced by a fountain' (Millet 2001: 139). As she walks through the terrace of the cemetery she

FIGURE 12.5 'I no longer remember clearly our first exchange of glances. But there were quite a lot of them, I remember that – several accompanied by a faint smile.' (Camus 1981: 56)

describes the ambiguous space between the horizon and the photographic lens. Millet compares the photographer's gaze to an 'opaque and transparent veil' that clothes her nude body in open spaces, while the lens of the camera itself holds her back from the edge of the cliff. Even the notion of a cemetery is ambiguous in that it is both profoundly private yet also a place for locals to stroll.

Millet's novel is laced with suggestive verbs, from 'open' and 'closed' to references to gates in Paris (as synonymous with bodily entry points), thresholds and penetration. The suggestive metaphors of 'stuffed' or 'filled' spaces connect Millet's body with the world around her as in Maurice Merleau-Ponty's body–world duality. 'Space rarely opens up to us in one go,' she states, suggesting the slow raising of a curtain in the theatre. Our relation with the world around us informs (in the language of both Bataille and Merleau-Ponty) our own sense of self. Millet describes this as the union of time and space that form a perfect architecture (Millet 2001: 122). The result is that she both brings the whole world into her body, and the experiences of her body into the whole world.

Camus' *Tricks: Twenty-Five Encounters*

In 1978, during an era that marked a break from the rigours of modernism, one year after Richard Rogers and Renzo Piano's Pompidou Centre was completed, and seven years after artist Vito Acconci linked life, the body and art by masturbating in public, French writer Renaud Camus described the dark alleys, obscure woodlands, shadowy hillsides and backrooms where men meet one another for sex. Over six months Camus attempted to write down every single casual sexual encounter. The English translation reduces the original thirty-three tricks to twenty-five (Camus 1981). The chapters which were removed contained the hardcore tales in the baths, and the references to 'fuck rooms'. In the intervening years, since the publication of the first edition in 1979, Camus included twelve more encounters that were published in the second edition of 1982, bringing the total number of tricks to forty-five (Camus 1987). However, all of these additions are excluded in the English version of the text.

Camus establishes a set structure for each trick. Each *récit* begins with the date, an introduction, a first view, a conversation, leading to a detailed description of the sexual encounter that comes to a climax (or several climaxes), before reaching a conclusion. Barthes suggests that we do not read to find out how the story ends, since we know how it ends (Barthes 1977: 163). His 'death' of the author takes on new meaning with the orgasm that provides the climax of each story after which the *dénoument* brings it to a close. Occasionally one trick interrupts another in a *mise en abyme* like a different instrument playing the familiar leitmotif that runs through the novel from one refrain to the next. When Camus interrupts his story of one trick to tell about another, the narrator's voice is constantly being intruded upon, and intruding on, itself.

Camus' novel may be read as a Barthian 'tale within a tale' with inserts of other stories 'penetrating' into others, while the story goes back and forth in a purely Barthian manner. There are many 'voices' although each is Camus' own: the tale itself, his commentary after it, and the interruptions. Interjections are in italics between square brackets to signify the different 'voice'. For example, in Trick Fourteen, 'Jean-Marc Laroque', a long introduction about meeting the trick in Cannes is interrupted with a comment on how he has just telephoned while the author was writing those words. Some pages later, another interjection, again signified with italics between square brackets, tells us that Camus is writing two weeks after the encounter and that Trick Sixteen (whose name is Walter) has just stepped out of the bath and walked naked in front of him to sit on the terrace. There are so many interruptions (often in the middle of a sentence), that the italics must alternate with plain text to signify Camus's 'voice', each with square brackets to show that it is an interjection. In one of the interruptions, Camus tells Trick Sixteen to stop interrupting as he is at work. From within yet another interruption comes a phone call from Jean-Marc Laroque himself, interrupting Camus' writing about him, or rather interrupting Camus' asking Walter to let him work so he can write about Laroque. By the end of these interruptions, we have three consecutive square brackets, to let us know we have once again returned to the main story.

> I went to piss and brush my teeth. Meanwhile, Jean-Marc undressed. [*Walter is now getting dressed. If I don't write this down immediately I'll forget that he's wearing a bright braided belt with tassels. (…).* [Interruption: he's getting dressed again after an absurd episode. He was leaving. I accompanied him to the door. He began kissing me. I told him to stop, [*Interruption: it's become a game. I repeat that I have to work. I am sitting at my desk: (…) The door is still open (…) and* [Interruption: new telephone call from Jean-Marc. Nothing special to tell me (…)] *noticing that I had an erection, he undid my fly, despite my protests (…) He sucked my cock while I was writing the previous page. (…)*] and that I had to work.]]
>
> *Camus 1981: 132*

The trick resolves itself, as do many others, with an explanation of whether or not Camus and the trick saw one another again, and an account of the next time they met Jean-Marc, when he interrupted Camus who was watching a film from which he could not tear himself away. The film is Marcel L'Herbier's *L'inhumaine* (1923). This story is of a 'man-eating' opera singer whose many lovers come to her villa, which is designed by Robert Mallet-Stevens and whose interiors are carefully crafted by designers whose work would feature in the 1925 *Paris exposition des arts decoratifs*. The comment that the film makes on modernity, as breaking free from restraints of the past, echoes Camus' own (Camus 1981: 122–46). The structure of the text evokes Tschumi's *Architecture and Disjunction* in which architectural

FIGURE 12.6 'You come into a very messy room. On a table to the right, in front of a window, are a lot of papers, scraps of writing, some crumpled up, unfolded letters, notes, memoranda, pencils, blotters, books lying open and face down, an ashtray overflowing with butts. At the far end, to the left, is a kitchen, the door ajar.' (Camus 1981: 46)

sequences presuppose an 'implied narrative … already there' as well as a dream space where stairways, halls and doors both open and closed, constantly insert themselves in one's path (Tschumi 1996: 162).

The maid's room

Camus describes the back rooms, bedrooms, the garden shed and the shadows of the bushes, as containers for the activities that took place within. His prose lingers around places, streets, outside the club, the bar, the smoky dance floor, and he simultaneously explores how memory and sensuality intertwine. The friction sparks not just erotic desire but boundaries between inside and outside, home and away, visible and imagined, the cold light of morning in the question: will you spend the night?

Camus' domestic situation unfolds with his tricks. The 'maid's room', which belongs to a friend but he is permitted to use, remains the central character from the beginning of Camus' novel when he mentions it to Trick One, Walthère Dumas. It's not luxurious, he says, and one doesn't like to spend the night there. All this detail is clearly delineated in the first trick so that he has set the *mise en scène*. They then set off to Dumas's large studio flat, described as sparsely furnished, modern, containing nothing 'actively ugly' (Camus 1981: 4).

In Trick Two, we see that the maid's room is on rue Saint-Simon and that one must climb seven or eight flights of stairs to get there. 'We walked through the lobby of the building in the Rue Saint-Simon, the courtyard, and started to climb the service stairs. I'm sorry, it's always like this with maid's rooms. There's a long way to climb' (Camus 1982: 17). He relates this information to Trick Two, Philippe of the Commandos. The heating is not on, the sheets are cold, and the WC is in the communal hallway.

In Trick Three, he goes to a modern apartment furnished in a rococo Louis XV style complete with a copy of a tapestry from the same era, and the reader easily infers his distaste. Camus takes Trick Nine, Maurice, to the flat on the Rue du Bac that he shares with Tony. On the walls are a drawing by Cy Twombly, a *Dollar Bill* print by Andy Warhol, and some framed text by Gilbert and George, with whom he dines at their home on Fournier Street in Trick Sixteen (Camus 1981: 86; Camus 1987: 94). Later, during a trick in Italy, he expresses scorn for the velvet flock wallpaper, and kitsch gold frames for Romantic landscape prints on the walls of a Milanese apartment in a modern block. Camus' spatial evocations are anything but arbitrary; instead, they are the means by which he slowly introduces himself to the reader. We get to know Camus as we are introduced to his spaces. We read his views on modernity, his home, his taste.

The names of the bars and saunas that he frequents reflect his attitudes towards his environment. In Paris, the bar he frequents the most is the Manhattan and the sauna he visits is the Continental. The descriptions of the Continental evoke Jean

Baudrillard's space of seduction, the space between desire and the object of desire that must be crossed. In the Continental, a short passage through which one must pass to get from room to room offers opportunities to press up against others as well as to see who is arriving, since it contains the only dim blue light in otherwise darkened corners.

Sometimes, although he prefers to go to bed with his tricks, no bed is available. For example, in Trick Nineteen, Camus meets a man, Jim, at a bar. 'I would have liked to go to his place, but he did not invite me. He would have liked to go to mine, which was impossible' (Camus 1981: 193). They retreat to 'a recess formed by a door that opened onto the street' into which a little air managed to enter, freshening the smothering atmosphere around them (Camus 1981: 193).

Describing a trick in Cannes, Camus writes that he touches briefly, but profoundly, on our encounter with place as he 'walks' the reader through a square, by the sea, along walls and passages, and evokes feelings of danger when the way is blocked in a subterranean passage to the beach. A large person blocks the light, someone else stands at the other end and then suddenly unease and the feeling of entrapment turns to a caress. We, the readers, picture the square, the beach, the boulevard along the sea, but only when we encounter others there do we enter Camus' world (Camus 1987). Camus lays out possible options of which we can choose one or another as the relation between reader and writer. As Foucault describes, '[t]he space of our primary perception, the space of our dreams and that of our passions hold within themselves qualities that seem intrinsic' (Foucault 1984). Only by traversing these intrinsic qualities of space described poetically in our imaginations, do we ground ourselves in the textual description.

Conclusion

The construction of space is dependent on our understanding of the commonplace, a word which indicates the importance of location. Places are described subjectively as they are experienced in these texts. They are 'spaces of participation', and the descriptions are not 'erotic', or metaphorical; these places, although often well detailed, are prosaic. One senses there is not a curved wall or satin sheet in all their sexual experiences. In fact, as Camus describes, the changing of cold sheets in the maid's bed each time he visits, sleeping in the 'wet spot' or the overhanging light that his tricks try to make more atmospheric by draping cloth over it, and the very unromantic sun that shines in the window each morning, define his tricks. The architectural contribution in textual descriptions provides both 'background' meaning spatial configuration, and 'background' meaning the claims of everyday life.

Neither writer portrays their experiences in terms of longing or sensuality. Millet likens an approaching anonymous group encounter to an approaching conference and anticipates it with the same apprehensions and feelings of relief when it

FIGURE 12.7 'Early one afternoon Claude came home to the apartment
– a big bourgeois apartment we had just moved into – and
into the spare bedroom near the front door. He interrupted a
copulation that I had been unable to resist.' (Millet 2001: 132)

is over. Camus has a horror of eroticism. His book, he claims, provides a picture of a 'particular aspect of a specific existence', one that exists in a defined time (Camus 1981: foreword). Other writers spatially evoke the erotic: Pérez-Gómez, Luce Irigaray and Hélène Cixous in their descriptions evoke the sensuality of the caress, and the seduction of the imagination. Millet and Camus avoid these references: their descriptions primarily describe emotionless sexual contact, but nonetheless evoke spatial responses and spatial description. Even in *plein air* they are 'caressed' by the breeze, and their bodies, whether alone or intertwined, are constantly aware of the surroundings. Millet concludes with a discussion of the body and the image, while Camus' text ends in Exile, the name of the bar in which he is tricking.

Camus' descriptions of the street, the stair, the WC, the maid's room, the cold sheets of the bed are a parody of Nicolas Camus de Mézieres' carefully composed, sensuous rendition of the architectural seduction (Pelletier 2007: 94). Millet's many words for enclosed space evoke her own gender and Camus' cut up text is a metaphor of penetration. Like Camus' text, Millet's novel offers a similar stroll through favourite haunts and a description of atmosphere as boundary, letting action unfold or providing a stage or foundation on which it can take place.

Neither Millet's nor Camus' textual descriptions of architecture are examples of Jean Baudrillard's desire, the space in-between, nor of Barthes' seduction, the text that can lead one astray. Both writers engage architecture as real spaces where events took place, yet places are described subjectively. In more than one place, Millet describes both her adventures and fantasies (which converge) as unrolling like a film. She frames things in her mind, cinematically setting the *mise en scène*.

Millet's professional writing looks at space in art, and at utopian spaces, as well as the blank spaces in abstract art, the white on white, and the spaces in-between found in Barnett Newman's paintings. She suggests that phenomenology and the primacy it accords to perception is a real panacea for theorists of modern art and criticises those who reduce art to a simple function of communication that theorists turn into an equation. Jean-Luc Marion's *Le phénomène érotique,* which expounds on Merleau-Ponty's body–world duality, enables us to interpret the relationship between architecture and ourselves in order to find points of contact between ethics and poetics, that is, interposed, or mediating between what we feel is right morally and what we feel is right linguistically, visually or materially (Marion 2007: 129). Both writers utilise the objectivity of Cartesian coordinates to reference the subjectivity of the narrator's position with that of the other or others: up, down, to the left, the right, face to face, across from one another, below, above. The activity is described in these terms of movement in space and by reference of where one body is situated in regard to another. One person is 'here', while the other 'over there'. The transformative experience of ethical action is analogous to the actuality of the encounters in metaphor. The narrators are true participants unlike the remote spectator.

If architecture may be explained it must also be experienced. Millet states that each home 'elicited a specific way of looking at it' (Millet 2001: 99). For example, an architect friend with a *pied à terre* on the top face of a new building on the rue Saint Jacques on Rive Gauche, is so high up that the view from the bed is directly into the sky. While Millet's novel both moves from place to place and from one person or body part to another, or several, and Camus carefully explains each Trick individually, both expound on our experience of the world through our bodies.

The spatial directionality of up/down, in front/behind, makes sense if we project ourselves into the positions described. We, and our experience of the world, cannot be separated from our bodies, nor one body part from another (Merleau-Ponty 1962: 154–73). As Merleau-Ponty suggests, the unified experiences of the senses and perception take the body parts detailed by Millet such as mouth, legs, waist, thighs, cunt, cock, buttocks, and combine them into the reciprocity between our bodies, movement and the world. The world of our imaginations is limitless, expansive and directly related to our experiences. These are unfolded or explicated and what has been unfolded is then recapitulated (Dilthey 1985: 227). Taken together, each individual encounter through its ipseity constitutes a complete lived experience (Merleau-Ponty 1962: 233). Experience is both a noun and a verb, that is, both the completed event and the process of experiencing. It is an activity generated by a subject or that which happens 'to' the subject and echoes Millet's suggestion that we should be keen to put aside academic dogma and prejudice and enjoy life.

Note

1 *Si l'une des significations du mot 'espace' est le vide, si lorsqu'il est employé sans qualification il evoke priorétairement un ciel pur ou un desert, l'espace exigue est presque aussi automatiquement vue comme un espace plein* (Millet 2001: 155).

References

Barthes, R. (1977) *Image Music Text*, London: Fontana Paperbacks.
—— (1979) 'The Metaphor of the Eye' in G. Bataille, *Story of the Eye*, London: Penguin.
Bataille, G. (1987) *Eroticism*, London, Marion Boyars.
Camus, R. (1981) *Tricks: Twenty-Five Encounters*, London: Serpent's Tail.
—— (1987) *Tricks; 45 Récits,* Paris: Publishing House.
Dilthey, W. (1985) *Poetry and Experience; Selected Works, vol. V*, Princeton: Princeton University Press.
Foucault, M. (1984) 'Of Other Spaces' in *Diacritics vol. 16 no. 1*, Ithaca: Johns Hopkins Press.
—— (1985) *The Uses of Pleasure; The History of Sexuality vol. 2*, London: Penguin Books.
Marion, J. L. (2007) *Le phénomène érotique*, Paris, Flammarion.
Merleau-Ponty, M. (1962) *Phenomenology of Perception*, London: Routledge.
Millet, C. (1993) *Le Critique d'Art s'Expose*, Paris: Editions Jacqueline Chambion.
—— (2001) *The Sexual Life of Catherine M.*, London: Serpent's Tail.

Pelletier, L. (2007) 'Genius, Fiction and the Author in Architecture' in *Architecture and Authorship*, London: Black Dog Publishing.

Pérez Gómez, A. (2006) *Built Upon Love; Architectural Longing After Ethics and Aesthetics*, London: MIT Press.

Tschumi, B. (1979) *Architectural Manifestos*, London: The Architectural Association.

—— (1996) *Architecture and Disjunction*, London: MIT Press.

Photographs of Paris by Florence Falzone.

13

'THERE ARE DIFFERENT WAYS OF MAKING THE STREETS TELL'[1]

Narrative, urban space and orientation

Inga Bryden

In this essay I will investigate the notion that paths through the city can be thought of as stories as well as maps (de Certeau 1984). I will be looking at the intersections between representations of urban space in literature from the late twentieth century and the first decade of the twenty-first century (notably, an anthology of short stories concerned with European cities, and texts by Iain Sinclair and Jon McGregor) and cultural criticism, primarily cultural geography and architectural theory. The focus is on the concept of narrative as both construction and means of orientation, in relation to both the literary text and the urban landscape. How do writers construct the stories of the urban landscapes their characters inhabit, and what are the narrative aspects of architecture, or the architectural process? In discussing selected literary texts, I will consider the specific strategies which writers use to represent architecture and urban space; how they make their streets 'tell'. The key themes of the chapter are thus the connections between form and space, and structure and story. What are the connections between literary form and architectural form (or space) in these texts? In what ways do the structures of the texts reflect the construction of, and ideas about, the spaces the authors are writing about? Finally, what links the roles of the writer and the architect in the realisation of the narrative/form?

There is a strong tradition, in a western context, of representing (or attempting to represent) the city/urban space in literature, and a critical history of envisaging the city as a text, or in narrative terms. A passage from Robert Wilson's novel *Eureka Street* (1998), about Belfast, draws attention to this identification of streets with stories: 'Whether in the centre itself or the places in which people put their houses, the city's streets, like lights in neighbours' houses, are stories of the done, the desired, the suffered and unforgotten … The city is novel' (Wilson 1998:

215). Literary theory has long drawn on spatial terminology, such as structure and form. Indeed, structure is an architectural concept. In the realm of cultural geography there has been a more recent move away from the notion of space as an inert container to the sense of space as 'process', as something linear to be narrativised. Writing about space and place incorporates a more literary language, referring to composition, textuality and stories, as Maria Crossan points out (Crossan 2006: xi). Moreover, not only have cultural geographers been more inclined to study literary texts, they have, crucially for this discussion, shown a particular concern 'for recuperating the spatial practices and bodily performances that may be detected within them' (Scott 2004: 28). In other words, the materiality of the text is brought to the fore.

In contemporary urban literature particularly, and in urban theorising, there is also an acknowledgement of the impossibility of ever being able to fully represent a given city or capture the complexities of the 'urban experience' (characterised, where the western industrial city is concerned, as continuous movement, the rhythms of which shape the [inter]connections between bodies, space and architecture). 'Urban theorising can spend forever,' point out Steve Pile and Nigel Thrift, ' … reassembling fragments of the city, but cities continually resist a meta-narrative … any claims to "know" what exactly is going on' (Pile and Thrift 2000: 303). It is the fragments (of buildings, memories) of the city which writers work with in attempting to assemble a narrative which makes some sense of those shards.

One aspect of the fragmented, polyvalent nature of the city, and a common metaphor in urban literature, is of the city as a 'babble of allusions', both architectural and linguistic. The 'babble' is represented as frustrating the order of sequential, linear narrative. The writer Penelope Lively captures the sense of disorientation well in *City of the Mind* (1991) when Matthew and Alice negotiate Charing Cross Road:

> all chronology [is] subsumed into the distortions and mutations of today, so that in the end what is visible and what is uttered are complimentary. The jumbled brick and stone of the city's landscape is a medley of style in which centuries and decades rub shoulders in a disorder that denies the sequence of time. Language takes up the theme, an arbitrary scatter of names
>
> *Lively 1991: 66*

As a site, then, of narrative and culture, the city is 'mobile … and monumental' (Tew 2004: 90). Given this, literary critics such as Philip Tew have argued that the contemporary city is represented predominantly as 'a world of multiple practical problems … fracturing or fractured relationships, and … inconsequentiality' (Tew 2004: 111). If this is the case, it suggests that narrative itself is necessary in order to make sense of the fractures in the edifice, perhaps becoming the sole means of linkage between fragments, or parts of the whole. Tew's assertion also raises the question of the need for orientation: for the reader of the text, the inhabitant of urban space and the visitor to the city. The challenge to writers to wrestle the city into a narrative form is more, though, than a question of reproducing topography or architectural features. Characters, their histories and their movement define urban space, as Wilson highlights: 'The men and women there are narratives ... And in the end, after generations ... the city itself begins to absorb narrative like a sponge, like paper absorbs ink ... The citizenry cannot fail to write there' (Wilson 1998: 215–16).

At this stage it is useful to consider further the extent to which the city is a text to be written, read and travelled through, as this reflects back on the literary representation of urban space. Roland Barthes argues that in understanding the city we must move beyond seeing spaces in terms of specialisation of functions (for example, the street as a homogenised unit) and 'decompose microstructures in the same way that we can isolate little fragments of phrases'. In this sense, 'The city is a writing. He who moves about the city, e.g. the user of the city (what we all are), is a kind of reader, who, following ... his movements, appropriates fragments ... ' Moving about a city gives the potential to 'find a different poem by changing a single line' (Barthes 1997: 170). In other words, narrative and the city offer potentiality; there are endless routes to take. As Peter Ackroyd has commented, the city 'is a form of literature in which the streets are the lines of a book which can never be completed' (Ackroyd 2001: 4).

What form, though, might the 'endless routes' take and what is the significance of the street? Streets as a system, a feature exaggerated on most maps, are 'the way maps become possible' (Harbison 2000: 126). However, cultural geographers (as well as sociologists) have drawn attention to what are termed 'desire paths': the use of unofficial routes, rather than devotion to 'cognitive mapping' (a phrase borrowed by urban theorists from experimental psychology) as a means of orientation (Tonkiss 2000). In this sense desire paths could be seen more as narratives of/through a city (regardless of whether or not it has already been mapped in the cartographic sense), and an acknowledgement that it is possible to know the city by working out a pattern, any pattern. Architecture clearly has a role in the literary representation of landmarks (buildings which themselves appear in conventional maps of cities), whereby characters may orientate themselves around a city.

However, cognitive mapping can also be understood as the process through which individuals orientate themselves in relation to society as a whole, as Fredric Jameson argues in *Postmodernism, or, The Cultural Logic of Late Capitalism* (1991). This social dimension to locating oneself is significant in relation to the literary texts discussed here, since characters, their histories, and the histories of communities or neighbourhoods define urban space. Perhaps most important for my argument is the notion that desire paths can refer simply to movement in urban space: the city 'houses a multitude of little spatial histories told by bodies moving within it' (Tonkiss 2000: 2). The narratives trace these everyday movements,

FIGURE 13.1 'Graffiti Route' (photo by the author)

which take place in relation to the built environment (interior and exterior spaces), though irrespective of whether routes have been mapped.

Crucial, then, to this investigation of writers' narration of urban space is the interaction between architectural forms and inhabitants; or, the extent to which one is prioritised representationally over another. I will now consider how urban space has been 'codified' by contemporary literary and cultural commentators (Lefebvre 1991: 269). Henri Lefebvre's concept of codification is concerned with the spatialities of representation, and more specifically, with the inseparability of space and social relations. This connects with the understanding of desire paths as 'spatial histories' as mentioned above. The writers discussed here use a range of strategies to represent architecture and urban space, or make their streets 'tell': describing topographical and architectural features (exteriors); focusing on characters, their histories and movements through space; prioritising walking as an aspect of psychogeography; highlighting perspective, or spatial epistemologies; describing microcosms or the interiors of buildings, and emphasising materialities.

It is the signifying space of the street itself which can be thought of as drawing these aspects of urban space together. The street is symbolic of collectivism – a communal space – whilst being made up of individual buildings and stories. It can also be expressed in terms of its materiality: the public space where detritus gathers and objects can be found as evidence of everyday culture. Significantly, the urban or suburban street is also liminal – the space where people pass through – and as such, is the starting point of narratives. In this conceptualisation, materiality (exteriors of buildings; objects found) is the clue to the hidden lives of others. Furthermore, as Ross King summarises, 'the street … promises freedom: anonymity, drifting, the cornucopia of displayed commodities, limitless contingency, boundless choice … ' (King 2000: 97). Ultimately, streets or roads offer potential;[2] they are 'wishes or proposals for journeys and demand to be travelled over' (Harbison 2000: 126).

Writers can exploit 'streetness' to highlight the narrative potential of urban space, whilst simultaneously emphasising the link between identity and place, between the individual and the social. Interestingly, 'streetness' in this sense became a generic convention in literary representations of London after the Great Fire of 1666. Cynthia Wall points out that as houses were being rebuilt and lived in again, 'the literature repeopled the streets, filling in those blank spaces' and literary characters' identities became increasingly constructed by place. Moreover, characters are 'more determined to construct their own or others' identities from place (or series of places)' (Wall 1998: 115–16).

The street as a locus for the urban encounter and the epiphanic moment (or revelation of character) is particularly in evidence in the contemporary urban short story. Indeed, numerous critics have observed that the city and the short story, as opposed to other narrative forms, are 'apposite bookfellows' (Crossan 2006: x). This is because successful short stories don't aspire to completeness and admit that the insight they provide is fragmentary and momentary, echoing the acknowledgement by writers and urban commentators that a city is always a 'work in progress'. Ian Reid (1977) draws an analogy specifically with architecture when he refers to the short story's symmetry and unity of effect.

Decapolis (2006), edited by Maria Crossan, is an anthology of stories from ten European cities. The aim of the anthology is not to provide direct entry for the reader into the streets of named cities, but rather to construct a series of 'city-like experiences' (Crossan 2006: ix). Nine of the stories are translated into English, which means that access to these imaginatively constructed cities is further compromised by language. Translatability seems curiously appropriate for the subject matter, though, if we acknowledge that 'the architecture of the text that we encounter' is removed to a degree (Crossan 2006: viii). There is a seeming incompatibility between the often spontaneous nature of the urban experience – for example, the element of chance – and the structured and crafted narratives which repeat such coincidences. Spaces and the people within them are not fixed, rather, suspended for the duration of each narrative. This concept is emphasised in the half-drawn outlines of maps of the countries where the cities are located, which are included at the start of each story.

The 'chance' of city living, notably 'the encounter' with a stranger, occurs in many of the stories in *Decapolis*. In David Constantine's 'The Beginning' (set in

Manchester), the adult narrator recalls his encounter with a girl, 'M', on the bus, and his first encounter with a dead body which is being pulled out of the river Irwell below. Later, waiting upstairs for the number 64 bus to depart from Victoria Bridge, he opens M's gift of Wilfred Owen poems. The moment is crystallised via the narrator's orientation of self in relation to landmarks – Telephone House, Exchange Station, the cathedral and the river Irwell – which can all be seen from his position, alone, in the space of the bus: 'I believe all behind me was empty space' (Constantine 2006: 5). From this perspective the narrator is able to watch the drowned man being hauled out of the river, whilst also watching the police-men on a platform fixed to the bridge watching the efforts of their colleagues below. Constantine uses perspective, through the placing of the narrator in relation to specific buildings and space at this point, to precipitate narrative. The narrator experiences a rush of 'questions' about his personal and family histories: the build-ings were significant in his grandmother's youth and, in the present, are the catalyst for him to 'collect up' his grandfather (who was blown to bits in the war) from his grandmother's 'bits of story' (Constantine 2006: 9).

As Robert Harbison points out, a writer can place particular buildings in a book 'in order to provide the scaffolding of automatic organization' (Harbison 2000: 74). Landmarks are also the means of orientation, structuring space and narrative, in the story 'A Man of the Streets' by Jacques Reda, which has resonances of Edgar Allen Poe's short story 'The Man of the Crowd' (1840). However, in using the device of walking around buildings and through streets, Reda draws on the earlier psycho-geographical tradition of navigating the city (Coverley 2006: 59–62). The paths of the businessman narrator and Georges Louis (an 'indigent' or beggar) – the daily, routine routes they take around Paris – intersect one day by chance. However, as the dynamic of the 'relationship' unfolds, based on an 'intimacy' of non-communication, the story highlights the different relation each man has to the streets of the city. Georges Louis could have found his way around the 'labyrinth of streets' with his eyes closed and has a strong awareness of the relative situation of landmarks. Driven by the dictates of his stomach everything is rendered of 'more or less equal interest'. By contrast, the narrator feels 'out of place', only a 'hypothetical being [like the oth-ers] … behind the silent stone and glass facades' (Reda 2006: 16).

Built structures are far more than urban 'backdrop', though, in the majority of stories in this anthology. A key concept defining *Decapolis* as a whole is that cities are in transition, and that buildings – their façades and interior spaces – can be read as evidence of the past living in the present. In 'Something for Nothing' by Larissa Boehning (Berlin) and 'The First Day of the Fourth Week' by Agust Borgbor Sverrisson (Reykjavik) it is the central characters' explorations of disused factories – ordinary, abandoned buildings – which highlight the inevitability of change. After her father's death, the narrator of 'Something for Nothing' gives his collection of cameras to Uli, the man in a nearby photo shop – 'a confidant who'd just happened to come along' (Boehning 2006: 104). Uli then takes the narrator on a drive to a disused factory in East Berlin, and they walk around a room filled with workbenches, handling 'the tools, metal, engine parts' left in a jumble, as if abandoned in a moment after the fall of the Berlin Wall. Uli comments: 'That's how a state comes to an end ... deserted by everyone ... it happens so fast ... It's a nice image: the people simply leave everything behind' (Boehning 2006: 105). Such an image reminds us that 'the city's very physicality never settles into a single version' (Crossan 2006: xiii). In this narrative the writer has used a focus on the physical fabric of ordinary buildings and the objects within them to stress the dynamics of history and the mutability of the city. The connection between the individual and the wider social narrative is still retained via the narrator's memory of seeing how everything had been left on her father's workbench, as if he might come back, echoing the scene in the unpopulated factory. Bringing materiality to the fore to emphasise change is also strikingly evident in 'The First Day of the Fourth Week'. Having lost his job, the narrator finds himself alone at home during daytime: detailed description of the domestic interior and workings of the townhouse magnifies his sense of disorientation due to his changed situation. What should be an architecture of familiarity is represented as teetering on the edge of destruction. This sense of alienation is replicated in the streets of the city when the narrator visits the deserted company buildings where he used to work and wanders his usual routes, but this time with no purpose.

The city is similarly represented, as a place of constant reconstruction where the familiar can be rendered strange in an instant, in Emil Hakl's narrative 'The News and Views'. The narrator of this story walks through a familiar street in Prague, only to encounter a 'brand-new' yet 'ordinary urban hill' which has been formed from dirt from the pit dug up for a gigantic new Carrefour supermarket (Hakl 2006: 97, 96). Standing on the hill, the narrator muses that there is no reason to 'get upset over some insignificant details' or be disoriented by the daily routines of city living.

It is precisely the (observed) detail, of architectural and topographical features, the minutiae of everyday life, and the marks left by people moving around urban space, that are significant in Iain Sinclair's writing about/of London. A key strategy used by Sinclair, which allows intervention in the urban space, is the activity of walking. Indeed, walking through the streets of a city, a characteristic of psychogeography, is a prominent feature in urban literature. Seen as contrary to 'swift circulation', walking can cut across established routes and facilitate exploration of marginal or forgotten areas (neglected urban spaces such as the non-u-mental sites exploited by Gordon Matta-Clark, for instance).[3] These areas could also be defined in terms of the mythic or mysterious dimension of the city, beneath or beyond the 'everyday', but revealed by and through the everyday. Such a concept might be seen as a reinterpretation of the Surrealists' term 'deambulation', whereby 'automatic writing in real space' reveals the unconscious zones of the city (Careri 2002: 22).

The structure of Sinclair's *Lights Out for the Territory: Nine Excursions in the Secret History of London* (1997) – the chapters or accounts of nine separate, yet related, walks forming an interconnected, organic narrative – reinforces the notion that walking is the best way 'to explore and exploit the city' (Sinclair 1997: 4). This method of being in the streets is an antidote to adhering to authorised paths and the 'gonzo' notion of the city heritage trail (Sinclair 1997: 207). In other words, the desire path takes precedence over the conventional street map. Moreover, the writer, and his urban accomplice Marc Atkins, the photographer, have moved on from the concept of the *flâneur* (or stroller) to adopt the stalker as a role model: 'the stalker is a stroller who sweats, a stroller who knows where he is going, but not why or how' (Sinclair 1997: 75).

This sense of uncertainty is mirrored in the text's representation of walking through the different areas of the city: walking as narrative can be disorientating both geographically and culturally. Even when the narrator and his companion travel on a bus, the route taken seems illogical: 'I can't connect any of this with the elegant fiction of my map' (Sinclair 1997: 44). Inseparable, then, from the business of orientating oneself around the built environment is perspective. Sinclair uses perspective, or narrative viewpoint, to endorse ways of knowing space other than ocularcentrism or lineation (the basis for gridding social space). Instead, the street-level gaze allows the writer to challenge the official representation of the city (Coverley 2006: 12) whilst offering the alternatives of mobile, inclusive, simultaneous and potential spaces (Dixon and Jones 2004: 90–1).

Walking marks out territory and allows the 'fiction of an underlying pattern' to reveal itself (Sinclair 1997: 4). Indeed, what might be termed Sinclair's 'London Project' – to restore the psychogeographical position of the city via literary texts, documentary studies and films – owes a debt to Alfred Watkins' discussion of ley lines and the argument that 'lines of force' can be mapped between iconic buildings to reveal the latent relationship between institutions (Coverley 2006: 119). As Sinclair observes in *Lights Out*, 'London, we were convinced, was mapped by cued lines of energy' (Sinclair 1997: 85). Another way of formulating this is to say that built forms resemble the conscious mind, a network with a purpose; whereas ruins are the urban unconscious, the unknown or the city's memory. Rebecca Solnit usefully compares these 'unknown' areas or objects to the terra incognita spaces on maps (Solnit 2006: 89).

'Archetypal landscapes' are combined, though, in Sinclair's writing, 'with the cumulative listing of objects' (Tew 2004: 135). Walking is very much a material 'aesthetic act', whereby the writer is arguably 'constructing an order on which to develop the architecture of *situated objects*' (Careri 2002: 20). And it is the text of the streets which proves the most significant 'object': the urban space presents 'a delirium of coded information, hot text … ' which Sinclair collects (Sinclair 1997: 49). This 'cumulative listing of objects' creates a potential problem with the architecture of his books. As critics have asked, 'can he create the structures to sustain his sentences?' (Jeffries 2004: 20). In particular, graffiti becomes the 'constant' element – 'part sign and part language' (Sinclair 1997: 4) – marking the journeys

FIGURE 13.2 'Vanishing Point', drawing by Mark Harris

through streets. Graffiti brings with it an element of surprise – 'words to hold your attention … breaking the monotony of … environment' (Smith 2000: 87) – and, as Sinclair reminds us, 'has a half-life far in excess of the buildings on which they have been painted' (Jeffries 2004: 20). At the same time, the representation of graffiti in *Lights Out*, for example, draws attention to the textuality of the city and to narrative as a construction holding together the fragments of urban space.

The notion that marks made, or traces unconsciously left, have resonance beyond the built architectural form is explored in Jon McGregor's novel *If Nobody Speaks of Remarkable Things* (2002). Indeed, the text could be read as an exemplification of Walter Benjamin's notion of the buildings of a city as places where human subjects leave traces, so that the interior spaces of a row of houses, for example, are altered both materially and psychologically (Benjamin 1986: 155–6). *If Nobody…* is an invocation of the life of a city in an unnamed, rather rundown street. The lives of the unnamed inhabitants (who are known by the number of the house they occupy) intersect via narrative description of ordinary everyday activities. In other senses the lives are unconnected, until an accident in the street becomes a crystallising moment (and a structuring device of the narrative) whereby shared witnessing creates an encounter (without contact) which reverberates into the future and the past. As the first-person narrator recalls: 'That's the way I remember it, with this single weighted pause, the whole street frozen in a tableau of gaping mouths' (McGregor 2002: 9). There is a link here with the stories in *Decapolis* ('Beginning' and 'Something for Nothing') which use the witnessing of the aftermath of a traumatic incident to give a momentary structure to the narrative and highlight the desire for intimacy in the context of a city. The text is also similar to *Lights Out* in that the seemingly ordinary, everyday things are significant, or 'remarkable': detail is magnified. At the moment of the accident in the street the narrator sees 'all these moments as though they were cast in stone, small moments captured and enlarged by the context' (McGregor 2002: 8).

Detailed description of a relatively small portion of urban space characterises the various strategies used by McGregor to represent the city 'architecturally'. The textual strategies also underscore how different characters try to come to terms with the momentary 'coming together' in the street, and indeed with the apparent randomness of urban life. In this way the writer reveals the tension between an acknowledgement of transience – that built forms and the street are temporary habitations – and the desire to leave one's mark permanently.

One of McGregor's strategies involves architecture directly, as a means of reflecting on the instability of the built environment. The young man who sits on his garden wall 'outside number eleven', for example, spends his time drawing a very detailed picture of the street, 'trying to get the correct perspectives and elevations, trying to capture all of the architectural details' (McGregor 2002: 58). He wonders what the people who first lived there would make of the houses now, 'shunted into the poor part of the town, broken up into apartments' (McGregor 2002: 59). The mark-making is an acknowledgement of the desire to connect one's identity with place, in the way that graffiti can be read as an assertion of individual ownership and identification: we can all 'divide London according to our own anthologies' (Sinclair 1997: 142).

A high proportion of the narrative of *If Nobody…* is focused on the details of interiors; the microcosmic spaces of the city. The first-person narrator articulates the desire to leave a permanent mark of human dwelling in buildings and urban spaces: 'I wanted to leave a note for the next tenant, leave a trace of myself behind … to go back years later and find a plaque with my name on it screwed to the wall' (McGregor 2002: 65). In a broader sense there is an interweaving of written text, narrative and the street: the words on sodden newspapers 'glued to the wet street' have the potential to 'soak into the stone … yesterday's stories imprinted like cave paintings, like a tattoo' (McGregor 2002: 66). Another strategy McGregor uses, emphasising the materiality of urban space, is concerned with collecting objects from, and images of, the street. The boy from number eighteen is an 'archaeologist of the present' gathering 'urban diamonds' – in other words, collecting finds from the street (McGregor 2002: 153). He represents the need to 'fix' transience in the form of photographs, his polaroids capturing 'the soap opera of the street corner marked out in [the] rain-faded initials and abbreviations' of graffiti and layers of torn posters (McGregor 2002: 30).

All the literary texts I have discussed depict the exterior and interior aspects of urban environments (neighbourhoods, streets, buildings, rooms) as sites of lived experiences and as places marked with visible traces of the passage of time, and of bodies moving through them. We could assert that writers and architects are inter-ested in the formation of an imagined literary/architectural space. Yet it is useful to consider this further and reflect on, as mentioned in the introduction, what links the writer of the city and the architect, in the realisation of the narrative/form. In *Architecture as Metaphor* Kojin Karatani defines architecture as the 'will to construct', a metaphor which he sees pervading thinking across disciplines, including literature and city planning. More significantly for this discussion is Arata Isozaki's comment in the introduction that since 1968 architects have been left with a 'loss of subject' – the disappearance of the 'grand narrative' such as 'architecture as construction' (Karatani 1995: xii). I would suggest that both contemporary writers and architects are responding to this in their realisation of narrative and structure. The response takes the form of a resistance to meta-narrative, or to providing any overarching explanation of the city. Implicit in this is a sense of the mutable and fragmented nature of urban experience, and of the impossibility of representing a city as a unified whole. At the same time, narrative is the 'bricks and mortar' necessary to both guide the reader around the city and ensure a degree of rootedness in place. Sinclair alludes to this with the comment 'the serial city is a manageable concept' (Sinclair 1997: 44).

It can be suggested that the texts focused on here are concerned with establishing some kind of relationship between the parts and the whole, between microcosmic and macrocosmic spaces. As Sophia Psarra discusses, conceptual ordering, spatial narrative and social narrative are fundamental to how buildings are shaped, used and perceived (Psarra 2009). For the writer and the architect, then, the relation of the individual self (part) to a communal identity (whole) is important. In 'The End of Modernity, The End of the Project?' Gianni Vattimo elaborates on this by arguing that writers and architects occupy an intermediary zone – between 'enrootedness in a place – in a community – and an explicit consciousness of multi-plicity'. This is the 'new monumentality', where self is recognised in shared values and in distinguishing 'marks' – that is, where one is. Interestingly, Vattimo draws attention in a broader sense to the 'rhetoric' of cities. If urban planning takes into account the cultural traditions of communities, its 'rhetorical aspect' means that the work of the contemporary architect is redefined (Vattimo 1997: 154).

Rather than rely on architectural landmarks as a means of orientation, can we look to a narrative of ordinariness, to a series of what Michel de Certeau terms 'rented spaces' and the movement of individuals through those spaces (de Certeau 1984: 103)? In this sense mapping becomes a form of story-telling or narrative, rather than adherence to mapped routes or streets. Contemporary urban literature may articulate a 'consciousness of the problematic of everyday life', although this isn't necessarily a negative position to take (Tew 2004: 111). Narratives of ordinari-ness can resist anonymity and inconsequentiality. Indeed, while McGregor, Sinclair and the writers of the stories in *Decapolis* represent familiar built environments, these may also be the context for 'extraordinary' encounters and realisations. The texts discussed here are all, in some way, concerned with what one might term the 'heroics' of the small; attempts to reclaim the importance of 'small things'. Physical detail is prioritised and thus noticed, as is the use and adaptation of space within/without a particular built form. Furthermore, the microcosmic is connected to the macrocosmic, and it is the connections (through movement, narrative and embodiment) that are ultimately seen to be crucial, rather than the overall masterplan or iconic structure.[4]

Such a view challenges the notion of a twenty-first-century 'city of bits' whose 'places will be connected by logical linkages [constructed *virtually* instead of physically], rather than by doors, passageways and streets' (Mitchell 1996: 24). In Wilson's *Eureka Street*, the citizens and streets of the city 'attend upon narrative' (Wilson 1998: 216). Are cities nothing more than a complex web of stories? Stories can be told in literary or architectural form, but both require a participatory audience for them to be fully realised. Architecture (here, the urban landscape) is materialised and 'inhabited' through the spatial tactics of individuals and the practices of everyday life (Till 2004: 355). The literary texts I have explored encourage, through the journeys the narrators and characters take, a kinaesthetic response to place. By extension, the reader is immersed in the city as a body of practices, becoming a member of the participatory audience.[5] It is the street which is most 'telling' in this context. In a newspaper article from July 2010 Joe Moran observes that 'in a society fragmented by free-market globalisation but still suspicious of state solutions, a lot is being invested in this idea of the street as the model for a vibrant civic life' (Moran 2010: 29).

Notes

1 Tonkiss (2000).
2 A potential for action or narrative visualised in Giorgio Chirico's painting *Melancholy and Mystery of a Street* (1914).
3 The architectural language of the 'anarchitecture' movement, which included Gordon Matta-Clark, included the use of empty buildings and undeveloped places, and the revealing of hidden construction. See *The Observer: Century City*, 1 February–29 April, 2001: 20.
4 In his discussion of the development of Edinburgh's waterfront, Terry Farrell argues that any masterplanning exercise 'should engage with existing and future communities' and that the 'common good' is the necessary 'glue that binds' and connects different 'nodes of interest' (Farrell 2008: 46).
5 An exhibition at the Victoria and Albert Museum, London, running until 30 August 2010, aimed to recreate such an immersive environment. '1:1 – Architects Build Small Spaces' is an exhibition of seven site-specific structures which aims to embody narrative space (moving beyond the dominance of the visual).

References

Ackroyd, P. (2001) 'The Life of the City', *The Observer: Century City*, 1 February–29 April: 4–5.

Barthes, R. (1997) 'Semiology and the Urban', in N. Leach (ed.) *Rethinking Architecture: A Reader in Cultural Theory*, London: Routledge.

Benjamin, W. (1986) 'Paris, Capital of the Nineteenth Century', in *Reflections*, trans. E. Jephcott, New York: Schocken.

Boehning, L. (2006) 'Something for Nothing', in M. Crossan (ed.) *Decapolis: Tales from Ten Cities*, Manchester: Comma.

Careri, F. (2002) *Walkscapes*, Barcelona: Gustavo Gili.

Constantine, D. (2006) 'The Beginning', in M. Crossan (ed.) *Decapolis: Tales from Ten Cities*, Manchester: Comma.

Coverley, M. (2006) *Psychogeography*, Harpenden: Pocket Essentials.

Crossan, M. (ed.) (2006) *Decapolis: Tales from Ten Cities*, Manchester: Comma.

de Certeau, M. (1984) *The Practice of Everyday Life*, California: California University Press.

Dixon, D.P. and Jones, J.P. (2004) 'Poststructuralism', in J.S. Duncan, N.C. Johnson and R.H Schein (eds) *A Companion to Cultural Geography*, Oxford: Blackwell.

Farrell, T. (2008) 'It's A Shore Thing', *RIBA Journal* 115, 6: 42–6.

Hakl, E. (2006) 'The News and Views', in M. Crossan (ed.) *Decapolis: Tales from Ten Cities*, Manchester: Comma.

Harbison, R. (2000) *Eccentric Spaces*, Cambridge, Mass.: MIT Press.

Jameson, F. (1991) *Postmodernism, or, The Cultural Logic of Late Capitalism*, London & New York: Verso.

Jeffries, S. (2004) 'On the Road: A Profile of Iain Sinclair', *The Guardian Review* 24 April.

Karatani, K. (ed.) (1995) *Architecture as Metaphor*, trans. S. Kohso, Cambridge, Mass.: MIT Press.

King, R. (2000) 'Habitation', in S.Pile and N. Thrift (eds) *City A-Z*, London: Routledge.

Lefebvre, H. (1991) *The Production of Space*, Oxford: Blackwell.

Lively, P. (1991) *City of the Mind*, London: Andre Deutsch.

McGregor, J. (2002) *If Nobody Speaks of Remarkable Things*, London: Bloomsbury.

Mitchell, W.J. (1996) *City of Bits: Space, Place and the Infobahn*, Cambridge, Mass.: MIT Press.

Moran, J. (2010) 'A Legend in its Lunchtime', *The Guardian* 17 July: 29.

Pile, S. and Thrift, N. (eds) (2000) *City A–Z*, London: Routledge.

Psarra, S. (2009) *Architecture and Narrative: The Formation of Space and Cultural Meaning*, London: Routledge.

Reda, J. (2006) 'A Man of the Streets', in M. Crossan (ed.) *Decapolis: Tales from Ten Cities*, Manchester: Comma.

Reid, I. (1977) *The Short Story*, London: Methuen.

Scott, H. (2004) 'Cultural Turns', in J.S. Duncan, N.C. Johnson and R.H Schein (eds) *A Companion to Cultural Geography*, Oxford: Blackwell.

Sinclair, I. (1997) *Lights Out for the Territory: Nine Excursions in the Secret History of London*, London: Granta.

Smith, S.J. (2000) 'Graffiti', in S. Pile and N. Thrift (eds) *City A–Z*, London: Routledge.

Solnit, R. (2006) *A Field Guide to Getting Lost*, Edinburgh: Canongate.

Sverrisson, A.B. (2006) 'The First Day of the Fourth Week', in M. Crossan (ed.) *Decapolis: Tales from Ten Cities*, Manchester: Comma.

Tew, P. (2004) *The Contemporary British Novel*, London: Continuum.

Till, K.E. (2004) 'Political Landscapes', in J.S. Duncan, N.C. Johnson and R.H Schein (eds) *A Companion to Cultural Geography*, Oxford: Blackwell.

Tonkiss, F. (2000) 'A–Z', in S. Pile and N. Thrift (eds) *City A–Z*, London: Routledge.

Vattimo, G. (1997) 'The End of Modernity, The End of the Project?', in N. Leach (ed.) *Rethinking Architecture: A Reader in Cultural Theory*, London: Routledge.

Wall, C. (1998) *The Literary and Cultural Spaces of Restoration London*, Cambridge: Cambridge University Press.

Wilson, R.M. (1998) *Eureka Street: A Novel of Ireland Like No Other*, New York: Vintage.

INDEX

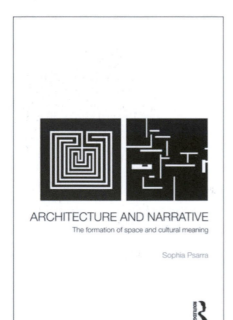

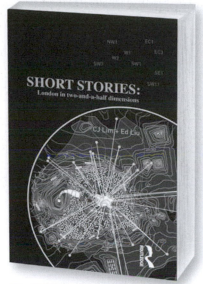